Complete
Handbook of
Basketball Drills

Other Books by the Author

Co-authored with Dr. William A. Healey

Basketball's Ten Greatest Defenses

10 Great Basketball Offenses

*The Winning Edge in Basketball: How to Coach Special
Situation Plays*

Complete Handbook of Basketball Drills

Joseph W. Hartley

Parker Publishing Company, Inc.
West Nyack, New York

© 1981 by

PARKER PUBLISHING COMPANY, INC.

West Nyack, N.Y.

Library of Congress Cataloging in Publication Data

Hartley, Joseph W
    Complete handbook of basketball drills.

    Includes index.
    1. Basketball coaching.   2. Basketball—
Training. I. Title.
GV885.3.H367   796.32′32   80-28724
ISBN 0-13-160945-9

Printed in the United States of America

DEDICATION

TO:

Treasury of Memories of all the close Ones
And the Good Times

Acknowledgments

It would be impossible to acknowledge by name everyone to whom the author is indebted in the production of a book such as this one. Certainly every coach that I had, that I have come in contact with throughout the years, has in some way contributed to the material within these pages. Especially to the players, the young men I have coached, I owe an eternal debt of gratitude. I cannot mention each by name, but they should realize that they are in these pages.

It gives me a great feeling to know that, as a coach and a teacher, I have in some small way contributed to the success pattern in the life of an attorney, an astronaut, a professional athlete, a coach, a salesman, a farmer, a soldier, a teacher, a school administrator, a doctor, a surgeon, a dentist, a plant manager, a factory owner, and to others in other professions and occupations as well. They all seem to have been successful. I know of none who are failures. They all stand as a tribute to the character-building qualities of the American athletic and basketball traditions. I acknowledge them and especially thank all of them for their contribution.

Some associates and some players have been closer in their association than others and as a result they have been more influential in my thinking, my coaching, and naturally have had a larger part in determining what I finally put into these pages. To all I express gratitude and thanks.

Joe Hartley

How This Book Will Help You

Basketball coaches are always seeking better ways to coach, to teach—some way, some drill that will enable the coach to instill or impart a new technique or fundamental to his team, or to some particular player on the team. Thus the stream of basketball coaching clinics, workshops, and basketball camps each year. Here coaches exchange ideas, and usually all are avidly seeking a better way or a new way to teach a fundamental.

I was an avid clinic attender, always seeking better ways to teach the various fundamentals and techniques of the game. Throughout the years, I collected many drills for each situation. The thought occurred that to put the best of these together—to compile the treasures into a single volume—would be a real service to the coaching profession.

I have selected what, in my opinion, are more than 250 of the best drills—the treasures so to speak—for each fundamental or technique. I consider myself a drill master. I have used most of these drills in my coaching. These are the drills that I found to be valuable and productive in the development of basketball players.

Drills are important in basketball. They are the tools that a coach uses to develop his players and to mold a team. Therefore, drill selection and use becomes important. This book will help you in this process. Several drills for the development of each fundamental area are given. In view of the importance of drills, it is no wonder that basketball coaches are constantly seeking new ones that will help them in their teaching.

Basketball is a game that can be broken down into parts, or phases. This makes the use of drills possible. A phase of the game can be taken and broken down into a drill phase. By doing this, a particular need can be developed, or improved, thus adding to the overall team improvement. It is a technique of improving the whole by using the part method. The coach analyzes the team. Certain phases appear weak, or show the need for improvement. By the proper selection of drills, and their proper use and application, these areas can be improved and developed.

During the course of a season, if a coach uses the same drills every day, players tend to tire or to become bored with certain drills. It is good and refreshing to change drills every two weeks or so, at least in certain areas. This change can relieve boredom, add new interest, and give cause to keep the team mentally alert—something new has been added. A new drill, but one that emphasizes the same fundamental teaching. Thus, the coach has a constant need for the input of new or additional drills for his team in the course of the long basketball season.

The drills in this book will be helpful to the coach who is constantly searching for new ones. My toughest assignment was selecting the treasury—those that are the best.

Joe Hartley

Contents

How This Book Will Help You   9

Key to All Diagrams   14

1 Drills for Receiving and Passing the Ball - 15

Passes That Need to Be Taught   21
The Two-Handed Push Pass   22
The One-Hand Push Pass   31
The Baseball Pass   33
The Hook Pass   37
The Bounce Pass   41
The Two-Handed Overhead Pass   43
The Flip or the Hand-Off Pass   46
Lob Passes   48
Special Passes   49

2 Drills for Teaching the Dribble - 50

The Dribble Play   50

3 The Shot — Drills to Teach Shooting-68

Special Notes on Shooting   68
Shots to Teach in Basketball   69
The Lay-Up Shot   70
The Jump Shot   79
The One-Hand Set Shot   86
The Hook Shot   89
The Free Throw   94

4 The Pivot — Drills to Teach Pivoting - 102

5 Drills for Body Balance, Stops, Starts, Change of Direction - 111

The Change of Pace Is Hard to Teach   112

6 Individual Defensive Drills - 121

Importance of Individual Defensive Play   121
Factors to Consider in Formulating a
    Defensive Philosophy   122
Factors Contributing to Poor Defensive Play
    and Teaching   123
Developing the Defensive Attitude   124
Defensive Ideas to Emphasize Continually   125

7 Team Defensive Drills - 142

Guarding the Player Without the Ball   151
Drills to Teach Switching   157
Zone Defense Principles   159
Combination Defenses   162

8 Defensive Rebounding Drills - 171

Defensive Rebounding   171

9 Fast Break Drills - 183

The Fast Break   183

10 Offensive Rebounding Drills - 201

Offensive Rebounding   201

11 Individual and Team Offensive Drills - 210

Individual and Team Offensive Drills   210
Fakes and Feints   216
Team Offensive Drills   224
Drills for Out-of-Bounds Plays   229

12 Pregame Warm-up Drills - 233

Importance of the Pregame Warm-Up   233

13 Combination Drills (All-Purpose) - 245

14 Drills for Special Situations - 255

15 Preseason Conditioning - 264

16 In-Season Conditioning - 267

The Spot Run   268
Sit-Ups   268
Push-Ups   268

17 Post-Season Conditioning - 271

Index   273

KEY TO ALL DIAGRAMS

O = Offensive Players

X = Defensive Players

———➤ = Path of Player

– – – –➤ = Path of Pass

〰〰➤ = Dribble

——————⟨ = Screen or Rebound Position

———⌒➤ = Pivot or Roll = ⟩〰➤

˙O = Ball Starts Here

⟨⟩ = Offensive player breaks to here

X̲ = Defensive player breaks to here

—‖‖‖‖➤ = Staccato Steps

——————⟨ = Player zones or floats the area

〰〰➤ = Rolls the ball or a rolling ball

Drills for Receiving and Passing the Ball

1

Before a player can pass, shoot, dribble, or do anything with the ball, he must receive it with skill that will facilitate his next move. Ball reception is probably one of the most neglected fundamentals of the game. Ordinarily one would think that at the college or professional level, the player obviously would know how to catch, or receive, the ball. However, if the cause of ball turnovers were checked out, it would be found that faulty procedures in this fundamental would be the cause of a high percentage of the ball turnovers. Attention to this fundamental area is needed, not only at the junior high school and high school level, but at the more advanced levels of play also. There is always the need for review of the basic fundamentals at all levels of play.

Passing drills give the coach the opportunity to check reception techniques and procedures of each player. All activity of every game centers around the ball itself, and because of this the fundamentals of ball handling become very important.

Reception involves the position of the player's hands on the ball, and the action of the hands when holding the ball preparatory to making his next move, which will be either a pass, a dribble, or a shot. The player will have to receive the ball in a variety of positions. Ball reception usually implies good body position. The player has to take the ball wherever it comes to him, but in order to guarantee good reception, the player's first move should be to get good body control and to receive the ball properly so that the next move can be made without undue delay.

The correct position of the hands on the ball is important. The hands should be placed on the ball so that the palms are facing each other on opposite ends of the axis of the ball. (The axis should pass between the middle finger and the ring finger, close to the fingertips.) This position has the fingers and the thumbs spread evenly around the ball with the hands a little behind the center and slightly on top of the ball. The thumbs should point nearly in the same direction as the fingers. Avoid spreading the thumbs wide, as it will create tension in the forearm muscles.

There is a difference of opinion among coaches as to whether the palms of the hands should touch the ball. Certainly the ball should not be palmed, but it is hard to imagine catching the ball without some contact with the palms of the hands, at least with the very top part of the palms. The pads of the palms of the hand next to the fingers will nearly always touch the ball when it is caught. Attempting to catch and hold the ball so that daylight shows between the palms of the hands and the ball will create tension in the forearm muscles and cause the player to be less relaxed. However, always remember that the feel of the ball and the tactile sense of the ball always comes from the fingers—not the palms. The final touch, and direction given to the ball in passing, dribbling and shooting, is done with the fingers.

If the ball should be removed from the hands, and the hands left as they were when holding it (as described above), the position of the hands would closely resemble a large loosely formed funnel. The hands and arms should be held up in this position when the player is expecting to receive the ball. This kind of position forms a backstop for the ball and allows the fingers to brake and cushion the ball when it comes to the player.

The following are some coaching points for proper reception of the ball:

Coaching Points for Receiving the Ball

1. The player must have good body position. This implies balance—low base of operation with proper weight

carriage—so that the player will have needed mobility to give good pass protection.

2. The receiver should always be in motion when catching the ball. Usually he will be moving toward the ball, but may be moving away from it, depending on the situation.

3. Passers should avoid a stationary receiver. This player is a dangerous teammate. Do not pass to such a player as this player will usually meet the ball with stiffened knees, be in an upright position, and will not be in a position to protect the passing lane.

4. Position of the arms. The player should make his moves with the arms *up* and *away* from the body. If the player does not have his arms and hands up in position, his late moves to bring them into position to receive the ball will cause him to meet the ball with resistance. *The player will be a resister, not a receiver.*

5. Hand position. The hand position should allow the receiver to draw the ball slightly toward the body as the hands and fingers contact the ball. The ball should be caught with the fingers as much as possible. Be a receiver, not a resister.

6. Finger position. If the pass comes in below the belt, the fingers should be pointing downward. For passes coming in above the belt and higher, the fingers should be cupped and pointing upward.

7. Eyes. The eyes should follow the ball all the way into the hands. *Look the ball into the hands.* Many fumbles are caused by the receiver's losing sight of the ball before he catches it, or taking his eyes from the ball in anticipation of making the next move.

8. Use both hands. Only as a last resort should a player ever attempt to catch the ball with one hand. Move to receive the ball in both hands, because one-hand reception is not effective, and the player is not in position to make the next move.

9. After reception, the ball must be protected by holding it in close to the body and by extending the arms and elbows, and keeping it in such a position that it cannot be deflected easily by an alert opponent.

Poor ball reception is the cause of many fumbles. Here are some things to look for in eliminating fumbles:

1. Weak hands. Some players have naturally weak hands and thus a minimum feel for the ball. Individual drills to strengthen the hands can help, but in some cases, the player's hands are liable always to be weak. Drills that could be used: Finger pushups; push away from the wall drills, squeeze rubber ball for finger and wrist strength.

2. Poor arm position. This player carries his arms down, and consequently his hands are never in position to receive the ball. Instead of the ball and the hands moving in the same direction at impact, the late movement of the hands to get in position will cause movement toward the ball as contact is made. Result—stiff-fingered fighting the ball and resistance that causes fumbling.

3. Palming the ball. Stress catching the ball with the fingers.

4. Failure to look the ball into the hands.

5. Poor finger position. Keep fingers relaxed. Point downward to catch low passes. Point upward for high passes.

6. Poor body balance can be a contributing factor to fumbles. A slightly crouched position should be maintained with joints relaxed, ready for a sudden move in any direction. The weight should be distributed evenly over both feet. Knees should be flexed. The center of the weight should be carried on an imaginary line through the hips. The feet should be spread, but only comfortably so.

Habit Drills to Teach Ball Reception

Ball reception can be stressed on any passing drill. Here the coach can constantly check the reception techniques and fundamentals and constantly be making corrections. However, there are a few drills that are very specific for teaching proper reception of the ball. Finger pushup drills, push away from the wall drills, squeeze a rubber ball drill for strengthening fingers, hands and wrists have already been mentioned.

1. **Wall Drill: Diagram 1-1.** Most gymnasiums will have a wall that can be used by players. In the drill shown here, the players line up facing the wall or walls as shown. If more than one wall is available, use it. Each player has a ball. The player may start close to the wall, and work back for more distance. The player throws the ball against the wall and positions

himself to receive the rebound. The coach can check reception techniques. If the player works very close to the wall, very quick reaction and eye reception are required. By working close to the wall, a lot of ball handling can be accomplished in a short period of time. The player can work back from the wall, and throw the ball against the wall at differing angles, requiring quick movements to be in position to receive the ball. If the player starts the drill very close to the wall and PINGS the ball against the wall a foot or so from it, very close eye, finger and hand reception coordination will be required.

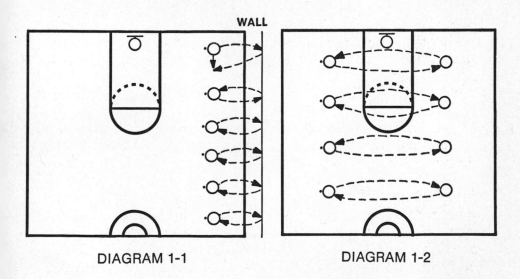

WALL

DIAGRAM 1-1   DIAGRAM 1-2

2. Two-Line Drill: Diagram 1-2. A very simple drill to check on ball reception is given here. Divide the players into two lines. A ball should be in possession of each two, and they pass the ball back and forth. Here the coach can check reception and passing techniques. Then, a variation can be added to this drill by having the passer intentionally pass low, high, or wide to the right or left so that the receiver will have to change position, and move to get the body into proper position to receive it. The coach will check the reception techniques, as well as body movements that properly place the body between the opponent and the ball. This will teach receivers also to be ready to move and receive the ball from different angles and positions. In so many basketball situations the ball does not come to the receiver in the perfect position, or from the perfect angle. The receiver must be able to adapt to this, and to quickly maneuver his body, arms and hands into reception position so that he can receive it and protect it from the opponent.

3. Multiple Ball Drill: Diagram 1-3. In this drill, more than one ball is used, usually two. Sometimes three can be used. There are five passers and one receiver. The five passers will keep the two balls moving to the receiver, who quickly returns it to another passer who does not have a ball. The passers help the receiver by not passing until he has released the ball he previously received, and is ready for reception. This gets the player acquainted with rapid fire reception and quick release of the ball to a teammate. It will require and develop intense concentration on the reception techniques and help the players develop and perfect eye-hand coordination. The drill will help the players develop split vision and proper passing speeds, and will teach them NOT to telegraph passes, to pass by defenders, and to concentrate on catching the ball. The players take turns in the passing and receiving positions.

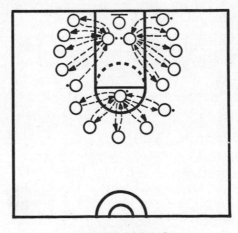

DIAGRAM 1-3

Drills to Teach Passing

There are a large number of passes that need to be taught to basketball players. Most coaches try to teach or expose their players to most of the variety of passes that can be taught. Some passes are special passes to be used in unusual situations. Usually most coaches end up concentrating their drills on three or four passes at the most, letting the other unusual passes take care of themselves. How many passes you teach and use will depend upon the type of offense you coach, and the passes required to make it functional.

Coaching Pointers for All Passes

The passer cannot always depend upon passing over the head of the defensive player who will be between him and the receiver. It is usually necessary to pass the ball *through* the defensive player, rather than *over* him. Consider these points.

1. First is the defensive factor. The closer the defensive man is to the passer, the easier it is to get the ball *through* him and past him.

   a. The farther away the defensive player is from the passer, the more time he has to react to the ball.

   b. The passer should never try to pass the ball by a player who is playing loose or sagging off in the defensive position.

2. Second—the defensive player's position must be analyzed. Ordinarily a defensive player will have one foot ahead of the other, the arm on one side raised—or he may have both arms to the sides.

   a. All defensive players are more susceptible to certain passing areas—such as over the top of the head, over the right or left shoulder, by the ear, or by the lower leg.

   b. In order to take advantage of the defensive player's weaknesses, the passer must master the basic passes in basketball.

PASSES THAT NEED TO BE TAUGHT

1. Two-handed push pass
2. One-hand push pass (Sometimes called the one-hand pro-pass)
3. The baseball pass
4. The bounce pass
5. The hook pass or the jump turn pass
6. The two-handed overhead pass
7. The flip or hand-off pass
8. Lob passes

9. Special passes
    a. Two-handed underhanded pass
    b. One-hand underhand pass
    c. Side arm hook pass
    d. Back hand flip passes
    e. Over the shoulder passes
    f. Special flips
    g. The drop-pass
    h. The hand-off
    i. The roll pass
    j. The behind-the-back pass

THE TWO-HANDED PUSH PASS

This pass is the most common pass in basketball. Sometimes called simply the *push pass* or the *chest pass*, it should be worked on a lot more than other passes, because it is used more. It can be used in more situations than any other pass, and can be made when the player is off balance. The guards should be masters of the bounce pass for getting the ball into the pivot player (some coaches use the bounce pass as a last resort), and rebounding players should have a good shoulder hook pass or a good baseball pass to get the fast break away, but every player *must* master the two-handed push pass. It is a pass that is ideal for the fast breaking team.

The position of the feet and the body are of no consequence in making this pass. It can be made from any position, but is usually made while the player is in the crouched or fundamental position, as he will be 90% of the time, if he is playing correctly.

Coaching Points for the Two-Handed Push Pass

1. Establish a *home position*. The ball should be held slightly above the waist with finger control. The elbows should be bent, and close to the body. The distance the ball is held from the body will depend upon the position of the defensive opponent. From the home position the player can execute an offensive move, as well as a pass.

2. Handle the ball in the fingers. The wrists first give the ball a slightly downward and backward motion, and

then upward to a full cocked position. The downward, backward, and upward motion is done almost in one continuous move.

3. As the wrists are uncocked, the fingers will move forward, giving power to the pass. The thumbs will move forward and under the ball. If the ball is held close to the body, it can be snapped quickly without any drawback motion.

4. The ball should be snapped by snapping the wrists and pushing with the arms. Give the ball reverse English with the thumbs. The force will come from the extension of the wrists and the inward snap of the thumbs.

5. On short passes little follow-through of the arms is needed. Make it more of a *snap pass*. On short passes the extension of the arms tends to telegraph the pass and to slow it up.

6. As the distance of the pass increases, the arm follow-through is advisable, since this motion gives force and direction. A step in the direction of the pass can give added distance and force if it is needed.

7. When the force of the arm push is needed, follow through with the arms and hands parallel with the floor. The pass can be from belt to belt or chest to chest.

8. The player can follow through and follow this pass; he can reverse from it; he can fake and feint a lot from this pass.
Note: If a player throws a dead ball on this pass it may be because his thumbs are not far enough behind the ball on the pass. Failure to snap the wrists and to move the thumbs forward under the ball will also produce a *dead ball* action on the pass. This should be avoided since such a pass will be hard for the receiver to handle.

Advantages of the Two-Handed Push Pass

1. The player can feint and fake easily from the fundamental position usually assumed before making the pass.

2. The handling of the ball to make this pass from the chest is such that the player can execute an offensive

move other than a pass—a dribble-drive, or a shot. It adds more finesse to the player's movement.

3. The pass can also be executed from any position.

Disadvantages of the Two-Handed Push Pass

1. Players have a tendency to develop the fault of batting the ball. This may develop from the emphasis of quickly snapping the ball for some situations. Do not allow this.

2. The players tend to do *blind passing*—that is, looking one way and passing another. This can cause the player to violate the golden rule in basketball, which is: *Do not fake or feint a teammate.*

Habit Drills for Teaching the Two-Handed Push Pass

1. Two–Line Passing Drill: Diagram 1-4. In this drill, have the players line up facing each other about eight to ten feet apart. Practice the pass. You can analyze the players' techniques and make corrections. It is best to have one ball for each two players. After practicing at this distance, have the players take one step backward, gradually lengthening the distance between them, until finally the players can pass a distance equal to the width of the basketball court. Other passes can be practiced from this formation also, such as the baseball pass, the bounce pass, the hook pass or the jump-turn hook pass, the two-handed overhead pass, and all underhanded passes.

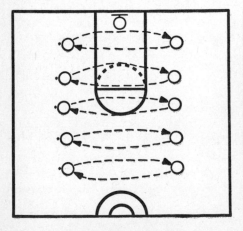

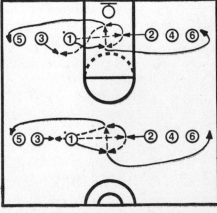

DIAGRAM 1-4   DIAGRAM 1-5

This could be used as a fundamental formation to teach beginners nearly all of the basic passes in basketball.

2. Double Exchange on a Single Line: Diagram 1-5. In the diagram, two single line formations are shown. You can run as many formations as you want or consider appropriate for the size of the squad. The players line up on a single line, with two groups facing each other. They should have about an equal number facing each other on each end of the line. With this drill, a considerable amount of ball handling can be accomplished in a short period of time. To start the drill, a player on the front of the line on one side takes the ball and starts the drill. All players work from a fundamental passing position—that is knees flexed, hips low, stance wide, etc. The pass—the two-handed push pass, is made from chest to chest. The distance the players start apart is at your discretion. The players are numbered in the lines to make for clarity in describing the movements in the drill. Player 1 starts the drill by making a two-handed push pass to Player 2 as he moves out to meet the pass. Player 2, after receiving the pass makes a pass back to 1 who has followed his pass. Player 1 will receive the ball at about half of the distance that was between the players when they started. After 1 receives the ball from 2, he now makes a hand-off or a flip pass back to 2 as they meet at about mid-distance from where the players were when the drill started. Player 2, after receiving the ball back from 1, now makes a pass to 3, the next player in the line behind 1. After this exchange, 1 and 2 go to the end of the line on the side opposite where they started. Now 3 and 4 repeat the drill, with the players constantly repeating and exchanging positions from one end of the line to the other. The main thing to remember in this drill is that after the double exchange between 1 and 2, and the hand back from 1 to 2, the ball is always returned to the point of origin, or to the side from where the first pass was made.

All the time the players run this drill, you should constantly check ball reception, passing techniques and fundamental body positions to make improvements in these ball handling techniques. This drill will provide a lot of ball handling in a short period of time. Enthusiasm for the drill can be generated by having contests to see how many exchanges can be made without a fumble or an error. Various games can be worked out to give enthusiasm to the drill. This drill could well be one to use for at least a short time every day in practice, especially with younger age teams where ball handling development is very necessary for improvement of the team.

This drill may be used also for the development of other passes, such as the baseball pass, the bounce pass, the flip pass and the hand-off passes. The drill could be started with a baseball pass by starting the players farther apart, returning a two-handed push pass, then including a flip, or a hand-off, a drop pass, or a behind-the-back pass, followed by a bounce pass that returns the ball to the point of origin.

3. Double Exchange on a Double Line: Diagram 1-6. This drill, to develop the two-handed push pass as well as other passes, is run like the double exchange on a single line shown in the previous drill, except that it is run on a double or a two line system. The players line up as shown, on two lines, facing each other. They may work in groups of six or groups of eight or more

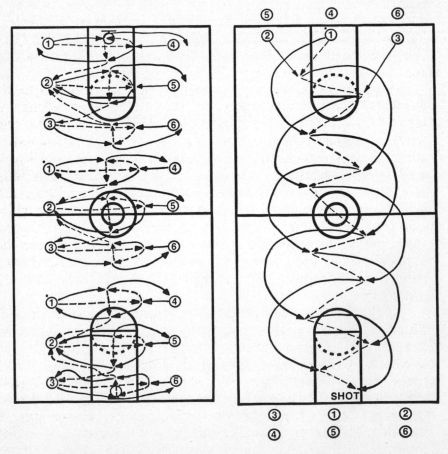

DIAGRAM 1-6   DIAGRAM 1-7

(must be an even number). Here we show squads of six. For one group or squad, 1, 2, 3, line up on one line, facing 4, 5, 6, on the other line. The two lines can vary the distance apart according to the passes being used, or according to the wishes of the coach. In each squad, the ball starts with Player 1, who passes to 4, who steps to meet the pass. Player 4 passes back to 1, who has followed his pass. Player 4 follows his pass, and always moves to the left of 1, since the ball is to be moved in this direction down the line. When 4 approaches 1, 1 gives him back a hand-off or a flip pass (could also be a drop-dribble pass, or a back hand pass if the coach wishes), and 4 then passes to 2, returning the ball to the line from which it originated. Player 1 will now go to the spot where 4 originally was, and 4 moves to 1's former spot. Now, 2 and 5 will work the double exchange pass system in the same way, exchanging places, and returning the ball to 3. Next, 3 and 6 will work the exchange pass system, exchanging places, and return the ball to 5, who is now in the position where 2 started. The drill continues back and forth in this manner. All the while the coach can check ball reception, passing techniques and fundamental positions and mechanics of the player.

Both of the Double Exchange Drills are readily adaptable to small squads of the varsity level, or to large classes where a large number of players can be accommodated in drills and where areas may be crowded. Both drills can be adjusted to small or large squads, and both give a lot of fast ball handling in a short period of time. They are drills that should be used daily to review and sharpen ball reception, passing techniques and fundamental body positions for the basketball player. The drills also give the players practice in meeting the ball and timing their moves for reception from a teammate. They can be adjusted to include a variety of passes used in the game, or may be limited entirely to the two-handed chest pass and a hand-off pass.

4. **Three-Man Grapevine Passing Drill: Diagram 1-7.** This drill is as old as the game. It is still good. Sometimes called the three-man weave, or the pass and go behind a player drill, it is an excellent drill to develop passing, ball handling and receiving while moving rapidly. It also helps to develop body movements such as changing directions and timing movements while keeping the body under control. A certain amount of footwork is involved and shooting can also be incorporated into the drill. The drill may be used the full length of the court as shown here, or it may be used for half-court drills. In the drill,

the ball starts in the middle with Player 1. Players 2 and 3 move in a diagonal direction down court and toward the middle of the court. Player 1 passes the ball to either 2 or 3, using the two-handed push pass, and cuts behind the player receiving the ball. In this diagram, 1 passes to 2 on his right. Player 1 cuts behind 2, and wide enough to be in the outside passing lane, before moving diagonally downward and toward the middle. Player 2 passes to 3, and cuts behind him, swinging to the outside lane and then diagonally downward and toward the middle lane. Player 3 now passes to 1, and cuts behind him as previously described. The players proceed the length of the court or half-court if desired. When the end of the court is reached, the drill may be culminated in a shot by one of the players. The players may return the length of the court, or they may be replaced by another team of three waiting at the end of the court. It is a good idea to designate a number of passes to be made by the three players as they traverse the distance; otherwise they will not make their cutbacks sharp enough, will travel more vertical distance down court, and will not move in sharp enough diagonally to get any body control and foot movements out of the drill. It is usually a good idea to require at least ten to twelve passes in traveling a full-court distance, or five or six passes for a half-court drill. In working the drill half-court, it should be run from the court division line at mid-court to the basket.

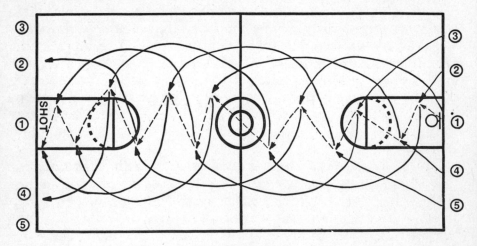

DIAGRAM 1-8

5. The Five-Man Weave or Grapevine Drill: Diagram 1-8. This drill is exactly the same as the one given in Diagram 1-7, except that it is done with five players instead of three. The ball starts in the middle with Player 1, and the other players line up as shown. Player 1 passes either right or left to the player nearest him. In this case, he passes to his right to 2, and then after passing to 2, 1 cuts behind two players, 2 and 3, before moving into the middle of the court. Player 2 passes to 4, and cuts behind 4 and 5, and then back toward the middle of the court. Player 4 passes to 3 and cuts behind 3 and 1. Player 3 passes to 5 and cuts behind 5 and 2. This continues down court with the pass to the nearest player and cut behind two movement until the court distance is traversed. The drill can be ended with a shot. The five-man drill has advantages over the three-man drill in that it requires more alertness from the players, gets them used to moving the ball under more crowded conditions, and requires more savvy and alertness in executing the cut back movements. Again, you should require at least ten to twelve passes on the drill in traversing the distance of the court, otherwise the players will flatten the drill out too much, cut almost entirely vertically, and not move back to the middle of the court with diagonal moves. This drill is usually liked by the players, moves fast, and gives a lot of good ball handling practice to players while on the move.

6. Four-Corner Passing Drills: Diagram 1-9. There are many variations to this drill, but this one is a good one to develop ball handling and player movements. It is especially well adapted to development of the two-handed push pass. This drill can be worked with two balls being kept in motion. The players line up as shown in the four corners. A ball can be started on two opposite corners as shown. The ball will proceed in the same way from each corner. Beginning with Player 1 in the lower left corner, 1 takes a short dribble to get moving, and passes to 4 moving out from the corner on his right. Player 4, moving out to receive the ball, passes it back to 1, who has followed his pass. After passing to 1, 4 breaks toward the corner on his right, and 1 passes the ball right back to him. After this pass, 1 goes to the end of the line behind the last player in the line where 4 moved out. The other players move up. Now 4 passes to 8, moving out from the corner on his right, and repeats the procedure that 1 has followed. In the meantime, 7 has moved out from the corner opposite where 1 started and is repeating this procedure on the corner to his right. Now the players continue the drill, moving two balls around the four corners in this manner. This drill gives good practice in receiving and passing the ball on the move. It also gives practice in passing and receiving while moving toward and from the ball. The drill should not always be moved to the right; after working the ball to the right a few minutes, the drill should be reversed, and moved to the left.

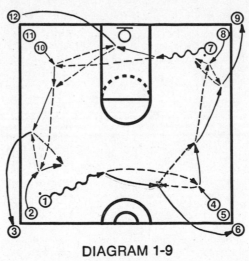

DIAGRAM 1-9

7. Passing Reaction Drill: Diagram 1-10. This drill is run on both sides of the court at the same time. Player 1 begins the drill by passing to 4 and then breaks full speed down the court. At the same time, 7 is beginning the drill on the opposite side of the court by passing to 10. Player 4 returns the pass to 1, who then passes to 5. Player 5 returns the pass to 1, who then passes to 6. Player 6 returns the pass to 1, who then dribbles in for a lay-up shot. On the opposite side of the court, the same pattern is run. The players in the passing positions on the court must be changed frequently so that all have the opportunity to have passing positions on the floor. The drill helps players develop skill in passing to a moving player coming toward them and moving away from them, and at the same time provides good ball handling development to the player passing and receiving the ball while moving rapidly.

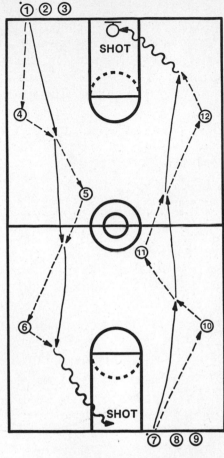

DIAGRAM 1-10

THE ONE-HAND PUSH PASS

This pass is sometimes called the "one-hand pro-pass." It requires the same fundamentals as the two-handed push pass. The pass is used to pass by or through an opponent. It requires finesse and adeptness, and should be mastered by all players. Time needs to be spent drilling the techniques required to become adept at putting the ball by the opponent to the receiving teammate. The player must learn not to telegraph the pass.

Coaching Points for the One-Hand Push Pass

The coaching points are very much the same as for the two-handed push pass except for the following:

1. The ball is held and passed the same way except that it is released from one hand with the opposite hand helping to hold and protect the ball prior to its quick release.

2. It is usually correct to say that it is a two-handed pass when released in front of the body and becomes a one-hand pass when released from the side of the body.

3. In order to make the pass, the player rotates the ball in the hands by allowing the passing hand to move behind the ball, and the other hand to move below the ball.

4. The fingers and wrists are used with a snap and a good arm follow-through.

5. The player should master the technique of making the pass with both the right and the left hand. This way, he can move the ball by the opponent to either the right or the left.

6. The pass can also be used by a shooter—in the air to jump shoot—if he sees a teammate in a better position. He merely pushes the ball off to a teammate—as he would push it to the basket on a shot.

7. The best use of the pass is for passing the ball by or through a defensive player.

Habit Drills to Teach the One-Hand Push Pass

Three-Line Passing Drill: Diagram 1-11. This is a drill that should be used every practice session possible. It gives the offensive player practice in putting the ball through and by the defensive player. The players line up in three lines as shown. The O players numbered one through eight are the offensive players. The X players numbered one through four are the defensive players. The offensive players on one line each have a ball. Player 1, with the ball, takes a dribble approach to X1, and fakes, feints or takes a drift step either to the right or left—and when getting a commitment from the defensive player—pushes the ball by him to 2, using a wrist flip with the one-hand push pass. The passer should never look directly at the receiver and should avoid telegraphing his passes. The drill is repeated on down the ball line with Players 3, 5 and 7. The players change positions in the lines to give each drill and practice in passing through the defender, in receiving, and in defensing the passer. The objective of the drill is to give the passer drill in passing by and through a defender, using the one-hand push pass. The drill will help the passer to develop creative passing ability. Later a defensive player could be added to compete with the receiver, and this can add a new dimension to the drill.

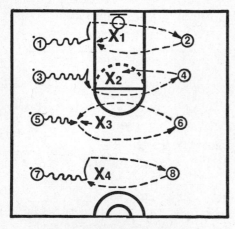

DIAGRAM 1-11

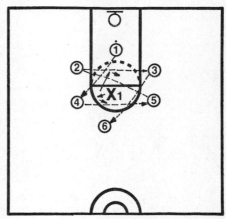

DIAGRAM 1-12

Bull in the Ring: Diagram 1-12. In this drill six players take positions around the circle. A defensive player called the *bull*, is placed in the circle. The players on the circle pass the ball over or by the defensive player as he tries to guard them and intercept the pass. If the bull intercepts a pass, deflects the ball, or ties up one of the passers, the player making the mistake must exchange positions with the bull. This drill can be worked well at all the circles on the court, and if need be, other circles can be formed. It can give good work in faking, feinting, and passing the ball through the defensive player. Suggested rules are that a player cannot pass to the player immediately next to him, nor can he throw over the bull with a pass that would be higher than the basket.

THE BASEBALL PASS

This pass has limited use—but it is of great value. It is a distance pass, especially useful and valuable in getting the fast break underway, and in hitting a fast cutting player on the way to the basket. It is also of great value in helping break the full-court pressing defenses. One well-placed baseball pass can shatter the press, and can give the offensive team an immediate down court offensive outnumbering the defensive situation and a good opportunity to convert on a scoring situation.

Coaching Points for the Baseball Pass

1. The pass is made just like the overhand baseball throw, or the catcher's baseball throw. The ball should be thrown from the ear straight from the shoulder with a snap of the wrist and fingers. The fingers should roll off the bottom of the ball.

2. In making the throw, do not wind up or sidearm the throw. If you sidearm the throw it will cause the ball to curve, and make it hard for the receiver to handle.

3. A right-handed player should start the ball back with both hands, over the right shoulder about ear level. At this point, the right hand will be behind the ball, and the left released. As the wrist is cocked, the body weight will be shifted to the right foot. The forward motion starts with the shifting of the weight to the left foot in a stride step.

4. The hand should stay behind the ball and not be allowed to turn, causing the ball to curve. (Keep the fingers under the ball.)

5. The arm should follow through with the corresponding follow-through of the right side of the body.

6. The player should learn to step either way—to the right or left—with the pass. It is most natural for the right-handed player to step with the left foot, and follow through with the right foot. Do not try to develop ambidextrous players with the pass. A right-handed player should make the pass with his right hand and the left-handed player should make it with his left hand.

Habit Drills for Teaching the Baseball Pass

1. The baseball pass can be incorporated in the double exchange passing drills given under drills for the two-handed push pass.

2. Have players stand and throw to teammates at the middle of the court.

3. Have two players at the foul line. One shoots the ball off the board; when he secures the rebound, the other runs down court in any path. Vary this path and the positions where he is to

receive the pass. The rebounding player must take the rebound, make a quick turn with head and eyes to locate the cutter, and then execute a baseball pass to the cutting player. This drill gives good practice habits in locating the receiver before committing the throw.

   4. Rebound, Pass, Shoot Drill: Diagram 1-13. The players line up as shown at each end of the floor. The first player in each line goes to the area near the free-throw line, and waits until the second player secures the rebound from a shot. (The coach or manager can put the ball on the board to start the drill.)

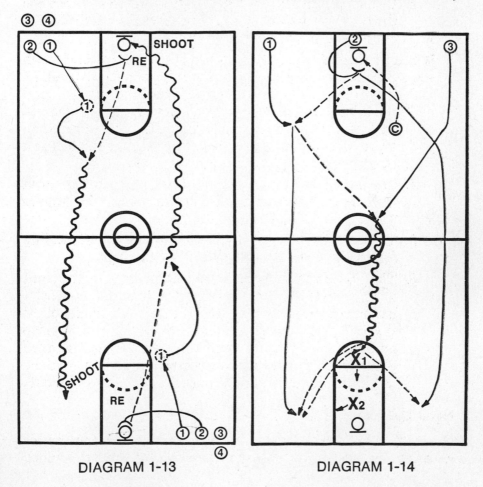

DIAGRAM 1-13   DIAGRAM 1-14

Then the player at the free-throw line breaks down the floor to receive a baseball pass from the rebounder. The receiver should break to different spots for the outlet pass, but should receive the ball before he gets to the court division line. After receiving the pass, the player should drive hard for the opposite basket, but should vary his shots, from a hard driving lay-up shot to different spots on the floor within shooting range, such as the top of the circle, the side or the free-throw line. The players keep the two lines moving, and will have to change positions so that they all get turns rebounding, passing and dribbling for the shot. As shown in this diagram, Player 2, after rebounding and making the baseball pass to 1, now becomes the next player to go to the free-throw line area to receive the next outlet pass from 3, the player next in line behind him. Keep two balls moving. The drill gives good fast action, and gives the rebounder good practice in spotting a receiver and getting off the pass. The receiver gets good work on moving to the outlet pass positions, receiving the ball on the move and driving hard downcourt for a shot.

5. **Combination Baseball Pass Fast Break Drill: Diagram 1-14.** This drill combines drill on the baseball pass with a fast-break drill. The players line up at one end of the floor in the three lines as shown. The coach or a manager puts the ball up on the board for a rebound. Player 2, in the center line, positions himself for the rebound. Players 1 and 3, by a prearranged signal, decide which one will break for the outlet pass position, and which one will break deep down court for a pass. In this diagram, 1 breaks to the outlet pass position. Player 2, after securing the rebound, must spot the receiver and whip a pass to him. Player 3 has cut straight down court for a distance to the mid-court area, and then breaks diagonally toward the middle lane of the fast break lanes. Player 1 immediately passes the ball to 3 just at the division line. Now 3 drives hard down court toward the basket at the other end of the court. Players 1 and 2 break hard and fast down the outside lanes as shown. Two defensive Players, X1 and X2, are placed at this end of the court to defend against the three fast-breaking players. When 3 approaches the area of the top of the circle, he holds up just enough to let 1 and 2 get into the play, and he may pass off to either player to take whatever option the defensive play presents to him. In this diagram, 3 passes to 1, and as the defense shifts on 1, he returns the pass to 3, who whips the ball to 2, who should have a shot. The offensive players follow hard for the rebound while the defense attempts to block out. The players change position so that all get turns at the various offensive and defensive positions. The players should mix the positions that

break shallow for the outlet pass and for the deep down court pass. This gives the rebounder more work on quickly spotting the possible outlet pass area.

THE HOOK PASS

This pass is sometimes alluded to as the *jump-turn* pass. It can be used by tall players to good advantage. The body must be between the opponent and the ball. The pass is especially effective off the rebound, on the sideline when crowded, and possibly in situations where the player has been trapped by a two-timing process in effect by the defense. The true hook is thrown with a sweeping motion and a comparatively straight elbow. It can also be thrown with the bent elbow, in which case it becomes much like a jump-turn baseball throw.

Coaching Points for the Hook Pass

1. As a general rule take a cross-over step to get away from pressure and jump high in the air to get over the defensive player. Only rarely should the pass be attempted without leaving the floor.

2. The right-handed player will take off on the left foot and jump high into the air. On the way up, turn the body to face the defensive man and the receiver. Both hands bring the ball up, at which point the ball may be thrown just like the baseball pass from above the shoulder and the ear.

3. Some variation in this will be noticed in players who fail to turn the body enough to face the receiver squarely, in which case the ball must be brought more over the head in an arm sweeping motion.

4. The ball should be released at the highest point of the jump.

5. The ball should not be palmed or cupped in the forearm—this results in loss of control.

6. Keep the body between the ball and the opponent. The player should alight in a well-balanced position, on both feet, feet even, facing squarely in the direction the pass was made and ready to move in either direction quickly.

Habit Drills to Teach the Hook Pass

1. The Dribble, Jump-Turn Hook Pass Drill: Diagram 1-15. The players line up on two sides of the court as shown. Player 4 on the left side starts the drill by passing to 1, who has moved diagonally down court and toward the basket. Upon receiving the ball, 1 continues to dribble diagonally toward the corner of the court on the left. After passing the free-throw line area, he jumps into the air, turns and executes the jump-turn hook pass, passing to 4, who delays at first and then breaks in a diagonal direction toward the right corner. Player 4 should receive the pass somewhere near the top of the circle, and then he dribbles fairly deep toward the corner and the baseline, where he now jumps into the air and executes a jump-turn hook pass to 1, who is now breaking toward the basket. Player 1 shoots, and 4 rebounds the ball and passes it back out to the original line where the drill is repeated. The players exchange lines. The drill should be run from both sides of the floor. When the players execute the jump-turn hook pass, the coach should check the fundamental coaching points, and especially the landing of the players after they have made the pass. The player should land with both feet even, well-balanced and ready to move quickly in either direction.

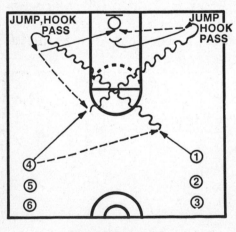

DIAGRAM 1-15

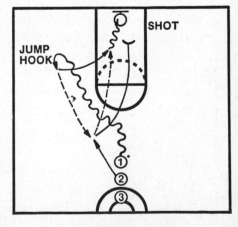

DIAGRAM 1-16

2. Single Line Hook Pass Drill: Diagram 1-16. In this drill the players form a single line at about the middle of the court. The first player in line, Player 1, dribbles down court and then veers either right or left and after reaching the area near the free-throw line extended, he jumps into the air, turns and locates the trailer, Player 2. Player 2 trails at some distance, and when 1 locates 2, he passes the hook, or jump-turn pass to him. Player 1, upon landing in good balance, ready to go in either direction, immediately breaks to his left toward the basket. Player 2 returns a pass to 1 breaking toward the basket immediately. Player 1 then dribbles in to shoot. Player 2 rebounds the ball and passes it out to the next in line, who repeats the drill. The players exchange positions to get drill at both positions. The drill not only gives work in developing the jump-turn hook pass, but places emphasis upon landing in balance, ready to move out immediately in either direction to receive a return pass on a drive for the basket.

3. Four-Corner Hook Pass Drill: Diagram 1-17. The four-corner passing drill can be modified to include the jump hook pass. In this drill, two balls can be kept moving at the same time by starting them in opposite corners. The players line up in the corners as shown. Starting in the lower left corner, 1 starts with a ball, dribbles out a short distance toward the opposite corner, then executes a jump hook pass to the next player in line, which in this case is 2. Player 1 takes care to land in balance so that he can take off immediately to his left, and the next corner. Player 2 immediately returns the ball to 1, who receives it on the move, dribbles a short distance and passes to 4. Player 4 now repeats what 1 did, using 5 as his receiver, and moving out to the

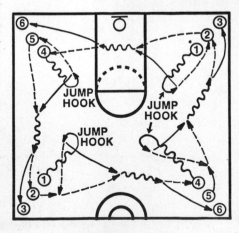

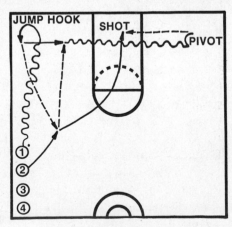

DIAGRAM 1-17   DIAGRAM 1-18

next corner. In the meantime, 1 in the top right corner has started the drill from that corner and the drill proceeds around the four corners with two balls moving continuously.

4. Side Line Hook Pass Drill: Diagram 1-18. In this drill, the players line up on one side of the floor as shown. Player 1, the first player in line, dribbles along the side toward the corner, and just before approaching the corner, he jumps up and executes the jump-turn hook pass, passing to the next player in line, Player 2, who has moved out toward the basket following 1 in a delayed move. After passing to 2, 1 lands in balance, and immediately breaks to his left, and 2 returns him a pass as soon as possible. Player 1 now dribbles just to the right of the basket area, does a stop and a reverse pivot, and feeds the ball to 2 driving in for a shot. This drill should be worked from both sides of the floor, and it brings into play the execution of the pivot, so that it could be classified as a combination hook pass, dribble, push pass, pivot, and shooting drill. Player 1 rebounds 2's shot, and returns the ball to the next in line to repeat the drill. The next line should be formed on the right side of the floor.

5. Defense the Side Line Hook Pass: Diagram 1-19. The players line up on both sides of the court as shown. On the No. 1 line, X1, a defensive player, lines up about even with 1. Player 1 takes the ball and starts a drive for the basket. Player X1's job is to turn the dribbler to the outside. Player 1, when turned to the outside, and when approaching the corner, executes the jump hook pass, passing to 2 who is breaking into the basket area. The players rotate lines, and take turns on defense. This is also a good defensive training drill, as it should teach the defensive man that when he is at least even, and on the inside, he should be able to turn the dribbler to the outside. The dribbler gets practice and drill in locating his receiver on the move to the scoring area, and in making the pass to him. This is a situation also where in some cases 1 could execute the behind-the-back pass to 2 coming into the basket area for the score.

6. Rebound, Hook Pass Drill: Diagram 1-20. In this drill, 1, 2 and 3 take the positions shown. Player 1 shoots the ball up on the board. Players 2 and 3 take positions in front of the basket in the rebound area. They start even, but jab and jockey for position in an effort to block the other out. The one who secures the rebound, hook passes it out to 1. The other player jumps on the one who secured the rebound in an effort to delay or prevent the outlet pass.

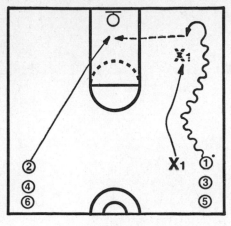

DIAGRAM 1-19

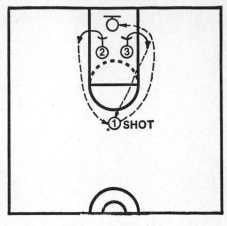

DIAGRAM 1-20

THE BOUNCE PASS

The bounce pass is a pass that can be used for a change of pace and by smaller players to advantage. Small players who cannot pass over or through the opponent can pass under with the bounce pass at times. The guards can use this pass to start the offense, or to work the ball through the defense.

Against zone defenses where the players have their hands up and arms spread, and against tall players where it is difficult to pass over or through them, the bounce pass comes in handy. It can also be used to feed the players cutting by the pivot post player.

The bounce pass is forbidden by some coaches because they feel that it is too slow and that it lends itself too easily to interception. When deception and fakes and feints are used in the execution of the pass, it can help the offense out of trouble spots. It has a definite place in the game.

Coaching Points for the Bounce Pass

1. The pass can be delivered with both hands, or with either hand alone. The player should master all three techniques.

2. The finger and wrist actions are the same as for the two-handed push pass, or the one-hand push, with impetus in a downward direction rather than forward or horizontally.

3. The eyes should not follow the path of the ball, but should be focused straight ahead for deception.

4. The bounce pass cannot (generally) be thrown too hard, if accurate, and if it reaches the receiver at the right height, because the floor will absorb the shock.

5. When the two-handed bounce pass is made, a *forward spin* or a *reverse spin* may be put on the ball. The reverse spin slows the ball and may be used to give the receiver a longer lead. A forward spin will cover more distance quickly and can be squeezed through narrower openings. It is also harder to handle.

6. The pass should be made so that the teammate receives it at the height of its bounce, or as it starts to come down. The height should be somewhere between the receiver's knees and his waist. Waist high is better.

7. If the bounce is too close to the receiver, it is hard to handle. The best place to hit the floor with the ball is about six inches to the side of the opposing guard, or approximately two thirds of the distance to the receiver.

8. The player will have to learn through experience the height the ball will bounce when it strikes the floor at different angles and with different force and spins.

Advantages of the Bounce Pass

1. The pass can be used by small players to pass under taller players.

2. It can be a very useful pass against zone defenses.

3. It can be very effective to feed players cutting in around, and by, the pivot post player.

4. It adds deception and change of pace to the passing game.

Disadvantages of the Bounce Pass

1. It is a slow pass.

2. It can be difficult to receive.

3. Because of the above points, the pass tends to lend itself to interceptions and ball turnovers.

Habit Drills to Teach the Bounce Pass

Most of the drills given to teach the other passes can be used to include bounce passes. All of the double exchange drills and three-line passing drills can include the bounce pass or be used to teach its appropriate and effective use.

THE TWO-HANDED OVERHEAD PASS

This pass is widely used by many teams that concentrate on a set offensive pattern and a deliberate game. Many coaches prohibit the pass because they feel that it commits the player too much—that once the player raises the ball above his head, there is not much else he can do except pass. For this reason the pass is not usually found to be in the repertoire of passes used by the fast-breaking, hard-driving team. The slower and more deliberate team will often use this pass to the exclusion of all others.

Coaching Points for the Two-Handed Overhead Pass

1. As the ball is held over the head, the hands should be slightly behind the ball with the fingers pointing straight up.
2. The elbows should be bent.
3. The wrists are cocked by allowing the fingers to rotate backward and downward. The length of this motion will depend upon the distance the ball is to be thrown.
4. As the ball is released, it is important to see that the hands follow the flight of the ball as far as possible to eliminate the tendency to throw the ball too low.
5. Release the ball with a quick snap of the wrists and fingers. A step forward with the foot on the strong arm side will give more impetus to the pass.

Advantages of the Two-Handed Overhead Pass

1. It is an excellent pass to execute from any position on the set deliberate offense.
2. The guards can use the pass to pass to the post man or the forwards in triggering offensive movements.

3. The forwards can use the pass to put the ball in to the post player, or to hit the guards cutting off the pivot post player.

4. The pivot post player can use this pass effectively after receiving the ball on a high post and turning to face the basket.

5. It is frequently used to advantage by the taller players..

6. It is frequently used by players receiving a *high pass* who want to make a quick return or pass off.

7. It can be used to maintain a passing position when the player is overguarded or crowded at the end of a dribble.

Disadvantages of the Two-Handed Overhead Pass

1. While holding the ball in the overhead position, the player cannot be an immediate threat to shoot or drive. In this position, many times the defensive opponent will move in wide, and belly-button close so that it is difficult for the player to do anything.

2. The player cannot do as many things from this position with the ball over his head as he could with it in a *home* position in front of the chest.

Habit Drills to Teach the Two-Handed Overhead Pass

1. **The Wall Drill:** The pass can be developed by the use of the wall drill that is given in Diagram 1-1. This can be done anywhere a smooth wall surface is available. The player can begin very close to the wall and develop the technique of raising the ball over the head and executing the pass against the wall with a snap of the wrists, forearms, and fingers. When the player develops passing ability and can give more impetus to the ball, he can be moved back from the wall to develop the passing ability at longer distances. Later, a restraining line can be drawn at a distance from the wall. The players retain their position behind this line and a contest can be held to see which member of the group can execute the greatest number of passes in a given time. This drill may be used to develop all passes and the distance of the restraining line may be varied according to the pass that is being used. The player is not to cross the restraining line.

2. The Star Passing Drill: Diagram 1-21. Five players are placed in star formation. The two-handed overhead pass is practiced. The player cannot pass to the player next to him. This gives each player a definite player to whom he must pass, and all passes will be the same length. This drill can be used to practice other passes as well. Many variations and contests can be worked from this drill formation.

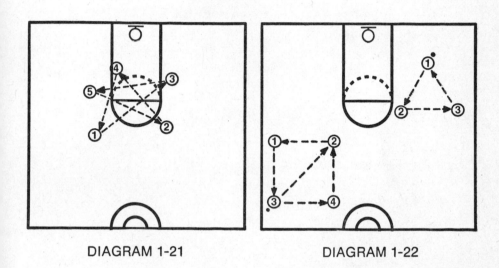

DIAGRAM 1-21   DIAGRAM 1-22

3. The Square and Triangle Passing Drill: Diagram 1-22. This diagram gives two formations that may be used to advantage to develop the two-handed overhead pass, as well as other passes. In the square drill, the players place themselves in a square formation and pass the ball around the square or across the square diagonally. In the other, the players pass the ball in a triangle formation. These drills are advantageous where the squad members are small and a large number of balls are available, and such small grouping can give more individual practice. From these formations—circle, line, star, triangle, and square formations—competitive elimination pass drills may be held to develop interest and competitive team spirit. Groups can compete against each other to see who makes the most passes within a time limit. Also, players may be eliminated from the drill as they make bad passes or fumble a pass that should have been properly received. The squad with the most players surviving, wins. This drill can be faulted in that the decision which eliminates a player in many cases is a matter of judgment of the coach, and of course the poorer players who need the drills the most are the first to make errors and be eliminated.

THE FLIP OR THE HAND-OFF PASS

Who Uses It

1. The pivot post player to feed cutters
2. Any player who has executed a quick stop and turn, and desires to feed a cutter
3. A forward feeding a guard on a guard-forward play maneuver
4. Any player who has a cutter going by a post-screen situation

Coaching Points for the Flip or the Hand-Off Pass

1. On the flip or hand-off, there should be no spin on the ball and it should be given to the receiver at waist or chest height.
2. The flip or hand-off should not be thrown at the receiver, but rather just flipped into space at the proper height for the oncoming player to pick it off, or receive it.
3. The receiver is not to take the ball out of the hands or off the hand of the passer. The passer flips it to the receiver with a snap of the fingers and wrists. The hands and arms are kept out of the way.
4. Do not platter the ball—or hold it out in such a manner that the receiver must take it from the hand or hands of the passer.
5. The player should learn to accompany the flip passes with a variety of fakes.
   a. Fakes should be made with the head, the shoulders, the eyes, and the ball.
   b. Usually, a high fake or a fake up means a low pass, and a fake down means a flip over the shoulder. Likewise, a fake to the right is usually followed with a flip to the left, and vice versa.

Habit Drills to Teach the Flip or Hand-Off Pass

The flip or the hand-off pass can be included in all the double exchange passing drills previously given.

1. Guard-Forward Drill: Diagram 1-23. The drill shown here is a good one to teach the flip hand-off pass exchange that would be typical of a guard-forward play. The guards and forwards line up in the guard and forward operational areas on each side of the floor as shown. The two sides can take turns working the drill. Player 1, in the first line, passes to 3 in the forward position. Before making the pass, 1 should make a good head and shoulders fake to his left. Player 3, before moving out to receive the ball, should make a good jab step to the inside, and then move out to receive the ball from 1. After passing the ball to 3, 1 then fakes a drive to his left, and veers right to the outside of 3. As 1 cuts close to the outside of 3, 3 fakes and then gives 1 the flip pass. Player 1 takes the ball and dribble drives for the basket. Player 3 executes a reverse pivot, and flares out toward the lane and the basket. Player 1 may drive all the way to shoot, pull up short and jump shoot or he may pass back to 3 who can shoot. The second and fourth line now run the drill to that side of the floor. Various options and variations can be worked from this drill.

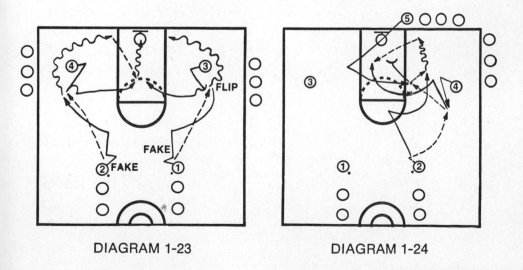

DIAGRAM 1-23   DIAGRAM 1-24

2. Split the Post Drill: Diagram 1-24. The players line up in five lines as shown—the guards in two lines on each side of the floor, and the forwards in two lines on each side of the floor, while the pivot-post players line up under the basket area. The play is initiated by the guard who may pass to the forward, and the forward in turn passes to the pivot-post player, 5, moving into the pivot-post area. The forward and the guard then do a split play over and by the pivot-post player. As the guard and forward fake and drive by the pivot-post, he fakes, and feeds one of them a flip pass. The player receiving the ball drives for the basket, or pulls up and jump shoots, or he passes off to his teammate or back to the pivot-post player, who moves to follow the play after he feeds off. If the first play is by the second and fourth side, the next play will be by the first and third line. The player who passes to the pivot-post player has the priority of the first cut by the post. Player 2 could pass directly to 5, in which case he would fake left, and veer right over the post. Player 3 would hold after faking right, and then cut over the post off the tail of 2.

LOB PASSES

Lob passes are somewhat dangerous to use. Such passes, by the nature of the lob, take longer to get to the receiver, and give defensive players time to intercept, or to get into position to draw a charging foul from the receiver. It is hard to judge the timing of the pass and to get accuracy with it; it requires practice.

When to Use the Lob Pass

1. It can be used in getting the ball into the pivot-post player, especially when he is coming out aggressively to meet the pass.
2. It can be a very valuable pass to use in feeding the post player who has reversed a defensive player playing in front of him.
3. It is a good pass to use when any player has reversed his defensive player and has the floor clear ahead of him.
4. Sometimes it can be used to hit a player out in front on a fast break.
5. It is a pass that can be used to inbound the ball on some out-of-bounds plays around the offensive basket when the team needs to take advantage of a player with extreme height or exceptional jumping ability.

Habit Drills to Teach the Lob Pass

Many of the passing drills already given can be used to incorporate the lob pass. The circle drills and the four corner passing drills can be used. The Split the Post drill given in Diagram 1-24 can also include designated times and situations to use the lob pass.

SPECIAL PASSES

All passes should be taught even though they may be little used. Some of the little used passes that need to be reviewed and taught at times are the one-hand underhand passes, two-handed underhand passes, the side-arm hook passes, back hand flip passes, over the shoulder passes, special flips, the drop pass, the roll pass, and the behind-the-back passes. Some of these, especially the behind-the-back passes, are what could be classified as advanced techniques and are to be used only in special situations.

The more of these special passes that a team and its players can master, the better it will be. The team should strive to learn all of them, and then must understand when and how each pass should be used.

Habit Drills to Teach Special Passes

The special situation passes can be worked into the various passing drills previously given. The behind-the-back pass can be used in the drills given in Diagrams 1-15, 1-18, and 1-19.

Drills for Teaching the Dribble

THE DRIBBLE PLAY

Dribbling will do the player more all around good than anything else. The dribble is the best ball handling drill and because of this, practice sessions should include lots of dribbling work. Dribbling brings out the individuality of a player and can be used often in a close game. It is a good tool to use in a delayed offensive maneuver. In the closing minutes of a ball game, a good dribbler is important, especially in a close game, and the chances are that a team with a good dribbler in this situation will be able to protect its lead.

The dribble is useful in teaching the feel of the ball and in developing body balance, grace, and poise, perhaps more than any other drill or phase of work in the game.

The dribble can be easily overdone, however. A player who masters the dribble technique quickly and easily tends to become individualistic, and to monopolize the play. Nothing can be more destructive to team play than the excessive dribbler. While you must teach the dribble and perfect the dribble techniques of all your players, you are also faced with the task of teaching the proper use of the dribble—what it is for, and when it should be used.

When to Use the Dribble

1. Use the dribble to take the ball away from the defensive basket before the man with the ball can be tied up by opponents. Ordinarily, only one or two dribbles are necessary to get away from this danger area, and then the dribbler should pass to a teammate as soon as possible.

2. Dribbling is used to advance the ball to the defense, and at times to draw a defensive player away from the basket.

3. It may be used on short drives toward the basket to get away from an opponent. The best example of this is when a player has received the ball from the pivot player as he cuts by on a short drive to the basket.

4. The dribble should be used to advance the ball on a fast break when the player with the ball is ahead of his teammates.

5. The dribble may be useful in getting the ball away from congested areas, after jump balls, for example.

6. It may be used to get away from an opponent or to make a clear drive to the basket when no one is ahead of the dribbler.

7. The dribble can be used to delay the play so that proper timing can be secured in order to get a pass to a teammate.

8. *The dribble should never be used if a pass can be made.*

Coaching Points for the Dribble

The dribble probably has more coaching points than any other fundamental in basketball.

1. Start the dribble well out from the body so as to get a running start, and so that the player will not bump into the ball with the body, knee, or toe and lose control of it. In a fast get-away, place the ball out four to six feet in making the start.

2. *Feel and push the ball with the finger tips.* Do not slap at the ball or bat the ball. The ball is bounced. The fingers should be cupped and well spread as the ball is bounced with a wrist motion, with the elbows and forearms rising and falling very little.

3. *Keep the head up*, with the eyes on the field ahead. This is the most important fundamental of the dribble. The player who dribbles with his head down, never being able to see his open teammates, is a detriment to the team.

4. To dribble for speed, and with a clear field ahead, dribble high—about hip to waist high.

5. When protection is needed, dribble low—not over knee high—keeping the body low to protect the dribble. To get the body low, flex the knees and keep the hips low. To a certain extent the height of the dribble will depend upon the height of the player. Tall players generally have more trouble dribbling for protection.

6. *Protect the dribble with the body.* When dribbling, always keep the body between the opponent and the ball, or keep the ball to the side away from the opponent. In order to do this the player must be able to dribble with either hand.

7. The dribbler should always be in position so that he can stop, pivot, turn, shoot, or pass. When he stops he should be in a crouched position over the ball and not upright. This will give the necessary protection to the ball and will prevent the dribbler from moving his pivot foot.

8. When making a pivot, and starting a dribble, never start a dribble on the inside—use the outside hand and start the dribble so that the body will be between the opponent and the ball.

9. The shoulders are a great factor in protecting the dribble. They can be kept ducking and dipping to protect the ball.

10. When dribbling on the right side of the floor and going to the right, keep the ball on the right side of the body, and when going left, dribble with the left hand and keep the ball on the left side of the body. Make it a rule to give the ball protection at all times.

11. When starting a dribble, be sure that the ball leaves the hand before the pivot foot is lifted from the floor. (It is a rule violation, traveling, to lift the pivot foot before the ball leaves the hand to start a dribble.)

12. The player must be able to pass off from the dribble while going at high speed, without hesitating or

breaking his stride. This is important—for the instant a teammate is open, the dribbler must deliver the ball to him. (This is definitely an advanced skill, and must be developed.) You will need special drills to do this—with a little practice the players will pick this skill up readily.

Habit Drills for Teaching the Dribble

1. **Two-Line Whistle Drills: Diagram 2-1.** Since you use a lot of two-line drills to teach passing, two-line dribbling drills will fit into the drill routine very well. The players line up in two lines—the full width of the court or more if space is available. All the players on one side of the floor have a ball, and when you blow the whistle once, they come out dribbling toward the opposite sideline with the right hand. When you blow the whistle twice, the players stop, flutter, and back up with the dribble. When one whistle is repeated, the players change hands with the dribble by doing a cross-over from the right to the left hand, and advancing toward the opposite sideline again. Repeat a series of one and two whistles in a series of stops, starts, fluttering, backing up, crossing over from right to left, or left to right as they advance across the floor. Always—one whistle is GO, and if out on the floor, cross-over and GO, while two toots of the whistle is STOP, flutter, fake, and back up with the dribble. As the players near the opposite sideline, blow the whistle three times and the player dribbling now passes the ball while on the move to a teammate waiting on the sideline. Now the drill is repeated with the players next in line dribbling over to the opposite sideline and returning. All the while the drill is going on, check the players on their dribbling techniques—head up, eyes on the field down floor, dribble protected, and on the cross-over from one hand to the other, the ducking of the shoulder and a cross-over step to give complete protection to the dribble.

2. **Dribble—Meet Opposition Drill: Diagram 2-2.** This is also a two-line drill, devised to polish the dribbling technique of meeting an opponent, faking to go around in one direction, but crossing over from one hand to the other and going around on the opposite side. The players in line Number 1 all have a ball. The players in line Number 2 all advance to meet the dribbler somewhere near the middle of the court, giving the dribbler only passive resistance. On your signal, the players in line Number 1 all dribble out till they meet the opposition—

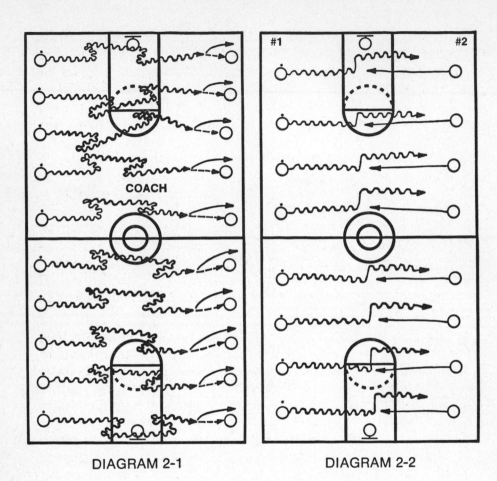

DIAGRAM 2-1   DIAGRAM 2-2

dribbling with the right hand. When they approach the
opposition player, they fake a movement to the right as if to go
around the opposition to the right, but with a change of pace or a
slowing up somewhat, the player dribbles up to the opposition
with the right hand, dribbling low for protection, and after
faking the dribble drive to the right, now whips the ball from
the right to the left hand, and ducks the right shoulder for
protection of the dribble. As the ball is crossed from one hand to
the other, the player also makes a cross-over step with the right
left across in front of the left leg. When this movement is made,
the ball now being dribbled with the left hand should be far
enough out and well protected by the dribbler's shoulder and
body so that the opposition defensive player cannot get to the
dribble. The player now dribbles around the opposition to the
left, and on over to the opposite side line, turns around, and still

dribbling with the left hand, dribbles back to the opposition player at the middle of the court. He now approaches the opposition player dribbling with his left hand, and as he approaches, whips the ball from the left hand to the right hand (after a fake left), ducks the left shoulder, does the cross-over step with the left foot and leg, and dribbles around the opposition to the right.

The players now exchange positions, with the Number 2 line becoming the dribblers, and the Number 1 line becoming the opposition. All the while you should check the techniques of faking, changing pace, crossing over with the hand from right to left, and left to right, the ducking of the shoulder and the cross-over step to keep the body between the dribble and the opponent. This drill develops, especially in the young player, the habit and the technique of protecting the dribble and maneuvering so that the body is between the ball and the opponent on the dribble.

3. The Chair Maze Dribbling Drill: Diagram 2-3. The purpose of this drill is to develop the use of either hand in dribbling, and to teach the player to switch hands on the dribble and to protect the ball when driving by an opponent. Three chairs can be placed in a row as shown about 10 to 12 feet apart and in as many rows as desired. If desired, other players may stand where the chairs are placed and give passive resistance to the dribbler as he approaches and drives around. (The players could be used for the maze instead of the chairs.) Each of the six dribbling players has a partner. Dribble relays could be held after techniques are developed, but when speed is emphasized, the players tend to neglect the proper technique of changing hands on the dribble, and protecting the ball as they drive around the chair object, or player, as it may be. If the player approaches the chair dribbling with the right hand, as the approach is made, the left leg should be back, and the ball should be whipped from the right hand to the left close to the body. As the ball is changed from the right to the left, the player makes a cross-over step with the right leg across in front of the left leg, at the same time ducking the shoulder for protection of the ball. The ball should be kept low and always with the body between the ball and the chair or opponent. After the above move, the player dribbles around the object (chair) with the left hand, and now approaches the second object dribbling with the left hand where the procedure is repeated, shifting the ball from the left to the right hand, and doing the cross-over step with the left leg and foot, going around the object dribbling with the right hand. Each player dribbles down each line and back in this manner. When the player returns, the partner now does the routine.

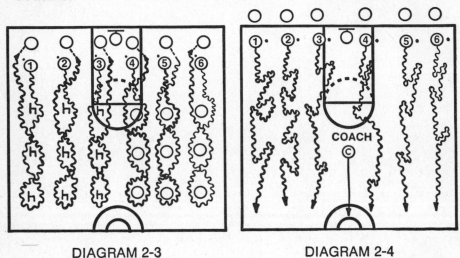

DIAGRAM 2-3   DIAGRAM 2-4

4. Follow the Coach: Diagram 2-4. In this drill, six players line up as shown, with one knee on the floor while dribbling with one hand. The players are given sight signals or clues on signal as to what they are to do, so they must keep their eyes on you out in front of them. First they will dribble with one hand, with one knee on the floor. At your prearranged signal, they change hand and knee, or come up on both feet and dribble up and down the floor, stopping, going back to one knee, dribbling with one finger, standing up again, forward, backward, changing hands on the dribble, changing pace, and so forth. This drill gives you a good clue as to how well the players keep their eyes on the floor ahead of them, as the quickness of their response to your signals will indicate how well they are watching and observing the floor ahead of them. Some players will be slower in their response to your signals, indicating that they respond to the teammates' reaction rather than your signals. All signals should be given with your hands and by what you do or indicate with your hands, such as down on one knee, change hands, dribble with first or second finger only, stand up, one finger GO, two fingers, STOP, three fingers, back up, down, up, etc. You can also indicate with motion of hands and arms when you want them to speed up, change pace, slow down, change hands, etc. This drill can be started with the players on the floor on both knees, and by having the players dribble with one finger, rotating the dribble with the first three fingers, then shifting to one knee, dribbling with all fingers, standing up to dribble, etc. The dribbling with the fingers one at a time will develop the feel of the ball being in the finger tips.

5. Tag Dribble Drill: Diagram 2-5. This drill can be done in two ways. The players usually like the drill. Place all the squad members on one half of the court. Designate two players with a ball to be "IT." They dribble and attempt to tag one of the other players who are confined to the limits of the half-court. If one of the other players is tagged by one of the "IT" players, they exchange places and the tagged player now takes the ball and becomes an "IT" dribbler.

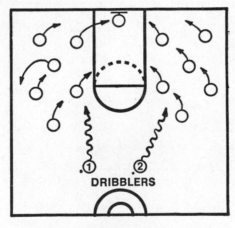

DIAGRAM 2-5

Another way to do the drill is to give each player on the squad a ball—if there are enough balls for the squad. Again, designate two players to be "IT." The "IT" players must hold one hand above the head while dribbling, and they attempt to tag one of the other players, all of whom are dribbling within the confines of the half-court. If an "IT" player tags another dribbler, the tagged dribbler becomes an "IT" dribbler, exchanging positions. Now the new "IT" player must raise one hand above his head, and attempt to tag another dribbler.

Variety and interest can be added to the drill by having "reverse dribbling" days, during which time those players who are right handed must dribble with their left hand, and those who are left handed must dribble with the right hand.

6. Dribble Lay-Up Relay: Diagram 2-6. In this drill the players dribble the length of the floor and using each circle as an object, they dribble with the outside hand as they go down the floor, and around the three court circles. Each player starts out with the right hand, going around the first circle, then as the middle circle is approached, changes over to the left hand, and goes around it, then changes over to the right for the last circle, and a lay-up shot. The drill may be run as a team relay, with each player required to make a lay-up shot after dribbling the length of the floor around the circles as shown, and then return the length of the floor in the same way, and make a lay-up shot on the return. The team that finishes first is the winner, of course.

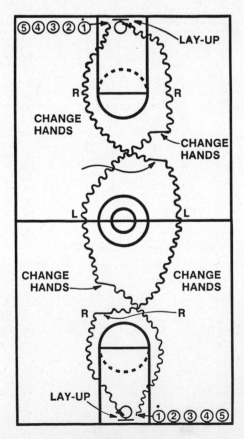

DIAGRAM 2-6

7. Four-Corner Dribble-Pivot Drill: Diagram 2-7. The players line up in the four corners as shown. The first player in each line has a ball. The manager or coach, standing at a central point from the four corners, gives a signal to start. The players in each line dribble directly at the manager or coach. Just before the dribblers reach him at the center point, the manager/coach calls out "RIGHT" or he may call out "LEFT." If he calls "LEFT," the players execute a one count dribble stop, pick.up the ball, and do a *reverse pivot* on their left foot, and pass the ball to the next player in line on the corner to their immediate LEFT. If the manager/coach should call "RIGHT," each dribbler executes a *reverse pivot* on his right foot and passes to the next player on the right. The next players in line repeat the drill. The dribbler goes to the end of the line to which he passes. This drill gives the players good work in dribbling, executing a quick stop, pass and pivot maneuver. You should check the players' footwork on the stop and pivot as well as their pivot and pass move.

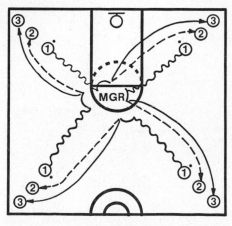

DIAGRAM 2-7

8. Circle Dribbling Drill: Diagram 2-8. Most basketball courts, in addition to the regular court circle markings, will have side courts and other auxiliary courts with free throw and jumping circles marked. These can be used to develop dribblers by dividing the squad into pairs and using the circles available, with one player being the dribbler and the other the defensive player. The offensive player must stay in the circle and dribble, using either hand and all his dribbling techniques to protect the ball from the defensive player. The defensive player should aggressively pursue the dribbler while the dribbler, with head up and eyes on the defensive player, constantly manipulates the body between the ball and the defensive player, giving good protection to the dribble. The players exchange positions after a determined time limit, or if the defensive player succeeds in deflecting the dribble, the players exchange positions.

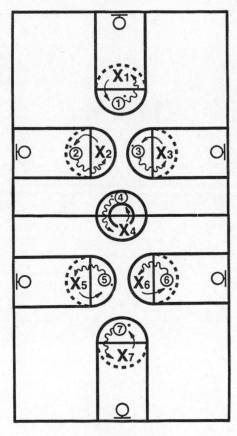

DIAGRAM 2-8

9. Roll Ball Out—Dribble in Shoot Drill: Diagram 2-9.

The players line up just outside the shooting range of the basket. Player 1, who has a ball, does a reverse pivot, keeping his body low on the pivot, and then, starting the ball well out from the body to get a good fast start, does a driving dribble into the basket and does a lay-up shot. After the shot, 1 recovers the ball, and *rolls* it out to the next player who repeats the reverse pivot and dribble drive to the basket. More than one ball may be used if desired, but if this is done, each player should start on a signal or be careful to take his proper turn to prevent crashing in around the basket.

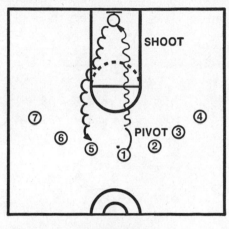

DIAGRAM 2-9   DIAGRAM 2-10

10. The Dribble Change-Up Drill: Diagram 2-10. In this drill the players line up in two lines as shown, one on the right side of the free throw lane, and the other on the left side. The players dribble as shown, the line dribbling to the right dribbles with the right hand and the line dribbling to the left dribbles with the left hand, until a point is reached near the sideline and the free throw line extended. When this point is reached, the dribbler stops, loosens up, or backs up slightly, continuing to dribble, and then does a fake as if to drive, and changes dribbling hands and direction as a cross-over step is made with a dip of the near shoulder (the one next to the defense). Now the dribbler makes a sudden dash with a change of pace on the dribble and drives in for a lay-up shot. Each player recovers his own shot, and rolls the ball out to the next player in line. The players change lines to get practice going both directions.

11. Dribble-Drive the Defense Drill: Diagram 2-11. This one-on-one setup is used to develop a feint in one direction, followed by a cross-over to elude the defense, and a drive for the basket. The defensive player, X1 is placed at the free throw line area facing the player with the ball. Player 1, with the ball, is instructed to dribble fast at the defensive player, and as he nears that area, he fakes, feints, or angles either right or left to draw the defensive player out of position. If the defensive player pulls with the feint, the dribbler then slows up just enough to get the defensive player with him, and then shifts the ball to the other hand on a cross-over away from the defense as a cross-over step is made, and drives for the open spot to shoot. The shooter recovers his own shot and rolls the ball out to the next in line.

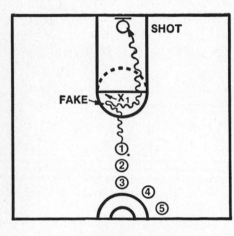

DIAGRAM 2-11

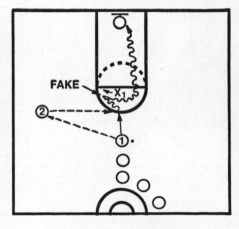

DIAGRAM 2-12

12. Pass, Return, Dribble, Drive Drill: Diagram 2-12. In this drill a third line is added. Player 1, with the ball, passes to 2, who may be either to the right or left of defensive X1 at the free throw line. After passing to 2, 1 advances toward the defensive player X1, and as he approaches the area near X1, O2 returns a pass to O1, who now starts with a dribble to the right or left and just enough to get X1 on the move. When a defensive declaration is made by X1, then O1 changes hands on his dribble with a cross-over step and drives to the area near the basket for a shot or lay-up. The player with the ball may take other options, such as driving straight in for a shot, if the defense refuses to declare on the first fake or dribble move, or if the defense drops back, he may shoot and follow hard on the rebound. If the defense counters every move, O1 can pass back to O2, cut for a return pass, fake and try to outmaneuver X1 again if he is sticking tight.

13. Four Ball, Four-Corner Dribble Drill: Diagram 2-13. In this drill the players line up in the four corners of a half-court situation as shown. The first player in each corner has a ball. Upon a starting signal they all start for the corner on their right with a dribble. Just before reaching the player in line in the next corner, the dribbler picks up the ball and does a one count stop, executes a reverse pivot on the right foot and hands the ball to the next player in the line. All the players dribble around the corners in this manner until you call "REVERSE." When this signal is given, the dribbler reverses direction and dribbles to the corner on his left, stops and does the reverse pivot on his left foot before handing off to the next player in line. After handing the ball off to the next player in line, the dribbler goes to the end of that line.

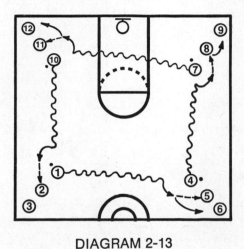

DIAGRAM 2-13

14. Speed Dribble Relay Drill: Diagram 2-14. This drill will help in developing speed on the dribble. Two teams of equal numbers are formed. They line up at each basket as shown. The first player in each line has a ball. On a signal, the first player dribbles the length of the court at full speed, makes a lay-up shot, and returns to the basket from which he started; he must make a shot there also. The next player in line now makes the trip. The team that finishes first is the winner. This drill usually generates a lot of exciting competition and can be a relaxer for the team when a fun night is needed. The player must make the lay-up shot at each end of the floor before the next player can proceed to do his trip on the relay.

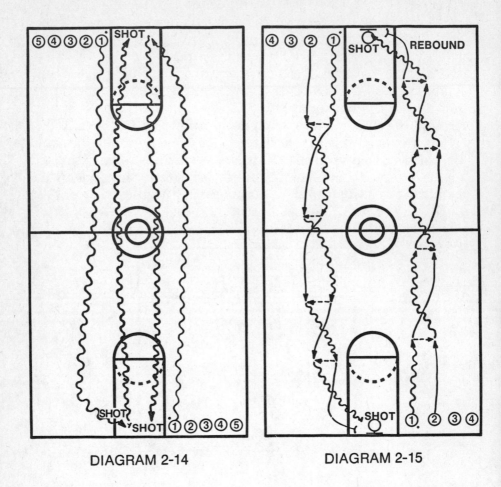

DIAGRAM 2-14   DIAGRAM 2-15

15. Trail the Dribbler Drill: Diagram 2-15. Often in basketball, the best play a dribbler can make is to pass to a trailing player. The dribbler must be aware of what is going on in front, at the sides, and behind him. This drill is to help develop an awareness of a teammate trailer, and to develop the skill of delivering either a drop-pass or a behind the back bounce pass to a trailing teammate. The players line up at each end of the court as shown. The first player in each line starts out fast with a dribble. The second player trails him closely, and at times lets the dribbler know by word of mouth whether he is on his right or left. After the dribbler has gone about one third of the length of the court, he slows up, and then either drop-passes to his trailing teammate, or gives him a behind the back bounce pass. The trailer now picks up the ball and becomes the dribbler, and goes about the same distance where the exchange is repeated. This exchange is repeated by each line about three or four times in going the length of the court, and the last one to become the dribbler drives in for a driving lay-up shot. The trailer recovers the rebound and delivers the ball to the next player in line, and both go to the end of the line at the opposite end of the court from where they started.

16. Pass-Off While Dribbling at Full Speed: Diagram 2-16. A dribbling technique that must be developed as soon as possible in every player is the ability to pass the ball to an open teammate while dribbling on the run at full speed. Unless this is drilled and worked upon, few players will develop this ability. This is definitely what might be termed an advanced skill or technique, but with some drill work it will be a skill that can be

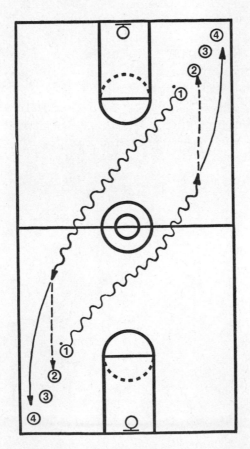

DIAGRAM 2-16

developed very rapidly in many players. In the beginning, in doing drill work on this skill, emphasize the necessity of making quick contact with both hands to make the pass-off from a dribble drive situation. Later some players can flip the pass-off effectively with one hand, either right or left, in an instant to a teammate who is open to receive a pass. In this drill, the players line up at opposite corners of the court. The first player in each line has a ball, and starts for the opposite corner with a fast driving dribble. When reaching the area near the court division line, the dribbler passes off from the driving dribble to the next player in line at the opposite corner, and goes to the end of the line. The next player in line repeats the process. Using this drill, a lot of dribbling pass-off at full speed exchanges can be done in a short period of time. To develop the pass-off from a dribble with the left hand, have the drill run from the opposite corners, and the dribbler must dribble out with the left hand and make the pass-off from the dribble with the left hand.

   17. Pass-Off from Dribble at Full Speed to Player on Reverse: Diagram 2-17. This is a further development of the skill explained in Diagram 2-16—the skill of passing off from a driving dribble to the teammate who is open. The players line up as shown, and O1 starts out with a driving dribble from the left side of the floor toward the right side. Player O4 fakes out to meet O1, and then reverses his direction toward the basket. O1 must pass-off to O4 from his dribble drive. He must deliver the ball instantly as O4 makes his reverse. Player O1 may make a direct pass or a bounce pass, and O4 will take the ball and drive

DIAGRAM 2-17

in for a shot. After running the drill from left to right, run the drill from right to left, and insist that the dribbler dribble with the left hand and make the delivery from the driving dribble with his left hand. In dribbling with the left hand, most players will need to make ball contact with both hands in delivering the ball on the pass-off. The players exchange positions on the drill so that all get work at both lines.

The Shot—
Drills to
Teach Shooting

SPECIAL NOTES ON SHOOTING

There are a few things that are important in shooting in basketball—important for any kind of shot.

1. *Finger Tip Control.* The tactile sense of the ball on a shot will come from the finger tips. Without this essential sensitive touch, the player never becomes a good shooter. The player who is a "palmer" never is even a fair shooter.

2. *Body Balance.* In order to be a good shot, the player must have good body control, and this implies balance and control of the center of gravity. With today's shooters there are many who release the shot from positions that appear "out of balance," but when analyzed closely, these players actually have perfect control and balance.

3. *Follow-Through.* A perfect follow-through is a necessity for becoming an artist at shooting. It is the final impetus on the ball that gives it the direction it needs to go into the basket. Who has ever seen a good shooter who did not have a good follow-through on the shot?

4. *The Target.* The player must look at the basket—before, during, and after the shot. The EYES *must* be focused on the target. This seems to be very important. Although outstanding coaches seem to disagree as to just what the target should be, all suggested focal points have merit. Focal points advocated by coaches range from the front of the rim to the hole, a point just over the rim, the center of the basket or the hole, a point six inches above the basket, and the center of the back of the rim. Arguments can be given for each focal point, but it all comes down to the fact that the shooting player must have his eyes focused on a target if he is to be consistent in his scoring.

5. *Confidence and Relaxation.* The player must be relaxed. Some refer to it as "controlled tension." It all amounts to a form of muscular effort without interference by tension—a relaxed effort. To accomplish this the player must have confidence. He knows the shot will go in, or come close.

6. The ball must be held out away from the body a reasonable distance (not an extreme or exaggerated distance, but well out) and high. Depending on the type of shot, the height should range from a point just under the chin to well above the head on the jump shot.

7. The jump shot is the dominant shot in the game today. It must be shot from well above the head.

8. Because of the development of the jump shot, some of the other shots that still have merit have become "lost arts." The best examples are the hook shot, set shots, and even the lay-up. These shots still have a place in the game and should be taught and developed.

SHOTS TO TEACH IN BASKETBALL

There are at leave five fundamental shots used in basketball today. They are:

1. The lay-up shot
2. The jump shot
3. The one-hand set shot
4. The hook shot
5. The free throw

The proper techniques of executing each will be presented in the order given, along with coaching points and habit drill for teaching and coaching. The two-handed set shot, long a dominant shot in the game, is now extinct. Due to the present day dominance of the jump shot, most of the other shots are becoming lost arts. The one-hand set and the one-hand driving jump in the air shot, which came into popular use following its introduction by Hank Luisetti and the Stanford University team during the mid 1930's, has now become practically extinct, due to the jump shot craze. Even free-throw shots are now being done with a jump shot, and many players in the game today cannot execute a lay-up shot properly, but must stop and jump off both feet to do the shot at close range.

Actually all shots could be categorized under four headings. They are:

1. *Under-Basket Shots.* This would include the lay-up shots, and the close in hook shots and other variations that result from driving into the basket from different angles and directions.

2. *The Pivot-Series, and/or Hook Shots.* These shots would include shots around the free-throw lane area that come from turn-around spin movements in pivot-post play, and hook shots that come from this type of play also.

3. *Floor Shots.* This would include the jump shot from out on the floor, and whatever set shots from a distance players might execute today. Aside from the jump shot, such shots are seldom seen in the game today.

4. *Free Throws.* Any shot from the free-throw situation. Today these shots range from various coaching techniques to the complete freedom of "let the player shoot what he does best."

THE LAY-UP SHOT

This is the shot that should be used in shooting close in, near the basket. It is usually executed after a drive or on the tail of a fast-break situation. The shooter "lays" the ball up against the backboard a few inches above the rim so that it falls down through the net. There are two basic types of lay-up shots. They are:

1. The underhand lay-up
2. The overhand lay-up

In the underhand shot the shooter lays the ball against the backboard *with the back of his hand facing away from his body.* It is a shoveling and/or a lifting technique.

In the overhand lay-up shot, the ball is brought to a position above the head, *with the back of the hand facing the shooter,* and the ball is pushed to the basket or the spot on the backboard. This shot gives more power and can be used where extra strength is needed. The power play of the shot makes its execution more stable when the shooter is fouled, or jostled in his movements. The young players who lack strength find this shot easier to get up to the basket.

The underhand lay-up shot gives a softer touch to the shot and can be used when a driving player cannot check his speed and he needs to lay the ball up softly.

Coaching Points for the Lay-Up Shot

1. The player must develop footwork that will enable him to drive at full speed to the basket without breaking stride.

2. The take-off on this shot is the most important factor. The distance the player takes off from the basket will depend upon the stride. Most high school players take off four or five feet from the basket.

3. On the take-off, jump as high as possible. Jump for HEIGHT, not distance.

4. When shooting the right-handed shot, take off on the *left foot,* raising the right knee and leg in the air to about a 90-degree angle with the body. This gives balance. On the left-handed shot reverse this procedure, taking off on the right foot.

5. Prior to the take-off the shooter will pick up the ball in both hands; if shooting right-handed, the left hand is used to steady and control the ball until it reaches a point slightly above the shoulders, at which time the left hand is released.

6. Release the ball at the highest point of the jump.

7. Do not English (spin) the ball. Just lay the ball up there softly off the tips of the fingers to a spot about ten to twelve inches above the basket and about two to four inches to the near side of the middle of the basket.

8. *Release the ball straight from the eyes.* On the *overhand* lay-up, the back of the hand should be toward the player's face, with the palm of the hand facing directly toward the basket. Finish by rolling the ball over the tip of the fingers, and as the ball is released, use a finger snap.

9. On the *underhand* lay-up, the shooting hand should move under the ball as the player starts to go upward. Roll the ball off the fingertips with a soft backspin.

10. The follow-through of the whole body should be in direct line with the basket, and the body in perfect balance.

Habit Drills for Teaching the Lay-Up Shot

1. First, have the beginner go through the motions of shooting the lay-up shot without the ball. Pretending to have the ball, the player takes one step with the foot opposite the shooting hand, jumps high into the air, and does the mechanics of the shot. This enables the player to concentrate solely on the footwork. Have the player do this both right and left. Players should be taught to shoot the lay-up shot both right- and left-handed. Players who have trouble executing the off-hand shot usually have trouble because of faulty footwork. Once the proper footwork is mastered, the right-handed player will have no trouble shooting a left-handed lay-up shot and vice versa; ambidexterity on the lay-up shot will develop easily.

2. Next, give the player a basketball and have him shoot the lay-up after taking one step with the foot opposite the shooting hand (sometimes referred to as the inside foot). Then have the player take three steps without dribbling and shoot, jumping off the foot opposite the shooting hand. Do this both right and left.

3. Next drill, have the shooter take one dribble and plant the foot opposite the shooting hand in the desired take-off position near the basket. Jump for height on the shot. Do this both right and left. Repeat this 10 to 15 times for both right and left sides.

4. **Single Line Lay-Up Shot Drill: Diagram 3-1.** The simplest lay-up shot drill of all—the players form one line. The first player dribbles in to shoot, the next player recovers the rebound and rolls the ball out to the next player in line who repeats the process. After dribbling in from one side, they next

form a line on the opposite side, and at various positions on the floor so that they get practice coming in on the shot from all sides and angles toward the basket. The players change positions so that the shooter and rebounder rotate positions.

DIAGRAM 3-1   DIAGRAM 3-2

5. Two-Line Lay-Up Shot Drill: Diagram 3-2. The players line up in two lines on opposite sides of the court as shown. One line takes the ball and dribbles in to shoot a driving lay-up shot. The other line rebounds the shot and rolls the ball out to the next player in line. Each player in the shooting line will dribble in and do the lay-up shot, first down the left side, then down the right side, and then down the middle. When coming in from the left side, shoot left-handed. From the right side, shoot right-handed. Practice coming down the middle, as well as driving in from various angles. The players exchange lines.

6. Dribble Straight in—Shoot Lay-Up Shot Drills: Diagrams 3-3 and 3-4. In Diagram 3-3, the players line up in the middle of the floor and dribble-drive straight in for the lay-up shot, coming straight in at the basket. The player should bank the shot coming straight in unless the coach prefers that the ball be shot just over the front rim of the basket. After the shot the player recovers the ball and rolls it out to the next in line. More than one ball may be used in the drill if desired.

In Diagram 3-4, the drill begins the same as the one in Diagram 3-3. A driver education pylon is placed about five to six feet in front of the basket. The player dribbles straight in at the basket, but first he dribbles in with the right hand, and as the

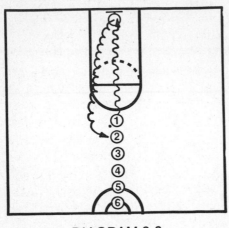
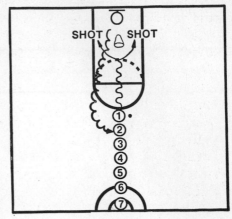

DIAGRAM 3-3   DIAGRAM 3-4

pylon is approached, he picks up the ball and takes a cross-over step with the left foot and leg in front of the body, and goes up for the lay-up shot, pulling to the right of the basket. The shot should be banked. After running the drill to the right, change so that now the player dribbles in with the left hand, and as the pylon is approached, he picks up the ball, and now does the cross-over step with the right foot and leg, leaping high in the air off the right foot and turning to do the lay-up from the cross-over step with the left hand. This pulls the player to the left of the center of the basket. The shot should be banked.

7. **The 1-4 Lay-Up Shot Drills: Diagrams 3-5 and 3-6.** This drill is called the 1-4 drill because the first and fourth player will come up for a shot on the drill. Furthermore, they will automatically rotate in their turns to shoot *unless* the number of players in the line is divisible by three. If the number of players in the line is a number divisible by three, the players will have to rotate positions to take turns shooting, rebounding, and passing. The player starting the drill dribbles in and shoots a lay-up shot from the right side; the second player follows to rebound the shot or pick it out of the net, and passes the ball to the third player, O3 in this case, who has gone to the free-throw line to receive the ball. Player O3, upon receiving the ball, executes a reverse pivot (the pivot is optional) and passes to O4 driving in for a lay-up shot. The ball should be passed to O4 so that he receives the ball just as he is ready to step with his left foot and go up on the lay-up shot. Insist that O2 use good form in grabbing the rebound and taking the ball out of the net, and in

making a good pass to O3. Insist that O3 pass properly to O4 driving for the basket. After running the drill from one side of the floor, the players reform the line on the opposite side of the court, where the drill will be repeated from the left side, and from where left-handed lay-up shots must be made. If the last player in line on the right side is a shooter, then the first player on the left side will fill right in as the next rebounder, etc., so that the line will flow automatically from one side to the other. After running the drill from the right and left sides, run it straight down the middle, and then down the middle with the shooter crossing over, first with the left foot for a right-handed shot, followed by the cross-over with the right foot and a left-handed shot. Next, run the drill from various angles and approaches to the basket. This drill is a good fast-moving drill and requires accurate passing and timing by the players, who will enjoy making it work.

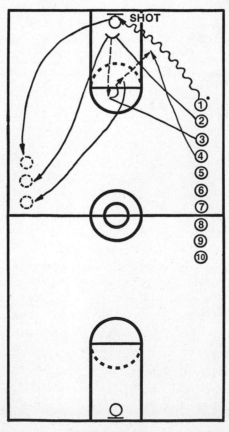

DIAGRAM 3-5

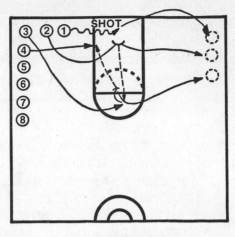

DIAGRAM 3-6

Diagram 3-6 shows the 1-4 lay-up drill being run from the corner and along the baseline. Again, the first player starts the drill by dribbling in to shoot. Player O2 rebounds the ball, and passes to O3, who has gone to the free-throw line. Upon receiving the ball, O3 does a reverse pivot (optional) and will pass to the next player, O4, driving in for a shot from this angle and approach to the basket. From this angle the drill should be done two ways. FIRST, the passer hits the shooter EARLY on his approach to the basket, and the shooter will, when coming from the left side, bank the shot with the right hand. When coming in from the right side on the early pass, the player will shoot with the left hand, banking the shot. SECOND, the drill from this angle should be done with the ball being passed to the shooter LATE, or as he arrives under the basket. In this case the shooter, when coming in from the left side, will do a reverse lay-up, planting his left foot and turning the body as he goes up on the shot to bank the underneath shot with his right hand as he comes under and turns. After running the drill from the left side, the players next form the line on the right side. When coming in from the right side, the shot is to be made with the left hand, both on the *early* and *late* pass situations.

8. **Three-Line Lay-Up Shot Drill: Diagram 3-7.** The players form three lines as shown. The ball starts with the middle line, and the middle line players will be the shooters.

Player O3 breaks down floor to a point near the free-throw line extended. Player O2, starting with the ball, passes to O3, who passes to O1, who has cut to a point on the opposite side of the floor and somewhat lower. After passing to O3, O2 fakes a drive straight in, and then cuts off O3 and goes to the basket where he receives a pass from O1 for the lay-up shot. Player O1 rebounds the shot, and passes the ball back out to the next player in the O2 line. Player O3 goes to the end of the O2 line, O2 goes to the O1 line, and O1 goes to the O3 line. The drill can be reversed to the other side for the left-handed lay-up shot.

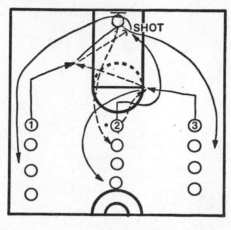

DIAGRAM 3-7

9. Down the Outside Drill: Diagram 3-8. The players line up in two lines on opposite sides of the floor as shown. Starting with two balls in each line, the players dribble in for a lay-up shot, taking turns. The player on the right side dribbles in with his left hand, faking straight in, then veering to his left, dribbles across the floor just outside the free-throw circle, and down the floor just outside the free-throw lane. He shoots the shot from just outside the lane with the left hand, banking the shot. The players on the left side of the floor do the same thing from the opposite side of the floor, but dribble with the right hand, and down the right side of the lane, shooting with the right hand. Each player recovers his own shot and rolls the ball out to the next in line and then exchanges sides.

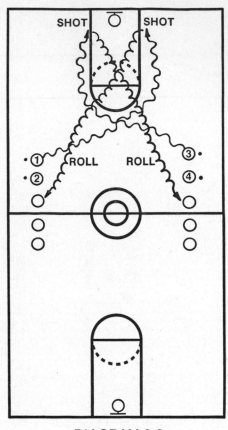

DIAGRAM 3-8

10. The Air Dummy Drill: Diagram 3-9. On this drill, get a few football "air dummies" for whatever number of baskets you will be using in the drill. One player, or the manager, or the coach stands near the basket with an "air dummy." The players line up on one side of the floor, and take turns dribbling into the basket for a lay-up shot. As the player comes near the basket, or as he goes up for the shot, the person with the dummy hits the shooter. The air dummy strike should be timed so as to be a surprise. The idea is to get the shooter used to contact and to train him to take contact without losing concentration on the shot. After dribbling in from the right side, the players line up on the left, then down the middle, and also coming from the baseline and at other angles driving to the basket. The air dummy could be used in some of the previously given drills, such as the one given in Diagram 3-8.

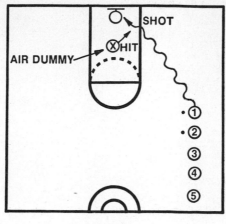

DIAGRAM 3-9

THE JUMP SHOT

The jump shot is the most effective and potent shot in basketball today; no other shot has changed the game to the extent that this shot has changed it. It is the most difficult of all shots to defense or guard, if executed properly. There are only about four things that can be done to defense the shot. They are:

1. Prevent the player from getting the ball.
2. When and if he does get the ball, drive him to his least favored shooting spots to shoot it.
3. When the player goes up to shoot, belly-button in on him and move a hand in front of his eyes and face.
4. Shout at him—distract him with the voice and hands.

To properly defense the shot the defensive player must know when the player is going to shoot and be able to jump up with him, and go as high as he does—a very difficult feat, and an impossible one if the shooter has good head and shoulder fakes.

The player must develop the mechanics necessary to shoot the jump shot from one of three possible situations. He must be able to shoot from a stationary position, at the conclusion of a dribble, and after maneuvering his opponent so that he has received a pass. From these situations it is very important for the player to master the mechanics of proper body balance, and to be able to maintain a strong and comfortable jumping position.

Among coaches there are two schools of thought or theories about the JUMP in executing the jump shot. The first is that the shooter should jump straight up with a maximum leap, as high as possible. The second contends it is best to shoot with a lesser jump—one that will not destroy the ease and rhythm of the shot. If the maximum leap does destroy the player's rhythm and relaxation, the height should be cut down. The player's jump should be one that gives him smoothness and relaxation without tension and strain. However, in situations where the player shoots from behind a screen, he will need as much height as possible.

Coaching Points for the Jump Shot

1. The strongest jumping position is usually found to be with the feet about shoulder width apart and aligned parallel to the direction the player is facing.
2. The knees should be bent, and the weight distributed evenly over the balls of the feet if body balance is to be achieved.
3. Jump straight up as high as can be done with smoothness and relaxation.
4. Carry the ball into position above the head and shoulders with both hands.
5. If right-handed, guide the ball with the left hand, either on the bottom or slightly at the side of the ball.
6. Get the hand and fingers of the shooting arm well behind the ball.
7. Release the ball at the peak of the jump with a forearm, wrist, and finger snap (unhinging of the forearm, and a snap of the wrist and fingers).
8. A right-handed shooter will take the ball above the head, and just over the right shoulder. The left-handed shooter will carry the ball just over the left shoulder.
9. Deliver the ball softly with a high arch.
10. Follow through and go for the rebound.
11. When maneuvering to receive a pass for the jump shot, or when coming off the dribble to get the shot, the player must control his center of gravity so that he can maintain balance and get the shot off properly. The player will have a tendency to glide in the direction of

the cut after starting the jump. This is a fault to be avoided.

12. When receiving the ball on a cut, or after ending a dribble, the player must square off and turn shoulders and feet squarely to the basket. This is no problem if the cut or dribble is straight at the basket, but if the movement is lateral, the player will have to turn on his foot nearest the basket and bring the one farthest away around so as to be squared away on the shot.

Variations in the Jump Shot

There are many variations of the jump shot today. Each player has his own version to a certain extent, such as position of the off hand underneath the ball or on the side, where the ball is started, height the ball is taken above the head, point of release, etc. Each player has to do what is comfortable for him and deliver the shot that gets the best results for him.

A very popular and effective style of the jump shot is the *fade-away* jump shot. It is difficult to learn and to teach. It is also very difficult to defend. Players should learn the regular jump shot before attempting to learn the fade-away shot. On this shot the shooter should fade in a direct line away from the basket while in the air. Fading to the side is to be avoided. When fading in a straight line away from the basket the player needs to concentrate on compensating for the distance of the fade-away in a direct line from the basket. If the shooter is fading laterally as well as away, he now must compensate for the fade-away in more than one direction, and this cuts his possibilities of hitting the target by a high percentage.

Habit Drills for Teaching the Jump Shot

1. Seven Basic Spots from the Outside: Diagram 3-10. The purpose of this drill is to develop proficiency in shooting the jump shot from the seven basic spots on the outside perimeter of the shooting and scoring area and/or maneuvering and driving from these spots and getting off a shot. The coach marks the seven basic spots as shown, and the players take positions on the spots. Each player has a ball. Various drills in shooting can be held with this drill. On a signal from the coach, the players take turns shooting from a stationary position and rebounding their shots. They can then rotate positions clockwise until the players have all shot from the seven positions. Various contests can be held: who made the most baskets out of seven shots, who hit the greatest number of consecutive shots, and who was the first to hit from all seven spots consecutively. Other games: all players must make three shots in a row from each spot—the player who goes the circuit first wins; shoot ten shots from all seven spots— record the number made, and the winner, the one making the highest number of shots, is the champ for the day and is to be rewarded.

DIAGRAM 3-10

If space is scarce and not enough baskets are available, the players may work in pairs from the seven spots.

After shooting from a stationary position, the players can then start maneuvering drills from the seven spots. Taking turns, the players work various fakes and maneuvers from each spot. From these spots the coach can work in whatever individual moves, fakes, and footwork he chooses. Suggested moves and fakes could be the following:

Fake left, dribble right, go up for a shot.

Fake right, dribble left, go up for a shot.

Double fake by faking left, then right, dribble left and shoot.

Do the rocker-step series using these moves:

Step at imaginary opponent with right foot, step back, drive right and shoot.

Do the same fake with the left foot, drive left, shoot.

Step at imaginary opponent with right foot, fake with head and shoulders as if stepping back—do a burst out drive and shoot.

Do the same with the left foot.

Step at opponent with right foot, step back with a short step, cross-over step with right foot and leg in front of the body, drive left and shoot.

Do this same move with the left foot and cross over and drive right and shoot.

Fake a drive—shoot.

Using this drill, the players get familiar with shooting from these spots, and maneuvering and shooting from these basic outside operational areas. Other games and drills can be worked from these basic spots. The drill could be started by having the players fake, or do one of the other maneuvers and dribble in for a lay-up shot. (A lay-up shooting drill can be done from the seven spots.) If you wish, call out each movement or fake you want the players to do each time around, and check them on their techniques. The drill moves fast, and the players usually enjoy it, depending on the enthusiasm you can generate.

2. Seven Basic Spots from the Inside: Diagram 3-11. This drill is much the same as the one given in Diagram 3-10, except that the shooting and maneuvering is done from the so-called basic spots from the inside. The players rotate the positions and shoot jump shots from the stationary position first, and then go to the maneuvering drills from the spots. In these positions, the same maneuvering and faking moves can be done that are used in the seven spots of the outside drill, and you can add the drill of having the players start with their backs to the basket. From this position, the players from each spot turn and jump shoot, or turn and make the fakes and maneuvers used on the outside shooting drill. A quick spinner series of fakes, jab steps, and a cross-over step series can be developed from these positions also. The shots made from spots, 1, 2, 6 and 7 should be banked off the backboard. From these spots hook shots, which will be discussed later, could be developed and practiced. Suggested game: Shoot ten shots from each of the seven spots— record score—reward winner.

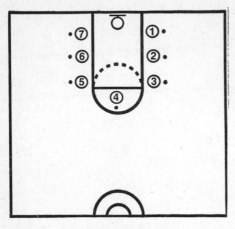

DIAGRAM 3-11

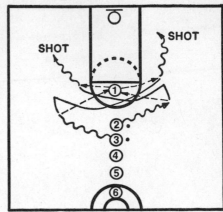

DIAGRAM 3-12

3. Pass to the High Post, Cut, Receive Pass Back—Drive Shoot: Diagram 3-12. The players line up in the middle of the court, and the first two players in line have a ball. (You can use more if you want to.) The first player takes a short driving dribble to the right or left, passes off to the high-post player in the outer half of the free-throw circle, fakes one direction, cuts off the post in a change of direction maneuver, and as he cuts off the post player, he receives a feed back of the ball from the post. The player now dribbles for a short distance and does the jump shot, then follows his own shot for the rebound. If he misses, he keeps putting the ball up until he makes the shot. After making the shot, the shooter rolls the ball out to the next in line. The players should drive to various spots on the floor for the shots, making sure not to shoot from the same spot every time.

4. Key-Hole Club: Diagram 3-13. The players take jump shots from each of the six spots along each side of the free-throw lane and from five spots around the circle beyond the free-throw line. The shots inside the free-throw line count one point, and those beyond on the circle count two points. If a player hits from all the spots in succession, and scores 22 points, he now belongs to the "KEY-HOLE CLUB"—a supposedly very exclusive club—and will be rewarded with a banner, a plaque, a ribbon, or recognition.

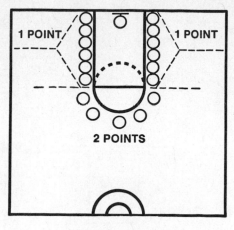

DIAGRAM 3-13

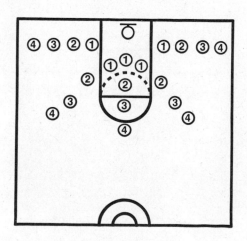

DIAGRAM 3-14

5. The Arrow Club: Diagram 3-14. The players take jump shots from the positions in front of the basket that form an ARROW as shown—four positions in each line. When a player hits from all the positions in succession, he belongs to the "ARROW CLUB." If in addition to the spots on the arrow in front of the basket, the player can hit from the eight spots along the base line, he becomes a member of the "DOUBLE ARROW CLUB." Rewards and recognition will be given for each.

6. The "Risk It" Drill: Diagram 3-15. The seven outside spots are marked, as well as spots 8 through 12 as shown. The players shoot jump shots from each spot. If the player hits the basket, he moves to the next spot. If the player announces, "I can make it," and hits, he moves up three places. If he misses, he goes down three places. The first player to finish the circuit of twelve spots is the winner.

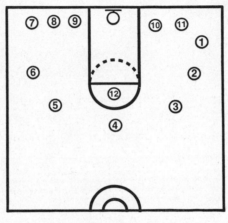

DIAGRAM 3-15

THE ONE-HAND SET SHOT

Set shots of any type do not seem to be a part of the game of basketball today. A two-handed set shot is rarely seen, and the one-hand set shot is almost extinct; however, the jump shot that is used almost exclusively in the game today is a variation of the one-hand set shot in that it is a shot executed from a different position and in a slightly different manner. The one-hand set shot can be effective from a longer range than the jump shot, and for this reason should be taught to players today. Almost always, in every game, there will occur situations where a shot needs to be taken from a range exceeding that of the effective jump shot. The one-hand set is the answer, and so should be included in the repertoire of shots to be coached, especially to junior high and high school players.

Coaching Points for the One-Hand Set Shot

1. *Footwork:* The feet should be well balanced, approximately shoulder width apart, the right foot a few inches

in advance of the left (right-handed shooter). The toe of the left foot will be pointed at a 30- to 45-degree angle to the basket or target.

2. *Balance:* The knees should be flexed, and the body weight distributed so that it falls within the base, and evenly distributed over both feet. The body should be erect, with no lean forward.

3. The ball should be held a comfortable distance from the body, just under the chin, or approximately shoulder height.

4. The back of the right hand (right-handed shooter) should be toward the shooter, with the left hand under the ball or slightly at the side for control.

5. *Eyes:* The player should concentrate on the target prior to the beginning of the shot, and as the ball is brought into position, the *eyes focus* on the target (suggest the target be the back half of the rim).

6. The wrists are broken to start the shot, as the ball is dipped slightly forward to obtain relaxation and rhythm.

7. Break the wrists and knees at the same time. As the shot is taken, the player should leave the floor slightly to insure better rhythm, relaxation, and coordination. (Some players may want more height as they leave the floor—if so this shot resembles the jump shot somewhat.)

8. The ball should be released from the fingers with an upward movement of the forearm, and a hinge-like action of the wrist. When the shot is started, the motion by the arm should be an upward vertical movement, not a lateral one. This gives a good arched shot and makes for a good follow-up position.

9. The wrist should be complete in a follow-through motion. When the shot is made in this fashion the position of the ball is good, because it is in line with the advanced foot, the shoulder, and the eye focus on the basket.

10. Keep the eyes on the target *before, during, and after the shot.*

11. The shot is made with the whole body. Follow through with the fingers, wrist, arm, body, and mind.

12. The shot should be made off-a-dime, so to speak. The take-off and landing of both feet should be approximately in the same spot. There should be no lateral gain in distance toward the basket or in toward the defense.

Habit Drills for Teaching the One-Hand Set Shot

Many of the drills that are used to teach the jump shot can also be used to teach the one-hand set shot. Specifically the drills given in Diagrams 3-10, 3-11, 3-12, 3-13, 3-14 and 3-15 can all be used to teach and perfect the one-hand set shot.

1. Move, Get Set, Shoot Drill: Diagram 3-16. The squad is divided into two groups with half the players stationed out-of-bounds, each with a ball in his possession. The other players are located anywhere on the floor in front of the basket. The drill is to teach the players to move, recover or receive the ball and "get set" for the shot. Before passing the ball to the shooter, the passer with the ball out-of-bounds calls the name of a certain player and then bounces the ball to a point which will force the receiver to change position. Upon receiving the ball, the shooter squares off to the basket, gets set and executes the one-hand set shot. You must supervise the drill and coach the players to get good position before attempting a shot. The passers recover the shots and step out-of-bounds and repeat the drill. The players change off on positions after you set a time for them.

DIAGRAM 3-16

THE HOOK SHOT

The hook shot has practically become a casualty of the jump shot. It is seldom seen in basketball any more. It is a lost art. So habitual has the jump shot become that players shoot it almost to the exclusion of all other shots, and will not take time to develop this very effective and artistic shot in and around the basket area. The shot can be very effective for tall pivot players and forwards who receive the ball with their backs to the basket in close shooting range. It is almost impossible to block or defend the shot. It also takes a lot of work and practice to learn to execute the shot properly and with a high degree of accuracy. Because the ball is received in a position with the back to the basket, the player will have little time for visual lineup on the shooting target, and so will have to develop a certain sense of feel for position in making the shot. While primarily used by big and tall pivot players, the shot has been effectively developed and used by many forwards and guards. Certainly right in and around the basket, all players should master the hook technique.

Coaching Points for the Hook Shot

1. The shot is usually started with the shooter's back to the basket. His first action is to set up the defensive player with a head and shoulder fake.

2. When receiving the ball with his back to the basket, the player should have his feet parallel and about shoulder width apart. This position will give him a good jumping and reacting position—a good base from which to start his action.

3. Each player will have his own variation and technique on the shot—each player will develop the shot to fit his physical personality. There is no standardized form on the shot.

4. The footwork of the turn for the shot is an important factor in developing a successful hook shot. The foot opposite the shooting arm (left foot for right-handed shooter) is the foot used for the pivot and turn on the shot.

5. On the step, turn and pivot, some players will step away from the basket to gain distance away from the

defensive player; others step to the side to gain ground away from the defensive player, while others will step diagonally to the rear and toward the basket with a good foot plant that screens the defensive player out, and gives the shooter a good rebounding position. The last-mentioned move is the preferred one for most players because of better rebounding position, and its movement toward the basket.

6. After catching the ball, most players will hold it at about waist height, and bring it in toward the body as the step and pivot is started.

7. The ball will be carried in both hands to a position for starting the shooting action, which will be about the height of the head. The arms will be extended more and the shooting hand will move under the ball—eventually the shooting hand will take over completely as the ball is extended out from the body on the turn and pivot.

8. The shot will be more accurate when the shooting action is started at head height. Starting it lower brings about a sweeping arc on the shot that requires more coordination and timing as to the exact release point of the ball.

9. Most hook shots are taken from the side, and the shot should be banked on the board. The player must get his eyes on the target early and as soon as possible after he starts his step and turn. He must concentrate on the target before, during, and after the release of the ball.

10. The ball should be released from the finger tips with the thumb providing support. The fingers provide the guiding action and when the ball reaches its highest point, the wrist and fingers will provide the final release force. The fingers should be comfortably spread to give an efficient guide and control. The ball should not be palmed or cupped in the wrist.

11. The ball should roll off the finger tips to give a soft backspin to the shot. A harsh wrist snap should be avoided.

12. The foot and leg on the shooting side (right leg for right-handed shooter) should be lifted and moved forward during the shooting action to bring about a turn of the body on the shot. This should be a smooth, rhythmic,

action and not a harsh, violent, or jerky motion. Stress smooth, rhythmic, motion on the shot.

13. The amount of body turn to effect the shot will vary with players, but it is best if the shooter turns almost completely toward the basket. This gives better rebound position and will also give the player a better line on the basket and a better follow-through on the shot.

14. The ball should be softly lofted higher than most shots, especially on shots in front of the basket that are not banked. The fingers continue in the line of the flight of the arc of the shot. The arm should be straight at the point of release of the ball and continues during the follow-through. The body will be erect at the release of the ball. On the final turn, the shooter should be squarely facing the basket.

Habit Drills for Teaching the Hook Shot

1. **Hook Shots Underneath the Basket, Right and Left: Diagram 3-17.** In this drill, every basket in the gym can be used. This is a good drill to use at the beginning of practice. Players are assigned baskets, and if there are enough baskets, have the players work in pairs at each basket. As soon as they come on the floor (or at another time if it fits your schedule better) the players start working right underneath the basket hooking the ball on right and left hook shots. Stress jumping on the shot and exploding in the air for height. The player first steps with his left foot, jumps high, turns into the basket and shoots right-handed. Don't let the ball touch the floor—catch it, then step with the right foot, jump high, turn body to basket and shoot with the left hand. Start out with each player doing this for 30 seconds to one minute and working up to three minutes or more. The players change off if you have more than one player at a basket. A score can be kept on who makes the most baskets in the allotted time. Points must be deducted if the ball is allowed to touch the floor. This drill is also a good conditioner. After working right under the basket for an allotted time, follow with the player taking the ball with back to basket, making a fake, taking one dribble away and shooting with the right hand, and then do the same move to the left. Teach the player to go both right and left with this shot close in to the basket. The drill also

helps develop ambidexterity on close in shots around the basket, and develops the proper footwork for right- and left-handed shooting.

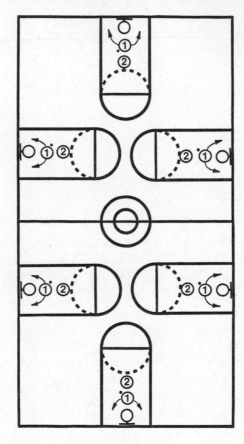

DIAGRAM 3-17

2. Hook Shoot from along the Lane: Diagram 3-18. In this drill the players line up as shown. Players O1 and O2 pass the ball back and forth, while O3 maneuvers to get open close to the basket. Player X1, the defensive player, gives passive resistance on defense. The ball is passed into O3 somewhere along the free-throw lane below the free-throw line and as near the basket as possible. Player O3, upon receiving the ball, fakes, maneuvers and goes either right or left for the hook shot. Player O3 may also dribble in around underneath the basket and behind it and come up with a reverse hook shot. The players rotate clockwise on the drill. Be sure to run the drill from both sides of the floor. If desired, O1 may pass the ball into O3 and O3 can be allowed to come as high as the outer half of the free-throw line to start his moves for the hook shot.

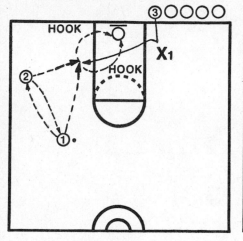

DIAGRAM 3-18   DIAGRAM 3-19

3. Getting Open for the Hook Shot: Diagram 3-19. This drill puts two defensive players on O1 in the free-throw lane area, and O1 must maneuver with fakes and feints to get open to receive a pass from O2, who may dribble and move about to make the delivery. Once O1 receives the ball, X1 and X2 must play behind him, and he dribble maneuvers as close as possible to the basket and shoots a hook shot. The players rotate positions clockwise.

4. Hook Shoot from Seven Basic Spots Inside: Diagram 3-20. The seven basic spots from the inside shown previously in Diagram 3-11 can be used to work on the hook shot as well. The players work and maneuver from all the basic inside spots as shown here. To illustrate further the better footwork needed in executing the hook shot, the number 2 spot is used. The shooter should step with the foot opposite the shooting hand in a diagonal direction toward the basket to gain distance toward the basket. The toe of this foot should point as much as possible toward the basket, not away from the basket. This gives the shooter a better rebounding position as well as a shot nearer the basket. This movement puts more pressure on the defensive player, and brings up the possibility of being fouled and making the basket also.

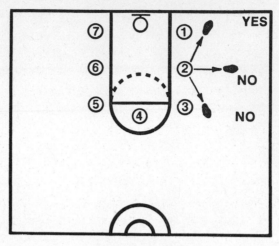

DIAGRAM 3-20

THE FREE THROW

So much could be said about the free throw that probably it would be best to leave most of it unsaid. Formerly all free throws in basketball were shot with the two-handed underhand shot. Then came the one-hand shot, and a change to a one-hand set shot on the free throw. Today most players use some version of the one-hand set, but with the jump shot being the only shot that most players can shoot, expect to see more and more jump shots from the free-throw line, or some version of the jump shot. There really is no such thing as a standardized method of shooting free throws in basketball today.

The free throw is different in that it is FREE—from the same spot and same distance every time. There is no defense. It is just a simple shot. A high percentage of accuracy should be expected.

Earlier in the history of basketball, on the average, 33% of all points scored were from the free-throw line. Today, due to various rule changes that have been made, and different officiating, somewhere between 20% and 26% of all points scored will come from the free-throw line. It is still a very important shot in the game and a vital factor in the outcome of most games.

Coaching Points for the Free Throw

General coaching points for the free throw will be given. Coaching points for the various methods will not be considered. Most players and coaches have their own style and method.

1. Within reason, teach the same shot to every member of the team.
2. There is no substitute for practice in free-throw shooting. The shot must be practiced until it is completely habitual and automatic.
3. Practice of free throws should not be mechanical and without purpose. How the player practices is more important than how many throws he tosses at the basket. Attitudes in practice must be the same as in the game—every shot is important.
4. Shoot free throws at the beginning of practice—break up scrimmages to shoot free throws—get some more shooting at the end of practice when the player is really tired.
5. Practice free throws under as near game-like conditions as possible.
6. The player should establish a thought pattern that will give complete relaxation and confidence. The thought pattern should be something like this: "I have hit thousands of these before, and I WILL hit this one."
7. Have an approach to the line and a pre-shot preparation that will help in concentration and bring about relaxation.
8. The player should place his feet exactly the same way every time he approaches the foul line. This will do three important things:
   a. Thinking of the placement of the feet will be a desired means of taking the mind off the pressure of the game and the shot, and thereby will give more relaxation.
   b. The distance from the basket is then always the same, allowing muscles to make foul shooting a reflex after much practice.
   c. The player will have assurance that he is back of the line.
9. The player should develop smoothness and rhythm on the shot. Any shot that is hurried and jerky will cut down on accuracy and control.
10. *Eyes:* The attention of the eyes should be directed to the pre-shot preparation phases until ready to shoot. Then

the eyes should be focused on the target (whatever point you establish as the proper target).

11. If the player is tired or has been running hard when fouled, he should take his time in approaching the line and regaining his breathing. One or two deep breaths will help relax the player.

12. Take advantage of the 10-second time limit in making the shot.

13. Just before making the shot, take a full deep breath, hold it momentarily, then exhale completely so that the body is in a completely relaxed position.

14. *Aim, direction and follow-through:* Try to reach the ball to the target. If the shooter stands in front of the basket and brings the ball up straight, the direction of the flight of the ball must be correct. A complete follow-through will contribute to control and accuracy.

15. *Spin:* The ball should leave the fingers in such a way that it will have a natural backspin as it leaves the hands.

16. *Distance:* If the shooter will stand directly at the foul line and put the same amount of energy into each successful shot, he cannot miss the basket. If the ball overshoots the target, the backboard will rebound the ball into the basket.

17. Proper consideration of these details of foul shooting will result in higher scores and more games in the victory column.

18. On all drills, be sure that players shoot no more than two shots without stepping back and readjusting their position in a new approach to the line. Be sure players rotate positions on shooting so that they will not develop a shooting pattern that does not exist in a game condition.

Habit Drills for Teaching the Free Throw

1. At the conclusion of hard scrimmages and conditioning drills, have the players divided into teams at the various baskets

and take turns shooting free throws. Have each player shoot until he misses or makes five in a row. Never shoot more than two at the line without stepping back and realigning position. Reward the team that finishes first—have a penalty for the losing team.

2. Another method or drill that can be used is having each team member shoot a set number of free throws each day. Start with 30 shots a day. Always shoot with a teammate. Record the shots made—day by day—week by week. Work out periodic awards to the best shooters.

3. Always manage to give a season's award and recognition to the best free-throw shooters on the team. Give trophies and get press recognition.

4. Research has shown that there is an advantage in having players shoot free throws in practice at a smaller than normal basket. Several firms manufacture a smaller rim device that attaches to the basket and reduces the size of the hole. This results in improved concentration in practice, and gives the psychological advantage of making the bigger basket seem easy during the game.

5. A free-throw ladder can be used as a motivational competitive device for fun and challenge.

6. Develop competitive games with free-throw clubs and free-throw contests.

    a. Have a "25" club—any player who hits 25 free throws in a row is a member.

    b. Also have a 35 club, a 50 club, etc., and give recognition to club members with awards, press recognition, trophies, etc.

7. **Nine Consecutive Shot Drill: Diagram 3-21.** Just before going in for the shower and at the end of practice, line up nine players from the varsity. (Any convenient number can be used.) The players take turns shooting one free throw. When all the players have hit one, and nine have been hit consecutively, the team may go. The players who miss and break the chain of consecutive shots will have to run laps.

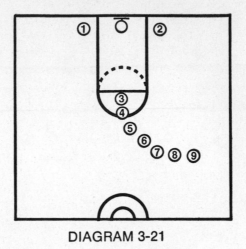

DIAGRAM 3-21

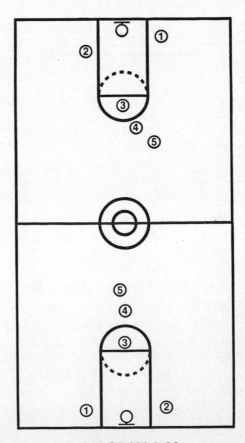

DIAGRAM 3-22

8. The Five Around Drill: Diagram 3-22. Teams of five players are selected for each basket. The players take turns shooting. The first round, each player must hit one shot. The second round, each player must hit two shots. (All five must hit two in a row.) The third round, each player must hit three shots. The fourth round, each player must hit two shots, and the fifth round each player must hit one shot. If a player misses a shot, the team must start over on that round until all have hit the required number of shots in that round in consecutive order. The team that finishes first is the winner. The losing team is required to run laps, or the winning team is rewarded.

9. Fifteen Point Free-Throw Drill: Diagram 3-23. On this competitive team drill, there are to be four players on each team, they line up alternately as shown, and during the shooting contest they will perform at the various positions as in a game, except for the player out-of-bounds, who remains out of the play until rotated into a playing position. Each player takes his turn

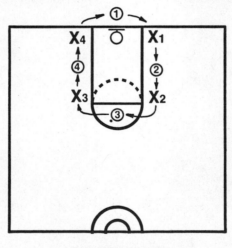

DIAGRAM 3-23

at the free-throw line and will shoot three free throws, being sure to step back and realign after each shot. The X's compete against the O's. The team to score 15 points first wins. Points are scored as follows. Each free throw hit counts one point. If the free throw is missed, the ball is in play, and each rebound secured, whether offensive or defensive, scores one point. If in a scramble the ball rolls out of bounds, the defense scores one point. If the team on offense tips the ball in, score two points. The players rotate clockwise after the third shot by each player.

Reward the winners. The drill helps develop free-throw accuracy and defensive and offensive rebounding play; the players should be checked by the coach on proper action in rebounding both offensively and defensively.

10. Free Throw Elimination Drill: Diagram 3-24. This drill is to be done right at the end of practice. The players line up at a basket. Each player is to take turns shooting one shot. When a player makes the shot, the player directly behind him must make the shot, or he is eliminated from the game, and must shoot 15 successful free throws at a side basket before he can shower. A player can be eliminated by either the player in front of or behind him. For instance, if the first two players, O1 and O2, miss the free throw, and O3 hits, then O2 in front of O3 is eliminated. If players O3, O4, and O5 hit, and O6 misses, O6 is eliminated. The game continues until only one player is left, and

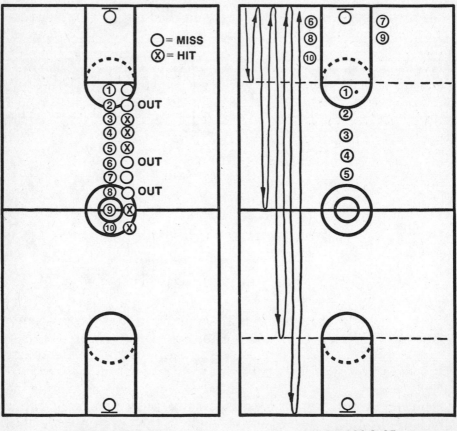

DIAGRAM 3-24   DIAGRAM 3-25

this player is declared the "Elimination Free Throw Champ" of the day. All other eliminated free throwers must shoot a set number of successful free-throw shots at a side basket before they can shower. The last player, "The Champ," shoots until he misses. Records can be kept too see which "Champ" hits the highest number of consecutive shots.

11. Run-Down, Run-Back Free-Throw Drill: Diagram 3-25. This is another good drill to be used at the end of practice. The team, whatever number it may be, gathers at one basket. Each player shoots two free throws. Set a percentage goal. If there are ten players and the percentage goal is 70%—the team shoots 20 shots—they must make 14 of the 20 shots. If the percentage goal is 60%, they must hit 12 of 20 shots. If they hit the percentage goal, practice is over and they may shower. If the team fails to make the percentage goal, they must do the run-down, run-back drill. To do this drill the players line up along the end line. On the whistle they first run to the free-throw line extended, touch the floor, pivot and return to the end line, touch floor, pivot, go to the division court line, repeat, then to the far free-throw line extended, repeat, then to the far end line and repeat. After the run-down, run-back, the team must repeat the shooting process. If they fail to make the shooting percentage, repeat the run drill again. Repeat until they make the goal, or you decide to be merciful.

4

The Pivot—
Drills to
Teach Pivoting

The pivot, a very important offensive fundamental, is accomplished by stepping in any direction with one foot, while the other foot maintains contact with a spot on the floor. The players should be drilled in its execution until they are fundamentally perfect. The pivot has two very important functions in a player's offensive maneuvering. They are:

1. To keep the player's body between the opponent and the ball and in this way give protection to the ball.

2. When used properly in many situations, it will gain distance for the player, enabling him to elude his opponent, or get by him.

Actually all pivots and turns can be classified under two categories. They are:

1. The forward pivot

2. The reverse pivot

In making the *forward pivot*, the pivot foot is established, and the shoulder opposite the pivot foot moves in a turn forward as the whole body is turned to face in the opposite direction.

In making the *reverse pivot*, the pivot foot is established, and the shoulder opposite the pivot foot moves in a turn to the rear as the whole body is turned to face the opposite direction.

All turns and pivots can be classified in one or the other of the above categories, and are determined by the direction in which the shoulder opposite the pivot foot turns or moves.

Coaching Points for Pivoting

1. In making the stop for the pivot, keep the body low, and the feet placed wide enough apart to form a firm base.
2. When the turn is made, always pivot away from the defensive player.
3. The body weight should be mostly on the pivot foot as the turn is made.
4. The turn should be made on the ball of the foot, rather than the heel. Notice where the player wears out his shoe soles. The shoes should be worn out on the balls of the feet rather than on the heels.
5. The pivot must be done with all possible speed.
6. As the pivot is executed, it should be done so as to keep the body between the ball and the opponent, and it should gain distance from the opponent.
7. The pivot can be executed with or without the ball. It is easier to make the pivot without the ball than with it. When made without the ball it is done for purposes of deception and to gain distance from the defensive opponent.

Habit Drills to Teach Pivoting

1. The drill given in Diagram 2-7, the four corner dribble-pivot drill, is a good drill to use in teaching the pivot.
2. The drills given in Diagram 2-9, and Diagram 2-13, are excellent drills to teach the fundamental techniques needed in the execution of the pivot.
3. The pivot can be added to or included in many of the shooting drills given in Chapter 3. The best examples are in Diagrams 3-5 and 3-6. The pivot can be included in these drills, and are given as optional.

4. A pivot can be included in the moves made from the seven basic spot shooting drills, Diagrams 3-10 and 3-11.

5. The Truck and Trailer Drill: Diagram 4-1. In the "truck and trailer" drill, the players line up in three lines at each end of the court as shown. On one end, the first player in each line, O1, has a ball. To start the drill, the player in each line with the ball starts down court on a dribble. After reaching the approximate area of the free-throw line extended, the dribbler, O1, picks up the ball, stops and executes either a forward pivot or a reverse pivot (you can designate the pivot if you wish) and

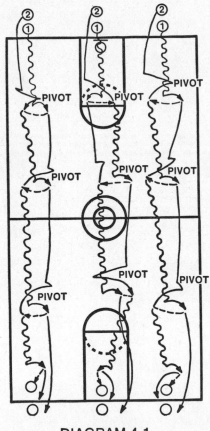

DIAGRAM 4-1

sets a post-feeder situation. The next player in line, O2, trails the dribbler, and after the pivot and post by O1, O2 fakes one way and cuts the other by the pivoting player. As O2 cuts by O1, he is given a flip hand-off pass by O1. Now O2 dribbles to about the division court line, where he now stops, pivots and posts for O1, who has become the trailer after feeding the ball to O2. Each line continues the length of the court in this manner, where they turn the ball over to the next two players who repeat the drill to the other end of the court.

6. The Three-Spot Pivot Drill: Diagram 4-2. Players line up in three lines near the court division line as shown. The drill is started by the player in the middle line, who dribbles either to his right or left in a diagonal direction toward the sideline and the baseline. When reaching a point about even with the player line on that side, he picks up the dribble, stops and does a pivot (can be either a forward or a reverse pivot) and posts for the player on that side. In this case, O2 starts down floor, fakes to the right and then cuts over the pivot post set by O1. O1 hands him a flip pass, and now O2 dribbles (with the outside hand) in a diagonal direction toward the opposite sideline, and when reaching a point near the O2 line, he stops, pivots and posts for O3, who has drifted slightly down court, and when O2 posts for him, he makes a strong fake to the left, and then cuts over O2's pivot post to receive the ball. Now O3 dribbles toward the opposite corner, and when reaching a point just below the free-throw line extended and about even with the O2 line, he stops, picks up the dribble, pivots and posts. Now, O1, who has drifted slightly down court, fakes a drive to his right, and then breaks sharply by O3's pivot post. When O1 receives the ball, he now does a hard dribble drive in for a lay-up shot. Players O2 and O3 follow for the rebound and pass the ball out to the next player in the O1 line. The players rotate lines, and the dribble from the O1

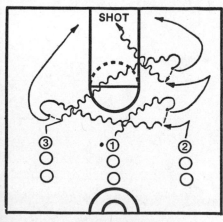

DIAGRAM 4-2

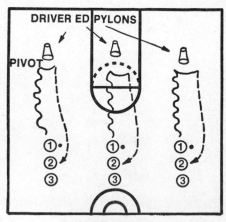

DIAGRAM 4-3

line should not always be started to the right. It should be rotated in starting right and left. The dribbler should always dribble with the outside hand. The drill gives good fundamental practice in dribbling, stopping, pivoting, posting, feeding a cutter by the post, and cutting by the post, as well as shooting.

7. **Single Line Pivot and Pass Drill: Diagram 4-3.** Place a driver education pylon or other obstacle on the floor as shown. The player dribbles to the obstacle, executes the stop, the forward pivot and then the reverse pivot. This is a good drill to use with very young players early in the season, who need emphasis in the mechanics of stopping and executing the various pivots.

8. **Pivot Drill in Formation: Diagram 4-4.** The players gather in any formation in front of you. Call the pivot you want them to execute, and they do the pivot on command. Examples of pivots—forward pivot on right foot, reverse pivot on right foot, forward pivot on left foot, reverse pivot on left foot, etc. In this situation you can check the footwork, body position, weight and turns to be sure the players are making the pivots properly and not traveling on the turns. It is a good early season drill, and excellent to use in teaching the very young players the proper pivoting techniques.

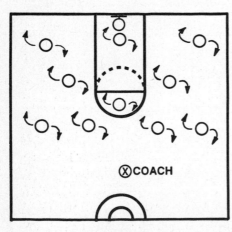

DIAGRAM 4-4

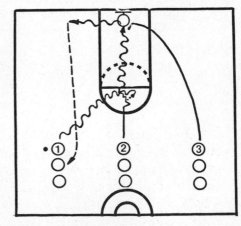

DIAGRAM 4-5

9. **Three-Line Pivot-Post Drill: Diagram 4-5.** The players line up in three lines at mid-court as shown. Player O1, with the ball, dribbles with the outside hand into the outer half of the free-throw circle, and making either a forward pivot or a

reverse pivot, sets a pivot-post. Player O2 drifts toward O1, and when O1 pivots-posts, O2 fakes one direction and cuts by O1 in the other to receive a flip pass and does a drive for the basket. Player O3 comes down the outside to recover the rebound, or pick the ball out of the net. He then does a quick dribble drive toward the side line and passes the ball back to the O1 line where the drill is repeated.

10. Defensive Pivot Drill: Diagram 4-6. The offensive players take positions on the floor with a ball facing the defensive players, in this case O's and X's. Upon your given signal, the X's attack the O's and the O's execute the various pivots to learn to protect the ball by making the proper pivot. The drill should emphasize the technique of keeping the body between the ball and the defensive opponent.

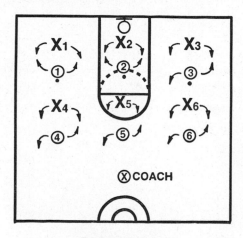

DIAGRAM 4-6

11. Four-Line Pivot Drill: Diagram 4-7. This drill has two offensive lines and two defensive lines. You may have as many squads as desired, or as room permits. The offensive line, the O's, lines up along a side line, the first player in line, O1, with a ball. The defensive players take positions in a line about 15 to 20 feet apart out on the court as shown. Upon a given signal, the O1 players all start dribbling at the defensive players in line X1. O1 fakes to go around X1 with his dribble, but the defensive player X1 is to turn the dribbler, who now pivots, and posts for O2, who is trailing O1. Player O2 cuts by O1 to receive a hand-off flip pass and now O2 becomes a dribbler and O1 trails O2. O2 dribbles at X2, and X2 turns O2, who pivots and posts to feed his trailing player, O1. O1 dribbles to the side line after taking the pass from O2. Now the X's become the dribbling pivot players and the O's become the defensive players and the drill is repeated as often as you desire or have scheduled. The drill is excellent for teaching the mechanics of the pivot, setting the post, feeding a cutting player from the post, timing in cutting by a pivot-post player and receiving the ball.

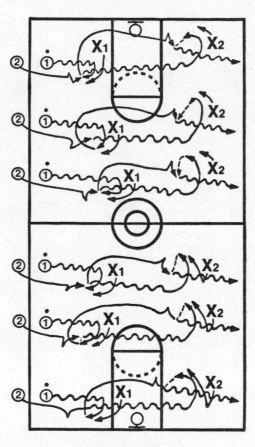

DIAGRAM 4-7

12. Four-Corner Pivot Drill: Diagram 4-8. This drill is similar to the four corner passing drill, except that the passer ends by doing a reverse pivot and post for the next player in line. The drill can be run with two balls. The players line up in the corners as shown, and they start at corners with O1 and O3. Player O1 starts with a fast driving dribble, passes to O2. Player O2 passes back to O1 who has followed his pass. Player O1 now dribbles past O2 and does a reverse pivot, and posts up for O2 who drives past him to receive the ball on a flip pass. Player O2 now repeats the drill with the O3 corner. Player O3 has done the same thing with the O4 corner, and the drill proceeds from corner to corner.

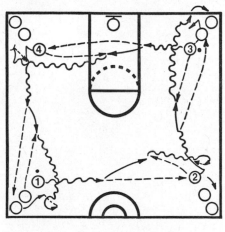

DIAGRAM 4-8

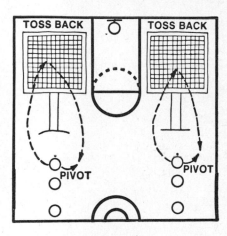

DIAGRAM 4-9

13. Toss Back and Recover Drill: Diagram 4-9. This drill can be run with a "toss back" machine or machines, if available. If the machine is not available, it can be done off a gymnasium wall. With the toss back machine, the players line up 10 to 12 feet from the machine. The angle of the machine is adjusted to get the correct toss back. The first player in line takes the ball and first with the right foot forward, passes to the net, executes a forward pivot on the left foot quickly, and getting the ball in line of vision, catches the return off the toss back. After three pivots on the left foot, the player then does three pivots on the right foot, starting with the left foot forward. The next player in line repeats the drill. The closer the players are to the toss back net, the quicker they must pivot and respond to the toss back. The slower players may have to increase distance from the machine, and take the toss back on the bounce.

If the toss back machine is not available, this drill can be worked fairly effectively from a gymnasium wall. The players take their places in lines about 10 to 12 feet from the wall. The first player, starting with back to the wall looking over a shoulder, will pass the ball so that it hits the wall hard enough and high enough to rebound back to the passer. After making the pass, the player pivots so as to face the wall and receive the bounce back off the wall. After pivoting three times off each foot, the player goes to the end of the line and the next player repeats the drill.

5

Drills for Body Balance, Stops, Starts, Change of Direction

In order to be an effective player on either offense or defense, the individual must have good body balance. The degree of stability the player has is dependent upon the center of the body weight, sometimes referred to as the "center of gravity," with respect to the base on which the body is supported. The base which gives this support is the player's feet.

Researchers have found that basketball players are able to move more quickly in any direction when they have taken a position with the feet spread at least shoulder width apart, and with knees flexed at least to an angle of 120 degrees, feet completely on the floor, with the weight distributed evenly on both feet. The expression "on the balls of your feet," or "keep on your toes" is not to be taken literally in basketball. The coach may be using such expressions to urge the players to "be ready," "be alert," and "be ready for action." In most situations, the whole foot, including the heel, should be on the floor to provide proper body balance.

In addition to pivoting, the footwork movements that need particular attention in basketball are starts, stops, changes of direction and changes of pace. To be effective in any of these movements the player must have good body balance.

111

In teaching coming to a stop, stress that the player may stop on either the "one" count, or on the "one-two" count, and with both feet even or with one foot in front of the other, *toes pointing straight ahead.* When going at full speed, it is best for the player to stop on the "one-two" count, with one foot in front of the other, and as this is done, the player almost sits down on the back heel, with the *weight distributed evenly over both feet.*

To start, the player should put all his effort into the first step—taking a long hard first step. There can be no hesitation or half-hearted attempt on this first stride.

THE CHANGE OF PACE IS HARD TO TEACH

Talk a lot about it to the players. This will cause the players to be conscious of the *change of pace.* The players who have a change of pace are usually the players who are relaxed and loose, and then all of a sudden—BOOM—they are gone. The player who has a change of pace will usually have three paces; They are: (1) a slow jog for position, (2) a speeding up for adjustment or timing and (3) the full burst of speed to lose the opposing defensive player. The excellent change of pace player will manipulate these three speeds or paces in various sequences to get a declaration from a defensive player, and then make his change of pace at a time of surprise to beat the opponent. The player can also start fast, slow up, then break away at full speed again. The procedure of starting fast, then slowing up just enough to get a declaration from the defensive player, followed by a sudden burst of speed will make it difficult for the defensive player to guard the offensive player.

A player who has no change of pace is easy to guard. The defensive player soon learns how much to loosen up on such an opponent. If the player has a change of pace, this cannot be true. The players who are loose and relaxed tend to get their opponents loose too. Talking is also a good tactic to use to get the defensive player to loosen up, and then when the defensive mind is distracted, the offensive player can dash by him. Actually, all the player has to remember about a change of pace is that it means slowing down when the player is in fast motion, and acceleration of pace when moving more slowly. It can be used by a cutting player without the ball or it can be used by a dribbler. Another important manipulation that can be used in the change of pace is the use of short and long strides. By changing the length of the stride, by entering into a series of staccato steps, and then suddenly bursting into full-length strides, the player can effectively change pace and leave the defensive opponent trailing.

Suggestions for Using the Change of Pace

1. The player should reduce his speed in certain situations to "set up" the defensive player for a change of pace.
2. The player should not move at one speed continuously, or at his fastest speed all the time.
3. The change of pace should be applied with quick starts, stops, and change of direction.
4. The player should use the change of pace at any time he can sense an advantage by using it.
5. Many times, the player can create openings in meeting the ball by changing pace. An opening in meeting the ball may not be there, but a change of pace can create such an opening.

Coaching Points for Body Balance, Stops, Starts, Change of Direction, and Change of Pace

1. *The head* should be kept directly above the midpoint between the two feet. The weight of the head can throw the player off balance. Keep the chin up, and do not lean forward—keep the trunk erect.
2. *Hands and arms:* Keep the hands and arms above the waist, and fairly close to the body. Keep the fingers spread and relaxed when not in possession of the ball.
3. Keep the body low in starting and stopping. Shorten yourself in height if you wish to start, stop, or turn quickly. Get close to your feet. The lower a player can get his center of gravity, the quicker he can pivot, veer, feint, stop, or start, other things being equal. Tall players should take special note of this.
4. Every joint should be flexed and relaxed, ready for a quick or sudden move or change of direction.
5. Proper body balance calls for equal distribution of the weight on the full soles of both feet. This does not mean on the back of the heels or up high on the toes or balls of the feet.

6. Carry the center of the body weight on an imaginary line through the hips.

7. The feet should be comfortably spread, and at least shoulder width apart.

8. Get the idea across to the player that in basketball he should learn to start instantly at full speed from many positions, in any direction and at the opportune time.

Habit Drills to Teach Body Balance, Stops, Starts, Change of Direction and Pace

1. Have the players stand in any formation on the court, with feet apart, knees and hips flexed slightly, back straight, head up. You stand in front, signal with your hands or voice, RIGHT, BACK, LEFT, or FRONT—whereupon the players dash suddenly five steps at full speed in the indicated direction. As the players stand ready to start, have them relax and loosen up by shaking arms and hands, weaving body slightly from side to side, breathing easily, taking in plenty of air.

2. Place two players, one six feet in front of the other, both facing the basket. The front player starts for the sideline or the endline. The back player is to try to beat him. Have the front player fake or feint to give him the feel of what a fake or a feint will do for him.

3. Jump Stop and Stride Stop Drill: Diagram 5-1. The players line up across the end line in six lines as shown. The drill is first done without the ball. The players start on your signal. After starting, on the first whistle, the players come to a jump stop (one-count), with both feet even. On the second whistle the players make a stride stop (one-two count), stopping with one foot in front of the other. On the third whistle, the players reverse direction by doing a forward pivot and sprint back to the baseline. The next group in line repeats the drill. The second time through the drill, the players, upon making the stop, execute either a forward pivot or a reverse pivot. You determine the pivot to be made on each stop. The player quickly does the pivot and returns to starting position awaiting the next whistle.

4. Jump Stop and Stride Stop Dribbling Drill: Diagram 5-2. This drill is exactly the same as Diagram 5-1, except that the drill is now repeated, but each player at the beginning of each line has a ball. On the whistle or signal the player dribbles out, and on the first whistle, comes to a jump stop (one-count) with both feet even. The second stop is again a

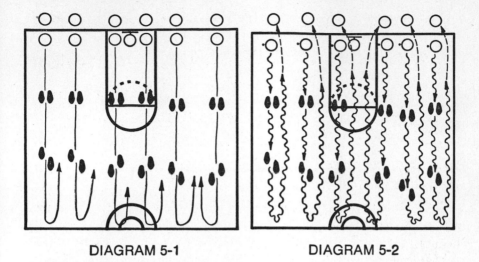

DIAGRAM 5-1   DIAGRAM 5-2

stride stop, with one foot in front of the other or advanced. Instead of stopping on the third whistle, the player reverses with the dribble, and upon the fourth whistle, the player passes the ball off to the next player in line, making the pass-off on the run at top dribbling speed.

5. Change of Direction Drill: Diagram 5-3. The players line up around the outside of a half-court situation with you in the center. Upon your signal, the players run along the outside boundary lines until they come to a corner. When a player arrives at a corner, he plants the outside foot firmly, fakes to continue, but now with body weight low, and evenly distributed

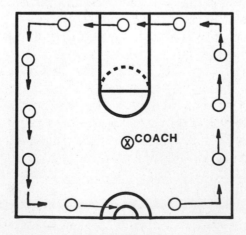

DIAGRAM 5-3

so as to control, the player steps off at a 90-degree angle with the opposite foot and goes in that direction, where the act is repeated at the next corner. First the players go around counterclockwise with the right foot always the outside planting foot. Then the direction is changed to clockwise and the outside planting foot would be the left foot, and the take-off at 90 degrees with the right foot. Check the mechanics and techniques of the foot planting, take-off on opposite foot, body weight distribution and control, head and shoulder fakes, etc. This drill can be used as an easy warm-up drill preliminary to other activities and as a general loosening up drill that incorporates running, jogging, change of direction, and body weight control.

6. **Change of Direction Shifting Drill: Diagram 5-4.** The players go up and down the floor in a series of shuffling and shifting steps that resemble the foot movements shown here. Each step is a fake and a change of direction shift with the body weight being controlled as the fake step is made in one direction and the foot take-off in another direction. The center of the body weight must be maintained within the base (area between the feet). The steps are accomplished by a skating slide-stroke as the feet are lifted off the floor and set down with a firm stomp, planting the whole foot on the floor. From this then, the opposite foot is shot out at a 90-degree angle, and also planted firmly on the floor. As the shift is made, extend the near arm in the direction of the shift. The players go up and down the floor practicing this shifting, fake, and change of direction, controlling body weight movement. The knees will be flexed, hips lowered, trunk erect and head up on the drill. This drill will help the player to get the feel of shifting weight in change of direction movements.

7. **Change of Direction Footwork: Diagram 5-5.** This shows the footwork needed for a change of direction and is the footwork that would be applied in the drills in Diagrams 5-3 and 5-4. The lead foot, sometimes called the outside foot (left foot in this diagram) is stamped down hard in a fake with weight being faked in direction of that foot, but actually under control and the center within the base established by the feet. The weight is quickly shifted as the back foot is picked up and started in the direction of a 90-degree turn. This move is especially good to use in maneuvering the offensive player to the inside and getting

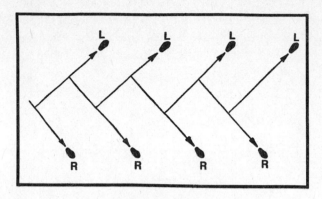

DIAGRAM 5-4

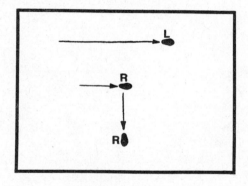

DIAGRAM 5-5

him unexpectedly between the defensive player and the basket for a center drive.

8. Forward Pivot—Hold-Out Drill: Diagram 5-6. The footwork on this change of direction drill calls for a forward pivot and a "hold-out" by the offensive player. Player O1 starts a dribble toward O2 who comes to meet the dribbler. The defensive player X2 plays O2 high to deny him a pass from O1. Player O2 plants his outside foot, pivots on the back foot to the inside. When he does this, he should get the defensive player, X2 on his hip or behind him. Now as he cuts to the basket, O2 should bring his inside arm up, and shoot it outward so as to completely block the defensive player out. Player O1 gives O2 a lead pass, which could be a bounce pass or a direct floater as he cuts into the basket on the reverse for a lay-up shot. Run the drill to both sides of the floor.

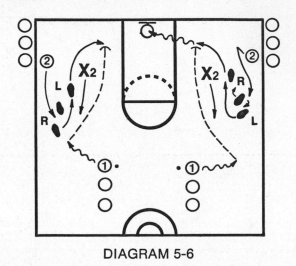

DIAGRAM 5-6

9. Change of Direction, Change of Pace Drill: Diagram 5-7. The players form three lines at one end of the court as shown. Take the players the length of the court by signals. For the first half of the court to the division line, the players change direction on signal from the coach, making the 90-degree direction changes on hand signals from the coach, and using the footwork previously described. When the court division line is reached, the players go into a slow jog, then with a fake, slightly speed up. This is then followed with a hard head and shoulder fake, and a sudden dash of full speed to the end line. This drill will help the players in the change of direction technique, and also give them the feel of the differing paces needed to develop the change of pace tactic.

10. Start, Stop Drill: Diagram 5-8. The players line up at one end of the floor in three lines. The first in line start on the first whistle. The first step should be a hard, full blast and decisive move to get away. On the second whistle the players stop. After the first line has made a start and a stop, the next in line start on a whistle. When they have cleared, the next group starts, and this is continued until all have gone the length of the floor with starts and stops. You may continue this back and

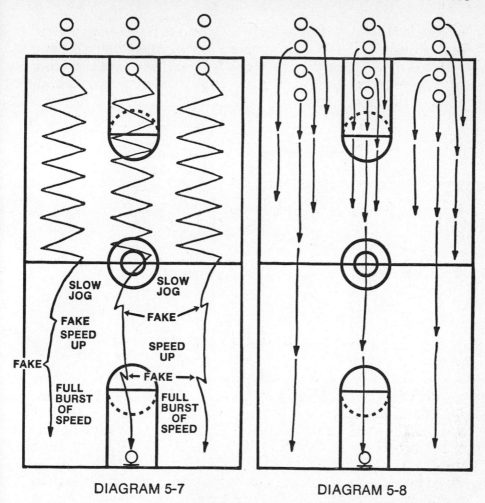

DIAGRAM 5-7   DIAGRAM 5-8

forth as long as it is advantageous. Check the players on their technique of starting and stopping. This can be used as a warm-up prelim to a full practice session after some stretching and other warm-up routines.

11. Imaginary Meet the Ball-Reverse Drill: Diagram 5-9. The players line up back of the baseline as shown. You and/or the manager or assistant coach take a ball in the positions shown. The players come out and maneuver to meet the ball outside the dotted line area, and back of the free-throw line extended. In the first rounds you never give the players the ball, but the players fake a reception or imagine they have it, pretend to drive on a dribble and shoot. In short, go through all the mechanics of receiving the ball, dribbling in and shooting, using proper footwork on reverses, change of direction, etc. After a round or two of this imagination drill, you and the manager or assistant coach can now pass the ball to the players when they shape up for reception, and they go in on a drive off the reverse direction for a shot.

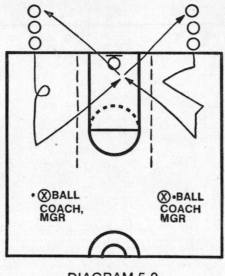

DIAGRAM 5-9

Individual Defensive Drills

IMPORTANCE OF INDIVIDUAL DEFENSIVE PLAY

A team cannot establish a sound team defense without individuals who are well-grounded in individual defensive fundamentals. Good team defensive play requires coordinated movements of individuals thoroughly schooled in solid individual defensive fundamentals. Probably your most difficult task will be to convince the individual team members of the importance of being skilled in individual and team defensive play. Defense has never been a popular word in basketball. Defensive play has appeal for only a few basketball players. The fans and the news media all popularize the scoring phase of the game. Consequently, the players and coaches seek to get recognition through this more popular phase of the game. Brilliant defensive play is seldom mentioned or eulogized by the news media and the fans. Even the coaches find themselves succumbing to the demands of the more popular phase of "the score" in the game, and as a result will be inclined to neglect the defensive concepts necessary to have a well-balanced and coordinated defensive effort from their teams.

In order to produce a sound defensive team, basic concepts must be learned by every player. Each team member must know and be able to perform the needed basic individual skills, and to use these concepts and skills in the manner necessary to make the defense function as a complete team effort. The individual moves of all players must be finely tuned and coordinated into a well-synchronized team effort if defensive play is to be successful. To secure such an effort, you have to sell the players on being enthusiastic and eager in working on both phases of the defensive game—the individual effort, and the team effort.

According to the rules of the modern game of basketball, every time a team scores, it must surrender the ball to the opponents. This fact has increased the importance of sound defensive play. When a team has lost the ball, the logical and best way to get it back is through aggressive and sound defensive play, rather than surrendering an easy score to the opponents. The rules makers in the game have struggled to keep a proper balance between offense and defense while retaining the fan and spectator appeal. The result has been an edge to the offensive phase of the game—the popular phase. Although the offensive phase and craze has a definite edge in present day rules, defense is still important. The defensive lag is due to the fact that being popular, offensive tactics and techniques have advanced more rapidly over the years. The defensive techniques haven't caught up, and probably never will.

FACTORS TO CONSIDER IN FORMULATING A DEFENSIVE PHILOSOPHY

When determining what the defensive attitude and philosophy should be in formulating your plans for coaching, you should consider the following points:

1. The team that is strong defensively is always a dangerous opponent. Being weak defensively places a great burden on offense, and being weak offensively places a great burden on the defense. The team should strive for balance in offense and defense.

2. The number of shots taken in a game by a team is much less important than the quality of the shots and the percentage of shots made. This should be the role of a sound defensive team—lowering the quality of shots taken by the opponents and thereby reducing their shooting percentages.

3. Defense is the stabilizer of the game. Defensive skill will be more consistent and have fewer "off nights" than the "shooting skills" of the game. If the team is sound defensively, the defense can carry it through the "off night" that frequently affects the more precise shooting and scoring skills.

4. The game of basketball requires both offensive and defensive play. You must work for balance in the game. Consider your predicament if the defense is poor, and a clever opponent plays a control game, forcing the team to spend most of the game time on defense—the team's weakest area.

5. A team with a good defense can control the tempo of the game. They can press, stop the fast break and force the opponent into errors, denying opponents the freedom of operating an unhindered offense—such a team will win.

6. If teams are evenly matched in material, the "edge" that the winner has usually comes from some source. Putting special emphasis on defense can provide the needed "edge," or it may overcome some "edge" that the opponent has. Since defense is neglected by so many coaches, the coach who emphasizes defense is more likely to have the "winning edge."

7. Having a sound defensive system will enable the team to handle late and last minute game situations when they are behind and scores are needed. Good defensive play is needed to combat control tactics often used by opponents in these situations. Without solid defensive play, no victory will occur.

FACTORS CONTRIBUTING TO POOR DEFENSIVE PLAY AND TEACHING

1. Recent rules changes favor the offensive player.
2. Officiating in most situations favors the offensive player.
3. The main objective of the game is to score, so most applause, recognition, and teaching is directed to this endeavor. Defensive play is neglected.
4. Defense demands hard work and requires intense concentration and determination; in return the player

receives little recognition for his effort compared to the scorer. This makes it hard for the coach to get the effort from the player.

5. Since the offensive player knows what he is going to do, the defensive player is at a guessing disadvantage. This can be discouraging to the defensive player, and is often used as an alibi for not being able to play defense well. A good defensive player will not accept this as an excuse for poor play.

6. The coach does not receive as much help in teaching defense as he gets in the offensive phase of the game. Most books, literature, games coverage, etc., have all been tuned to the offensive game, and the score—the basket.

DEVELOPING THE DEFENSIVE ATTITUDE

Although you encounter many barriers to teaching defense, there are many things you can do to overcome these barriers and to develop the defensive attitude.

1. The coaching plan must be organized so that defensive fundamentals have a definite place in the practice patterns and organization. The defensive part of the practice should be made to seem as important as the other phases of practice.

2. No player should be allowed to do less than his best on all defensive assignments and practices. The good or excellent scorer should not be allowed to loaf on defense because he can score.

3. Players who make good defensive plays should be singled out for praise and recognition as much as the scorers of the game. The fans, the community, the media should all get in on this act as much as possible.

4. Objectives and goals should be established for defensive play. Establish a quota for the number of points the opposing team should score, and allot points the individuals on the opposition team can score. Defensive players are then to be held responsible for holding opponents to or below the allotted scores. This can be done in scrimmages and practices as well as games.

5. Get the community to help recognize and praise defensive effort. If possible get a community organization to

sponsor a trophy for outstanding defensive performances over the season. Give trophies for the following:

a. The best defensive player of the year.

b. The most improved defensive player of the year.

Appropriate newspaper publicity and coverage should be given such awards. By a continuous campaign of your own, and with the cooperation of reporters and other people, you will find that in time your efforts to inculcate the defensive attitude will be rewarded.

6. You should overlook no opportunity to improve the defensive attitude of the team. You must develop in each individual a desire to play good defense. Individual pride will carry over to pride in good team defense.

7. There are many talented athletes who do not have the God-given talent to be awesome scorers. These players are good athletes, and can play superb defense. Any good athlete can play defense if he will concentrate on it. You should be sure such players get recognition for their talent. These players are needed, and recognition of their abilities and defensive accomplishments is another medium through which the coach can strengthen the whole team effort.

8. You should make the defensive phases of practice as interesting and active as possible. Get competition and recognition into the practice.

9. Do all possible things to relieve boredom of defensive play. Give recognition, make it competitive, demand perfection, develop pride in defensive accomplishment with every motivational device possible. Make defense a way of life with the players. Talk it, live it, work it, have fun at it, and defensive success will come in such a way that the players will realize that defense is winning for them.

DEFENSIVE IDEAS TO EMPHASIZE CONTINUALLY

1. Today, with the jump shot being the shot of the game—players hitting with deadly accuracy—put the emphasis on stopping the jump shooter.

2. Stopping the jump shot may mean at times doing what ordinarily would be considered unsound. Chase the jump shooter. Get in close to him.

3. Encourage the jump shooter to go where the defensive player can get help.

4. Play defense entirely with a "GO GET THE BALL" attitude. Put pressure on the ball at all times. Don't let the jump shooter have a decent shot. (Today nobody can shoot anything else, so if you stop the jump shooter, your defense is bound to be superb.)

5. Move in on the jump shooter with a wide stance and bellybutton closeness. Play him so tight he has to go around—then depend on help from teammates.

6. The most under-used weapon the defensive player has is the hands and arms. Think of the KARATE move with the hands. Move in on the shooter—get close to him—hug him—get hands up and moving from down to up positions. This does not mean throwing the hands forward or out to the extent of losing body balance. The hands and arms should be kept close to the body, but constantly moving to harass the opponent.

7. Continually emphasize the help situation on defense. Players help each other continuously. Some coaches refer to this as the "switch" or the "shift."

8. The second most under-used weapon on defense is the VOICE. A defense that talks is bound to be a tough defense. *The hands and the voice* are potent weapons to be used continually.

9. Learn how to stop the dribbler. What can the dribbler do to beat the defensive player?

   a. Most of the time he beats you in the direction he is going. Then get ahead of him in this direction—hustle and stop him.

   b. He may slow up, change pace, give a new burst of speed, or he may jockey, slow up, burst out, or give you a cross-over dribble.

   c. Get ahead of him, keep the hand down that will protect the cross-over dribble, and keep the other hand up with stance open to this side.

   d. If the dribbler reverses, *hustle and get ahead of him again.*

     e. If the dribbler bobs with head and shoulder fakes, do not move with such fakes. This is an invitation for him to drive you when you declare.

10. Work hard to teach vision on the weak side (peripheral vision). (The weak side is the side away from the ball.)

     a. Teach this philosophy. Nobody beats you to the ball.

     b. The defense must make the offense work every time they get the ball.

     c. The player must make constant adjustments as the ball moves so as to see the ball and keep position on his opponent.

11. Stress these three fundamental things on defense:

     a. Don't let the weak-side player beat you to the ball.

     b. Make the ball side player work to get the ball.

     c. Put the real heat or pressure on the man with the ball.

12. The defensive player guarding the person with the ball is the player on the spot. This is where the pressure must be applied. Only the player with the ball can score. The other four players have a responsibility to help the player guarding the person with the ball. If this player gets beaten, the other four must help.

13. Anytime a teammate gets beaten while guarding the player with the ball, the other four players must know how he got beaten. The other four have a responsibility to help this player as best they can. This was the player on the *hot seat*—the one who put the pressure on. If this player did not pressure the ball handler, the job was not being done.

     a. The basic philosophy—*everybody* helps the player guarding the person with the ball.

Coaching Points for Individual Defense

1. The important element in individual defensive play is body balance. The center of the body weight (center of gravity) should always be kept within the area of the base. The base for the defensive player is the feet.

2. The feet should be comfortably spread, and in most cases at least shoulder width apart. Some coaches prefer a boxer's stance (sometimes called a stride stance) with one foot in front of the other. Others prefer a square stance with feet parallel. There are times when both are advantageous to use.

3. Where the boxer's stance is used, either foot may be advanced, except in situations where the advanced foot could determine the direction the offensive player is to be maneuvered. The distance that one foot is advanced in front of the other will vary with each player. The player should have a natural feel in his stance.

4. Flex the knees, keep the trunk erect, with the hips low.

5. Keep the whole soles of the shoes of both feet completely on the floor. All moves are to be made from a solid base from the feet.

6. The weight of the body should be distributed over both feet evenly. If in a stride stance, and the body weight should have to favor one foot over the other, favor the weight being over the back foot.

7. Keep the hands and arms low, and working in close to the body. Work the hands and feet together. Out on the floor, when using the hands to cover, extend them straight up.

8. Never make a commitment with the hands except as the feet move.

9. The defensive player will use glide steps for establishing the path of defensive action in proper relation to the path of the dribbler or offensive player. The glide could be laterally right or left, or an oblique glide in either direction.

10. In making the glide or the shifting movement to stay with the offensive opponent, stress moving both feet at the same time. The distance between the feet may be slightly greater than during the original stance, but approximately the same. Do not move one foot and then the other. Never move one foot without moving both feet.

11. The head should not bob up and down on the glide or the shift, but should glide along evenly with the shift as both feet move. (Do not do the kangaroo shift.)

12. The feet should never be crossed in the gliding action.

13. Carry the hands and arms forward and to the side. Keep them close to the body. The height of the hands will depend upon the situation—being low on the dribbler and near full extension if there is threat of a shot.

14. Keep the hands close to the body (not reaching out) and the head should remain directly above the midpoint between the feet—keeping these body extremities close to the body and at midpoint on the base is very important to body balance.

15. Have all joints flexed to give relaxation. Be ready to move in any direction at any time.

Defensive Mistakes to Avoid

1. The player should avoid keeping the hands and arms in a high position out on the floor—so high as to take the heel of the back foot off the floor, or to bring the body up so high that the whole sole of the shoes of both feet would not be firmly planted.

2. The player should not stab downward at the ball with the hands, especially where the weight of the body is thrown forward, and in such a manner as to bring the sole of one or both feet off the floor. This kind of action causes the center of the body weight to be thrown outside the base—resulting in poor body balance, lack of stability, and inability to react to an opponent's actions.

3. The player should avoid jumping off the floor to knock the ball down on an attempted shot by an opponent out on the floor. Such effort seldom accomplishes its purpose, and leaves the player out of defensive position. More can be accomplished with less commitment by keeping proper defensive rebounding position.

4. The player should never, while on defense, stand erect, or upright without being in the defensive stance. To do so means the player is not defensive minded and that he is not alert.

5. The player should never rest or loaf on defense. Defense requires constant hustle, work, communication to be effective.

Habit Drills to Teach Individual Defense

1. The Defensive Shift Drill: Diagram 6-1. Drill 1. This formation can be used at the beginning of practice to do various defensive and warm-up drills. The players take the formation shown. Start with a leader or coach out in front, and do stretching exercises briefly. Then run in place, keeping the hands above the waist. Remember, basketball players should have the hands above the waist at all times. After running in place for a short time, hop on both feet. Do two hops and then jump for height. Take turns hopping on the right and then the left foot and on the third jump or hop on each foot, jump for height. Pretend to go up after a ball, bringing it down. Now do imitation jump balls—actually jump as if going up for a jump ball. Go over proper techniques and form for jump on a jump ball, and the coach should check constantly. Follow this with five push-ups on finger tips. Players should do five with ease. After this brief pre-practice warm-up the players should be ready for Drill 2 and the mass defensive shift drill.

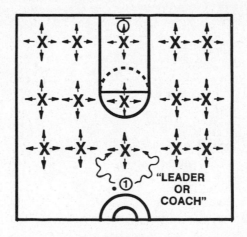

DIAGRAM 6-1

2. Drill 2: This drill should follow Drill 1, and using this formation, can be used in several drills to teach the mechanics and footwork of the defensive stance, the retreat step, the drop step, and the defensive glide. The players face the leader, and take the defensive stance as if guarding the leader with a ball.

The stance should be checked to see that the players are in the proper stance. Hands should be held with palms upward, arms bent, and both close to the body. In this drill the leader will call the direction of the shift by calling forward, right, back, left, etc., or he may point in the direction of the desired shift, and the players shift in the direction indicated. The leader should start out by doing the drill three minutes a day, then increase the time as the season goes along until the players are conditioned to do the drill to the time limit desired by the coach, perhaps 8 to 12 minutes per day. While the drill is being done, the coach should check the stance, the footwork, the glide, and the various defensive position techniques.

3. Drill 3: Using the same formation as shown in Diagram 6-1, the leader takes a ball, and each player in the formation takes a stance as if guarding the leader. It should be announced beforehand whether the leader is right-or left-handed, and the direction in which he is to be forced on his drive. The players take a stance accordingly. If the leader fakes only, the players retreat step, and immediately reverse into an attack step. If the leader drives to the side of the open stance, the players retreat step and do the defensive glide to counter the move. If the leader drives opposite the direction of the forward foot, the players retreat step, then drop step and go into the defensive glide to counter this move. The coach should check the mechanics of the footwork of the players. This drill should be worked in with drills 1 and 2 in timing the work done on the defensive techniques each day.

4. One-on-One Drill: Diagram 6-2. In this drill the players pair up and scatter about the floor as shown in this diagram. One ball is allotted to each pair, and one player takes the ball on the offensive and the other attacks the man with the ball, playing one-on-one against each other. The offensive player with the ball, using the rocker step techniques, and other offensive fakes and footwork, tries to outmaneuver the defensive player and drive around him. The defensive player is to prevent the offensive player with the ball from driving around him. The players take turns on offense and defense. The coach constantly checks to perfect the defensive techniques. If the defensive player makes his first and second moves properly, the offensive player will have a hard time driving around him.

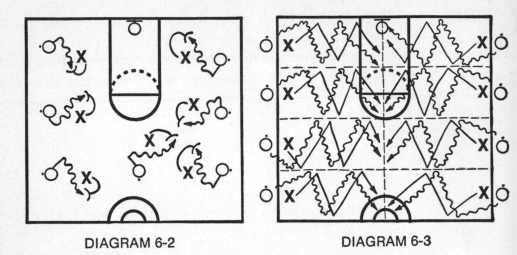

DIAGRAM 6-2   DIAGRAM 6-3

5. Defense and Dribble Drill: Diagram 6-3. In this drill the court is divided into imaginary lines as shown by the dotted lines. This is in reality a twofold drill, one player working on the dribble, and the other on defense. The player with the ball, starting at the sideline, works on the dribble and dribbles halfway across the court working on the cross-over, change of direction, change of pace, faking, etc., in an effort to beat the defensive player. The defensive player just works on maintaining position on the dribbler. He should not slap at the ball with the hands, but should keep one hand down to protect on the cross-over, the other hand up, with stance open to the side of the dribble, maintaining good defensive position. The players should work first at half speed, and then later at full speed. When the imaginary line at the middle of the court is reached, the players change off on offense and defense and work back to the side line. The whole court can be utilized in this drill.

6. One-on-One from Guard-Forward Positions: Diagram 6-4. The players position themselves at the two guard spots and in the forward operational areas as shown. The forward takes the ball in the forward operational area (all players work this spot as well as the guard spot) with his back to the defensive player. The defensive player reaches out and flicks the offensive player across the hips, and this is the signal to start. The offensive player turns, faces his opponent and goes into his jab steps, rocker moves, fakes, step backs, and drives to get the defensive player committed so that he can drive past him or around him for a shot. When the forward turns to face the defensive player, the defense moves to the attack and to defense the offensive player with the ball. This same drill is worked from the guard operational areas, except that the player with the ball does not turn his back to the defensive player. The players rotate positions and go from offense to defense in each position on the floor. The action is rotated from spot to spot while all the players observe the action with the coach constantly checking the defensive techniques. Various contests can be held and scores can be kept in a one-on-one contest to motivate the players and to give competitive interest to the drill. The "Defensive Drill Man of the Week" could be selected from contests using this drill, and some reward given each week. Place emphasis on the defensive player stopping the player with the ball.

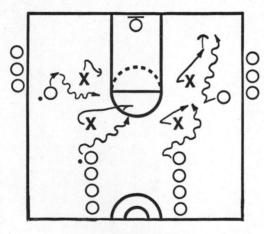

DIAGRAM 6-4

7. Defensive Footwork Drill: Diagram 6-5. This is another defensive footwork drill. A stop watch should be used. The players work for 10 seconds at a slow warm-up speed. This should be followed with 20 seconds at half speed, then followed with 30 seconds at full speed. The tempo should be changed by the coach's whistle. Player O is the offensive player. Player X is the defensive player. The drill can be run from the sideline to the middle of the court as shown in the diagram, or it could be worked with fewer players, working from the end line to the court division line. The defensive player hooks his thumbs inside his belt, and guards the offensive player without using his hands and arms, learning to stay with O, using footwork only. Player O, the offensive player, makes all possible maneuvers to elude the defensive player by starting, faking, stopping, changing directions, changing pace, etc., without the ball. The players take turns on defense and offense. After running the drill with thumbs tucked inside the belt, the drill should be repeated allowing the defense to use the hands and arms along with the feet. The drill may be run with, or without, the ball. The purpose: To learn to play defense with the feet and the mind.

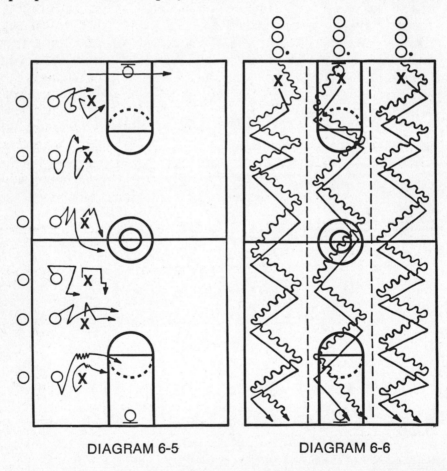

DIAGRAM 6-5   DIAGRAM 6-6

8. One-on-One—Full Length of the Court: Diagram 6-6. The court is divided into imaginary lines as shown so that each group has about one third of the court. Much like the defense and dribbler drill, the players work one-on-one the full length of the court going one-on-one, using only one third the width of the court. After going the full length of the court, the defensive player becomes the dribbler and the dribbler the defensive player, and they return the length of the court. The defensive player just slides with the dribbler, makes the necessary drop step movements, and changes direction as needed to slide with the dribbler when he does the cross-over.

9. **Seat-Tag Drill: Diagram 6-7.** The players are divided into offensive and defensive groups, with abilities about even. The objective of the offensive O players is to cross the division court line without being tagged on the seat. The O's line up along the end line under the basket. The X's, the defense, line up along the side line. Player X1 moves out to the top of the free-throw circle, and as soon as O1 moves into the free-throw land area on the court, X1 moves in to tag him on the seat. The sideline is out of bounds and O1 may use any maneuver he can to get around X1, such as fakes, feints, change of direction, change of pace. If O1 gets across the 10-second division line without being tagged on the seat, he is the winner. The defensive players, the X's, are to attack the O's with defensive stance, not crossing feet, etc., in an effort to tag the offensive player on the seat before crossing the line. The players rotate from offense to defense.

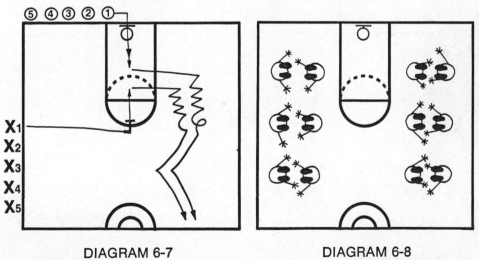

DIAGRAM 6-7   DIAGRAM 6-8

10. **Knee Tag Drill: Diagram 6-8.** In this drill the players are divided into pairs, of about equal abilities in quickness. The pairs face each other, and take a very low squatting position, almost a sitting position. They reach forward with the hands to touch the inside of the knee of the opponent. The opponent

dances to prevent the touching, and counters to touch inside of his opponent's knee. Each touch counts one point. When a touch is made, the player calls aloud his count or score. They dance and spar to touch. Highest score in a time limit set by the coach is the winner. Games and contests can be held with this drill— elimination tournaments—determining a winner of "Best Knee-Touch" or "Quickest Hands" player of the week. The drill helps to develop quickness of hands and feet and also helps to stress the importance of body balance, keeping low, and moving hands and feet properly on defense.

11. Quick Hands Drill: Diagram 6-9. In this drill the players line up as shown. The first two players in the line face each other in close, and standing low. The Coach tosses a ball between the two players—player with the quickest hands gets it. Two out of three would be the winner and the next two come up for their turn. The drill will help develop quick hands, footwork and body control needed to get in position for ball recovery.

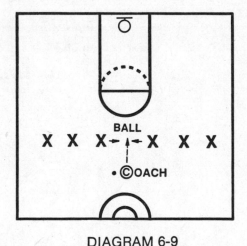

DIAGRAM 6-9

12. Defensive Lateral Glide Drill: Diagram 6-10. This drill is to make habitual the footwork of the lateral glide of the defensive player. The O players (offense) and the X players (defense) line up facing each other as shown. Player O1, the first player in the offensive line with the ball, dribbles laterally across the floor. Player X1 moves in on O1, and glides laterally in a wide defensive stance, keeping position on O1 as he moves across the floor. Player X1 moves both feet at the same time, and does foot movements necessary to keep position, and never crosses his legs in this glide. Player X1 also keeps hands moving in close to the body, but on the ball, with palms up. The dribbler should fake, bob, change pace in his move across the floor to give the defensive player some work in covering deception. The players go to the positions shown to make a change from offense to defense, and O1 rolls the ball to O2 where O2 and X2 repeat the drill.

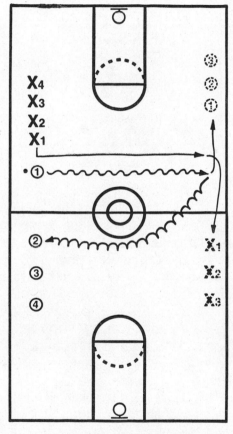

DIAGRAM 6-10

13. Catch the Dribbler Drill: Diagram 6-11. Two lines are formed as shown. Player O1 is given a ball, and starts a fast-driving dribble for the basket. Player X1, in the defensive line, is to run hard to catch O1, establish defensive position on him, and then turn his drive away from the basket. Once position is established, he goes into the defensive stance and glides with the offensive dribbler to keep position on him and to control the offensive dribbler. This is a good drill to teach the defensive player how to establish defensive position, once the dribbler has gained an advantage on him.

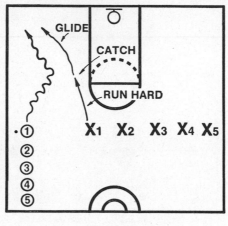

DIAGRAM 6-11

14. Sprint-Glide Drill: Diagram 6-12. This drill is combined with some conditioning to teach the lateral defensive glide. It also puts emphasis on the necessity of sprinting to establish position on the offensive player. The players line up along the end line as shown. On a signal the first player (X1) sprints from the end line to the court division line. Bending over, touching the line, X1 now glides laterally on the defensive glide to the opposite side line—and after touching the side line, he now sprints to the far end line, touches it, and glides to the opposite side line, touches it, sprints to the division court line, touches it, glides to the opposite side line, touches it, and sprints to the end line from which he started. As soon as X1 has cleared a comfortable distance, he is followed by X2, X3, and the others until all have done the drill.

15. Sprint-Glide, Return Drill: Diagram 6-13. The players line up as shown, paired up as offensive and defensive players, O's being offense, X's being defense. The offensive players sprint toward the opposite end line, as shown in this diagram, by O1. Player X1 sprints to head him off, turns him back, and X1 then glides back in defensive glide with O1. Player O1 returns part way, and then sprints again and again, and X1 repeats. This is repeated by each pair until the opposite end line is reached.

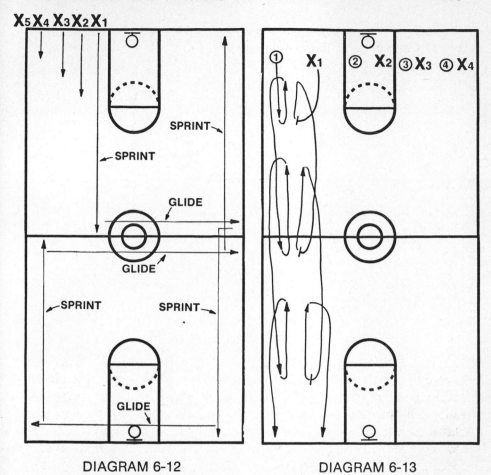

DIAGRAM 6-12   DIAGRAM 6-13

16. Reaction One-on-One Drill: Diagram 6-14. This is a good drill to develop reaction and aggressiveness in the players. The players form two lines near the court division line about 15 to 20 feet apart. You hold a ball and take a position equidistant between the players. You toss the ball out on the floor, and the first two players, O1 and O2, go hard to recover the loose ball. The player who recovers the ball immediately goes on a drive for the basket. The player who failed in the possession attempt must go on defense and hustle to stop the offensive player in a one-on-one play. The ball becomes dead when the offensive player scores, the defensive man recovers the ball, or it is lost out-of-bounds.

17. Defensive One-on-One Close-out Drill: Diagram 6-15. Both ends of the floor or all baskets can be used for this drill. The defensive players line up under the basket. The offensive

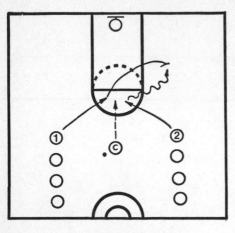

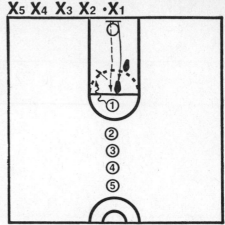

DIAGRAM 6-14   DIAGRAM 6-15

players line up out on the court as shown. When O1 reaches the free-throw line, X1, who has a ball, passes it to O1. Player X1 then advances quickly to defense O1 who goes on the offense in a one-on-one. Player X1 should approach quickly and aggressively in a proper defensive stance. Player O1 may shoot over X1 if he is slow closing in, or he may drive, using all his jabs, rocker steps, fakes, etc., to free himself for the drive to the basket. Player X1 will guard all offensive players before taking his turn at offense, and this goes on until all have taken their turn at offense and defense. Score can be kept for the individuals, or teams can be matched in a score and a defensive effort.

18. Two-on-One Drill: Diagram 6-16. In this drill, O1 with the ball passes in to O2 who is defensed by X2. Player O2 maneuvers from the forward operational area to beat X2. Player X2 plays his defense in an aggressive manner and is to deny the pass into O2 if possible. Player X2 must make O2 work hard to get the ball and should play with his inside foot forward, and almost on the line from the ball to the opponent, as shown in the diagram. Player O2 maneuvers to get the ball, and when he does get the ball, he tries to beat X2. If O2 gets in trouble or kills the dribble, he may pass back to O1 and start the drill over again. The defensive work of X2 should be constantly checked. In taking the stance or foot position shown, should O2 reverse the back side or baseline side of X2, X2 must turn to the inside, pivoting on the back and outside foot, face the ball, and play to break up the move in this way. Next on offense will be O3. Player O2 will be the next defensive player. In this drill the defensive player gets work on guarding the player with and without the ball. The coach or manager could be used to do the O1 feeder position if desired.

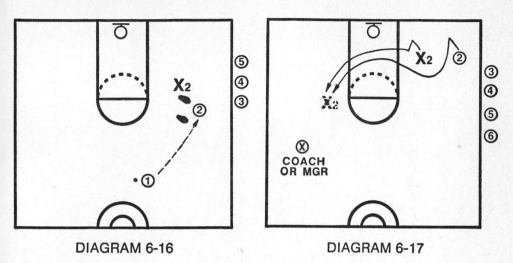

DIAGRAM 6-16   DIAGRAM 6-17

19. Guarding the Weak-Side Cutter: Diagram 6-17. This drill is to teach the defensive player to guard the player without the ball and to learn how to prevent the opponent from receiving the ball in a dangerous scoring zone, You, the manager, or another player, have the ball as shown in the diagram. Player O2, on the opposite side of the court, maneuvers and breaks toward the ball to get open for a pass. Player X2 must take a stance that will enable him to see the ball and his opponent, O2. He must not let O2 execute a reverse against him or break into the vital scoring area where he will be able to receive the ball. He can play O2 loosely until O2 approaches the areas where he could receive the ball. Player X2 should play at the side and in front of O2, if necessary, to prevent him from receiving the ball. At times X2 should face the ball, and screen O2 out of the play in order to keep him from moving to receive a pass. If O2 receives the ball in this area, then X2 defenses him in the best way he can. O2 may pass back to you or the outlet player, if he is countered. Player X2 should front O2 completely anytime he is below the free-throw line area to prevent a pass to him. At the free-throw line, and possibly a little higher, he should play O2 to the front and side toward the ball. The players rotate on offense and defense so that every player has an opportunity to participate equally on defense and offense.

7

Team Defensive Drills

The importance of individual defensive play has been stressed in Chapter 6. Once the individual has mastered the techniques of the fundamentals of individual defensive play, the key to having an excellent team defense has been found. You now have the weapons with which to build a team unit. It is conceded today that a good offensive player can beat a good defensive player in a one-on-one duel *most* of the time. To be effective, then, the defensive unit cannot rely on one against one defensive play. The players must be molded into an effective team unit. When the players are individually sound and well-schooled in defensive techniques, your job will be much easier, and can be much more effective, but the job of coaching defense is not complete until the five players learn to work together as a team unit and to be aware of the need to help teammates who are on the pressure spots. You must recognize that, although there are physical and psychological barriers that hinder the defensive teaching process, progressive coaching methods can build a highly favorable team attitude toward defense. The team defensive fundamentals, strategy, and knowledge must be organized into the coaching schedule and patterns as clearly and definitely as the offensive patterns. All uncertainties must be removed, and players must know their exact duties in the various defenses used in team play.

Basketball has been and still is a changing game. Once upon a time it was a cardinal sin for a defensive player to allow the opposing offensive player to go around him, or to cut the base line on a drive. In basketball today, the 15-, 18-, or 20-foot jump shooter is so effective he has to be stopped. This means moving in tight on these shooters—so tight that they can go around the defense on many occasions. The defensive player in many situations needs to chase the shooter so avidly that the shooter is encouraged to drive and go around and inside the defense where teammates can help.

Only the player with the ball can score. Only the player with the ball can shoot. The defensive player guarding the person with the ball is the player on the *hot seat*. This player, with his teammates collaborating, now plays defense with a go-get-the-ball attitude. Pressure must be put on "the point of the ball." The shooter must be stopped. Chase the player with the ball and encourage him to go in where the defensive player guarding him can get help. All the players on the defensive team must know where the ball is, who the defensive player is that is guarding the ball, and all the other four players must be prepared to help this player at all times. With this kind of attitude, regardless of the type of defense the coach teaches, an effective defensive unit should be possible.

Coaching Points for Team Defense

1. Your first task may be to eliminate boredom in defensive practice. Allow the defensive unit to fast break when they get the ball. Also work out a point system—the defense gets one point when they get the ball—the offense gets two points for scoring a basket. Make it as competitive and meaningful as possible.

2. You should work upon every idea possible to develop the proper attitude toward team defensive play. It should be a team effort to keep the player with the ball from scoring.

3. The greatest team weapon the players have is the *voice*. The players must communicate constantly with the voice. They can let each other know where they are, what is happening behind them, alerting each other to

trouble situations—always encouraging the defensive player guarding the player with the ball, and always being alert to help this player who must put the "pressure" on. The use of the voice will not happen—it must be coached continuously. The defense that talks is bound to be a tough defense.

4. Coaches will differ on whether they want to "switch" on screens, or "HELP" each other. Whatever it is called, it definitely will call for a "help situation" in many instances. The defensive player guarding the player with the ball will have to have help when he pressures the "point of the ball" and the other four defensive players should be prepared to give it immediately and effectively.

5. The defensive player guarding the offensive player with the ball should challenge him—rush him, square-off on him, over-play him, move in belly-button tight—get hands high.

6. You as a coach can, with your offense, dictate how the defense will play. But you, with your *defense, must* dictate how the opposing offense will play. To do this you cannot sit back and play a normal defense. You must do the unusual.

7. Use the element of surprise. You must be able to use many combinations of defense to survive in basketball today. Use full-court pressure defenses, man-to-man, combination defenses, three-fourths court press, combination zones and man-to-man, half-court pressure—be able to do it all, and do it. The day of multiple defenses is here.

8. Be sure your defensive team can and does recognize the important problems. The number one problem is to guard the player with the ball and especially the 15- to 20-foot jump shooter.

9. The second most important problem is to prevent the ball from moving into dangerous scoring areas. For defensive purposes divide the court into areas. See Diagram 7-1. Area A is to be regarded as a ZONE area. In this area always play between the offensive player and the ball to prevent passes into the area. In a normal defensive situation, divide the court into three areas,

Area A, B and C. Area A is a strict ZONE situation and considered the vital scoring area. Play between the man and the ball to prevent passes into this area. Expect to be effective in preventing this 70% to 80% of the time. In area B, pressure the ball excessively.

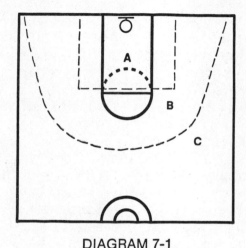

DIAGRAM 7-1

10. The third problem your players must recognize is the need to guard or cover the drive of the wing player, or the cut of the weak-side player in movements toward the ball. The player should never be able to break into area A ahead of the defensive player to receive the ball.

11. Be sure the team can cover these four situations on defense. Drill your players so that they automatically know how to cover each situation.

    a. The cross and roll by the guards, or the screen and roll-off cut in any situation.

    b. The split-the-post play.

    c. The pass and go either inside or outside for a screen play.

    d. The sucker play, or the simple pass and cut play.

12. Coach the team so that each defensive player will make his opponent work to get the ball. Recognize that when the opponent gets the ball, the defense changes—you are now guarding an opponent with the ball. You put pressure on the ball and you will need help.

Habit Drills to Teach Team Defenses

You can begin teaching team defense by first teaching the defensive responsibilities of two against two from the two guard spots, and from the guard-forward positions. Then pit three against three from the guard-forward and the pivot-post positions. Follow this with four against four—guard, guard-forward, and pivot-post position, and then add the fifth player—and develop the full team defense. By taking this approach the players learn their duties step by step, and their exact duties in given situations are more firmly imprinted and conditioned in their responses in defensive play.

1. Two against Two at the Guard Positions: Diagram 7-2. If O1 and O2 make a cross maneuver in Area C, outside the shooting range or effective scoring range, defensive players X1 and X2 slide through and stay with their assigned opponents. When O1 dribbles as shown, X1 goes with him. Player O2, cutting over the top of O1 to receive the ball and take away on a dribble, is outside the effective shooting range, so X2 will slide through behind O1, and go between X1 and O1. While doing this, X1 may need to drop off slightly to allow X2 to slide through. Here the use of the voice begins, and X1 and X2 communicate constantly, talking so that each knows what the other is going to do. Player X1 could say, "slide through, slide through, stay with him, etc." Player X2's response: "I have him, I have him." Player X1 could even aid X2 by placing his hands on X2's hips and guiding him through.

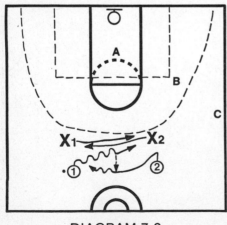

DIAGRAM 7-2

DIAGRAM 7-3

2. Two against Two, Guard Positions—Area B: Diagram 7-3. In this situation, the cross maneuver and exchange between the two guards must be handled differently. Player O1 drives the ball into area B, and into an effective jump-shot range. Player X2 cannot slide behind O1 and be effective. If he does, O2 can take the ball and have an open shot from behind a screen. Player X1 stays tight on O1. Player X2 moves with O2, and as O2 moves over O1 to receive the ball, X2 must "go over the top" with him, sliding in between O1 and O2. Here again, X1 and X2 communicate constantly, with X1 saying, "stick tight, stick tight, over the top, stay with him," etc. Player O2 responds with appropriate words such as, "I've got him, I'm with him," etc. If X2 should be bumped out of the play by an effective screen, then X1 must be prepared to step out on O2 immediately so as to prevent the effective jump shot from behind a screen. In this case X2 must drop back immediately to take O1. Constant talk keeps the assignments straight. If X2 sees he cannot effectively slide through over the top, he should call to X1, "Help, help" or "take him, take him," etc. Good defensive players are seldom screened, and by constant work, players can effectively manipulate the slide through maneuver "over the top" on screens within the effective scoring area.

3. Guard-Forward Maneuver: Diagram 7-4. Next go to a drill using the guard and forward operational areas or spots. Teach the proper defensive mechanics for those areas. This diagram gives a common guard-forward maneuver with O1

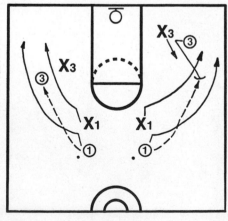

DIAGRAM 7-4

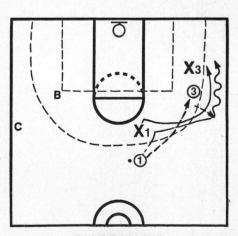

DIAGRAM 7-5

passing to O3 and cutting to the outside for an outside screen. If O3 is outside the effective shooting range for O1, then X3 should loosen up slightly and call for X1 to "slide through." Player X1 will slide through between O3 and X3 and stay with O1. Constant voice communication between X1 and X3 must be maintained.

4. Guard-Forward Maneuver: Diagram 7-5. If O1 should be an effective shooter from the side, or if the guard-forward maneuver should be executed deep inside area B, at a point and place where O1 would be in an effective scoring range with a jump shot from behind a screen, then the defensive maneuver should be executed with X1 sliding over the top of O3, and sticking very close to O1. This is an "over the top," stick tight maneuver. Should O1 be bumped off on the screen, here again X3 must be ready to help and move in on O1 if he receives the ball, with X1 dropping back quickly to pick up O3.

5. Guard-Forward Inside Screen Maneuver: Diagram 7-6. When the offense executes an inside screen as shown here, X1 goes with the opponent O1, the screener, and loosens up slightly in order to be effective on O1 if he should do a roll-away maneuver. Since X1 is not being screened, he should do most of the talking on this maneuver, calling to X3 to watch for the screen. Player X3 should fight his way "over the top" and around the screen so that he can stick tight on O3. If X3 cannot slide between O1 and O3, his next choice is to slide between O1 and X1 to stick as tight on O3 as possible. Voice communication must be constant.

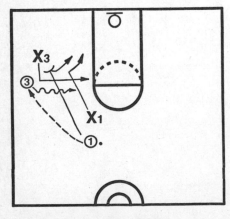

DIAGRAM 7-6

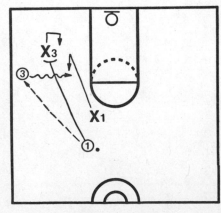

DIAGRAM 7-7

6. Guard-Forward Inside Screen: Diagram 7-7. If X3 is consistently screened out on this inside screen maneuver by the offense, then defensive players X1 and X3, with voice communication, go into a help situation. When X1 follows O1 to the screening situation, he drops off slightly, and when O3 starts his dribble off the screen, X1 takes him. Player X3 now steps back and into position to defense O1 on any move he may make on a roll-off. Should O3 reverse back, constant talk and maneuvers between the two defensive players should get a declaration from the dribbler, and they should be able to keep the help situation straightened out. This help situation should only be used when it is impossible for X3 to fight through "over the top."

7. Zoning Area A: Diagram 7-8. Before a team defense can really be effective, it must be able to prevent passes into area A, the "dangerous zone" or vital scoring area. All players should be schooled in this technique, and this drill should accomplish the objective. Players O1, O2, O3, and O4 pass the ball around rapidly in an effort to work the ball into Area A to O5. Player O5 works and maneuvers to get open, but X5 defenses him by checking, fronting, siding, stepping in front of him to block his moves—doing anything to prevent the pass inside to O5— anything that is within the rules. Player X5 must make every effort to stay between O5 and the ball to prevent a passing inside to the vital scoring area.

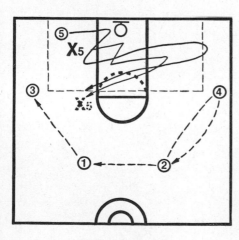

DIAGRAM 7-8

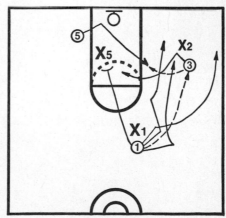

DIAGRAM 7-9

8. Three against Three: Diagram 7-9. After teaching two against two defensive maneuvers, go to three against three, using the guard, forward, and pivot-post positions on offense. Now the defensive maneuvers that must be used when the ball goes into the pivot-post position must be taught. If offensive players cut by the pivot-post player in screening maneuvers, the "over the top" principle of sticking tight must apply and be practiced. If screens are effective, the "HELP" situation must be applied—with the VOICE communication process being used to the fullest extent to be sure that assignments are straight, and that pressure is applied to the player with the ball. When O1 passes in to O3, he may take any of the movement options indicated, and scrimmage play progresses from there to give the defense all the possible options they would confront in an actual game situation. When either O1 or O3 pass into O5 at the pivot-post position, if they take the option of breaking past O5 to secure a screen, the proper defense is to be worked out so that defensive team assignments are clearly defined.

9. Four against Four: Diagram 7-10. For further development in mastering the team defense, now go four against four. Throw in the guard maneuvers and the proper defensing moves, the guard-forward moves, with proper defensing, defensing the pivot-post area (preventing passes thereto) and defensing moves made over and around the pivot-post, once the ball is passed into that position.

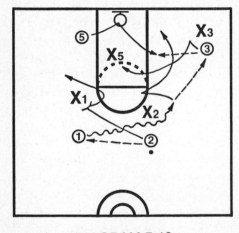

DIAGRAM 7-10

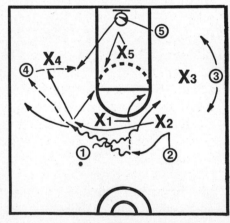

DIAGRAM 7-11

10. Five against Five: Diagram 7-11. Now the team should be ready to go five against five, with the defensive team movements being coordinated against the many complicated offensive moves. You now coordinate your defense as a team making sure all players know their assignments and what they must do to handle each situation as you, the coach, want your defense to handle it. Have the offense work the various situations that you want them to be especially adept at handling. Leave nothing to chance—be sure each team member knows what to do in each situation, and that all know how to help the defensive player guarding the ball—the player on the *hot seat*.

GUARDING THE PLAYER WITHOUT THE BALL

When the player with the ball passes off to a teammate, the position of the defensive player must change immediately. The defensive player should determine his play by consideration of *two imaginary lines*—one drawn from the ball to the player he is guarding, and the other, a line drawn from the same opponent to the basket. Immediately after the offensive player has passed the ball to a teammate, the defensive player drops off on the imaginary line from the opponent to the basket. The player now changes his stance so that he can watch his offensive opponent and the ball. The drop-off or fall away is often referred to as a *sag* or a *float*. In reality it is a *zone defense move*, and the application of a *zone principle*. The defensive player is playing both his opponent and the ball. The first move is a drop-off on the line toward the basket from the offensive opponent. The player will now make adjustments from this line toward the second imaginary line from the ball to the opponent. The distance the player SAGS will be determined by a number of factors such as his speed, the opponent's speed, the distance the ball is from the opponent, and the speed with which the opponents move and pass the ball. Alertness and acuity must be developed in these situations. The defensive player must not lose his stance when he does this sag, nor should the center of gravity be changed by standing up higher in a more relaxed position. The defensive player must remain low and in a balanced position, ready to play the opponent and to counter any offensive moves by the opponent being guarded. If the opponent should move into the vital scoring area, area A, the defensive player must maneuver into a position that will prevent the opponent from receiving the ball. Allowing the opponent to receive the ball in this area is equivalent to giving the opponent two points.

You should work hard to teach the players to use peripheral vision on the weak side (the side away from the ball). Anytime the ball is moved by the opponents (either a pass or a dribble), the defensive player must make constant adjustments in his position so that he will be able to see the ball, and at the same time keep position in relation to the opponent. Play the opponent through the ball. The defensive player must be ingrained with the philosophy and thinking that no opponent shall ever be allowed to break from the weak-side area and receive the ball in the vital scoring areas. This will often necessitate having the defensive player play in FRONT of the opponent and directly between him and the ball, while facing the ball. At other times it will involve watching the player by partially siding him in such a manner as to keep the player from receiving the ball.

11. Learning to Play the Triangle: Diagram 7-12. Have the offensive players move the ball around from player to player rapidly. The defensive players work on properly defensing the player with the ball (X1); on defensing properly to make the player on the ball side of the floor work hard to get the ball (X3) (note foot position of X3 shown); on defensing the weak-side player, and not letting that player break toward the ball, ahead of the defensive player, to receive the ball in the scoring area (X4). Note the dotted lines giving the two imaginary lines that the defensive players must be aware of and play at all times—the line from the opponent to the ball, and the line from the opponent to the basket. When the opponent *does not* have the ball, the defensive player must make adjustments in position between these two lines based on the speed of the opponent, distance from the ball, position of the ball, his own speed, speed of opponent's passing and the defensive application being made at the time. When the opponent *has the ball*, there is only one line

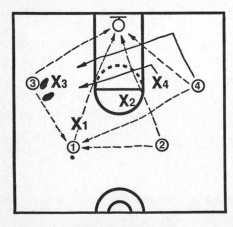

DIAGRAM 7-12

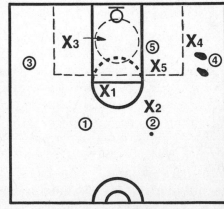

DIAGRAM 7-13

application to be made—the imaginary line from the opponent to the basket—and since his opponent has the ball, this defensive player must apply pressure.

12. Application of the Team Principle of the Sag: Diagram 7-13. Have the players pass the ball around the various positions, and develop the basic concepts of the weak-side float or sag as shown in this diagram. Player O2 has the ball. Player X2 guards him tight at the point of the ball. Player X4 plays O4 in such a manner as to deny him the ball or to make him work to get the ball. Defensive players X1 and X3 sag into the middle area of the court and toward the basket. They play almost a zone principle, but must drop straight back on an imaginary line from their opponent to the basket. They will then make adjustments, considering an imaginary line from the ball to their opponent, and adjust between these two lines so that they always keep their man and the ball in view. Player X1 must learn how far he can float or move away from O1. He must make sure he can quickly advance to the attack position on O1, should O2 pass to him. Player X5 plays in front of O5 and between him and the ball, since O5 is in area A. Should a floater pass be attempted over X5's head, X3 is responsible for the area behind him, and he must give help from the weak side. Player X3's sag is considerable, and again is determined by his speed, his opponent's speed, and how fast the opponents move the ball. Player X3 must be sure to know where the opponent, O3 is, and where the ball is. He is responsible for the dotted area behind him, should a teammate lose his opponent who breaks into this area. Player X3 must always make sure that O3 never breaks into Area A ahead of him toward the ball—always being ready to front him, and step in front of him to block him out. The front line on this defense will not be parallel at any time—note the positions of X2 and X1.

13. Covering the Pivot-Post Player: Diagram 7-14. Player X5 should play in front of and to the side of O5, if he should break high to meet a pass in the outer half of the free-throw circle. Player X5 in this case should front and side O5. Player X3 is responsible for the high passes over O5's head, should O2 float a pass into this area to beat X5 in his effort to cut off passes to O5 in the high position.

14. Movement of the Defense with the Ball: Diagram 7-15. You must coach the players to move and adjust their defensive positions as the ball moves. Player X1 must learn how

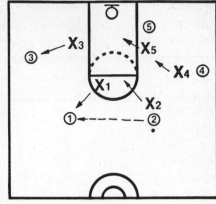

DIAGRAM 7-14   DIAGRAM 7-15

far to sag off so that O1 can be covered when the ball is passed to him as shown here. Player X2 drops off into the hole as shown when O2 passes the ball to O1. Player X2 should not turn his back, but should drop straight back immediately in order to keep both the man he is guarding and the ball in view. Players X4 and X3 will also vary their positions as the ball moves. When the ball moves from O2 to O1, X3 will tighten his position on O3 and make him work to get the ball. Now X4 can slide off O4, and will be responsible for the deep areas behind O5 should he advance to meet the ball.

    15. Rebound Coverage on a Shot: Diagram 7-16. If the offense should decide to put up a shot to give O5 the inside rebound position because of the way X5 plays in front to prevent

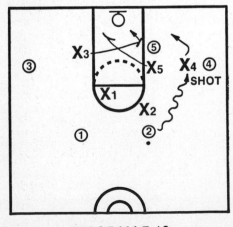

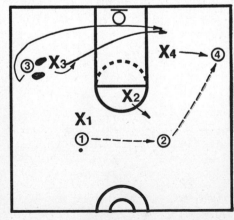

DIAGRAM 7-16   DIAGRAM 7-17

passes into the vital scoring areas, rebounding responsibilities must be practiced and established. If O2 should dribble as shown and put the ball up on a shot, then X3 should move in quickly from the weak side to block O5 off the boards. Now X5 should cross over to the opposite side to cover the rebound area on the side vacated by X3. Player X4 will block out and cover the right side, and as a result, the rebound areas will have the usual coverage.

16. Deny the Ball on the Reverse: Diagram 7-17. The defense should make an all-out effort to prevent the ball side forwards from receiving the ball. When O1 has the ball, note the foot position of X3 in his play to deny O3 the ball. If O3 should reverse and back door X3 on this move, X3 must play the ball, pivoting to the inside so that he can see the ball, and then move so that he is ahead of O3 as he comes up underneath the basket or inside area A. As the ball is passed from O1 to O2 to O4, X4 should move out quickly to the denial position on O4.

17. Deny the Ball Inside: Diagram 7-18, Phase 1. In this drill, the players move the ball around the horn, and the defense works on covering properly on both the ball side and the weak side. The players use peripheral vision, voice, talking constantly, making the offensive players work hard to get the ball. Note the foot position of X3 when O1 has the ball.

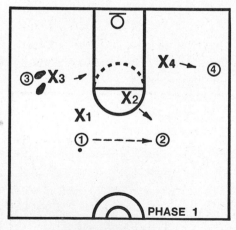

DIAGRAM 7-18

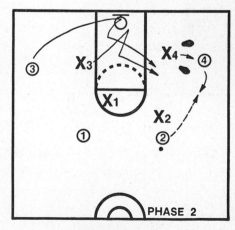

DIAGRAM 7-19

Deny the Ball Inside: Diagram 7-19, Phase 2. When the ball is moved from O1 to O2, X4 moves out to the denial position on O4, so as to prevent him from receiving the ball in a favorable position. When O2 and O4 receive the ball, X3 must change his position and must not allow O3, now the weak-side player, to maneuver so as to receive the ball inside the vital scoring area, area A. Player X3 must not allow O3 to move ahead of him in this area.

18. Sliding Through on Defense: Diagram 7-20. Use a four-man weave offense to teach the slide-through technique on defense. The four offensive players shown, O1, O2, O3, and O4 work the four-man weave, and the defensive players talk and slide through on the screens, keeping defensive assignments straight, and proper position at all times. On the slide-through, when the offensive weave is maneuvering outside the circle area, the slide-through should be one-man deep away from the opponent, but when the offense presses the defense back inside the top of the circle, the slide-through must "go over the top" tight with the opponent so that no player can receive the ball behind a screen and take an unmolested jump shot.

DIAGRAM 7-20

19. Deny the Trigger Spots: Diagram 7-21. Most teams will want to trigger their offense to the right side of the floor. Drill the defense in denying these trigger spots. Practice and drill on having the guards bring the ball across the court division line, and as shown here, if O1 is right-handed, and he brings the ball up floor on the left side, play the inside and force him to the left. A blind screen applied here with O1 going left will hurt less often than if he is allowed to go to his right. If the offense brings the ball up-court as O2 is doing on the right side of the floor, defense to the outside, forcing the player to the left. A blind screen with O2 going to the right can hurt the defense more often than it would with the player being forced left. Reverse this procedure for the left-handed player bringing the ball up-court.

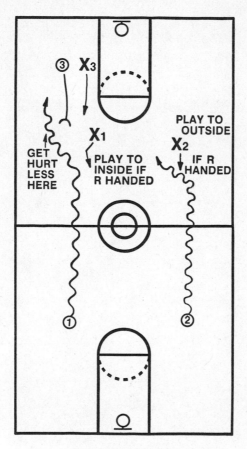

DIAGRAM 7-21

DRILLS TO TEACH SWITCHING

Many coaches prefer to "switch on defense" rather than to slide through, or to stick tight by "going over the top." If switching is preferred, then drills will be needed to teach proper switching. The four-man weave drill given in Diagram 7-20 may be used to teach switching also. The defense, instead of "sliding through" or "going over the top," will simply "switch" on the screens that are executed by the four-man weave offense. The four-man weave will present both the lateral switch and the vertical switch. Communication by voice is very much necessitated by a switching maneuver on defense.

20. Lateral Switch on a Lateral Screen: Diagram 7-22.
This is an example of a lateral screen. Player O1 starts a dribble
from near the court attack area, and dribbles fast over the top of
O5 in the outer half of the free-throw circle. Player X1 guards
O1 and as O1 dribbles by O5, X5 slides out to cover O1, and X1
drops back and slides onto O5. The switch maneuver is executed
by each defensive player sticking tight to his offensive opponent
until, with hands up and outstretched, X1 and X5 make contact.
Player X5 talks constantly to X1 and then calls the switch and
switches right onto O1 as X1 switches onto O5. Players O2, O3,
and O4 each have a ball and each is guarded by a defensive
player. They now follow O1 with a fast dribble so that there will
be a chain reaction of switches being executed. The drill is then
run from the opposite side of the floor.

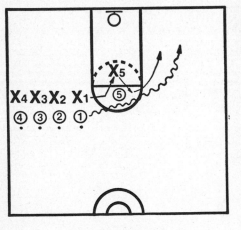

DIAGRAM 7-22

DIAGRAM 7-23

21. The Vertical Screen and Switch: Diagram 7-23.
Player O1 takes a ball at the position shown, and is guarded by
X1. Player O5 in a position down floor moves up to set a screen as
O1 dribbles toward him. Players X1 and X5 move with their
opponents, and when contact is made by voice and touch, they
switch, X5 stepping out on O1, and X1 quickly sliding in to
guard O5. Now O2, O3, and O4 repeat the process. Since the
purpose of the drill is to perfect the "switch" maneuver on a
vertical screen, you, the coach, check the defensive mechanics
constantly. If you like, two lines could be run on this drill—one
on the right side, and one the left, with the players rotating
offense and defense positions.

22. Switching on the Down Screen: Diagram 7-24. A common offensive maneuver from the box-one formation is the so-called "DOWN" screen. The players in positions O2 and O3 screen down for players O4 and O5. If the switching defense is used, the coach must drill on the execution. Set the offense as shown, and as O2 and O3 screen down for O4 and O5, the defensive players with communication by voice, at the proper moment make the switch, keeping assignments straight. If O1 dribbles to his right and passes to O5 and cuts over the top of O5 for a screen, another switch between X1 and X3 must be made. The switching defense does have weaknesses, such as switching a small defensive player to guard a much taller player, but it also helps the zone principle of allowing the defense to keep the larger and stronger players in a position next to the basket for better rebound position.

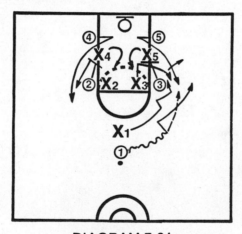

DIAGRAM 7-24

ZONE DEFENSE PRINCIPLES

Certain principles need to be applied when using zone defenses. Here are some to remember:

1. Attack the player with the ball when in your defensive zone area. Ignore other offensive players.
2. When there is no player in your zone coverage area, find the area that has more than one player in it, and move in to help on the extra coverage.
3. When there is more than one player in your zone, and none have the ball, cover the player nearest the ball.

4. Never allow a player with the ball to drive around you.

5. On a zone defense, keep the hands at least shoulder high.

6. Communicate with the voice; talk and keep in touch with teammates.

7. Concentrate on position, stance, and good, sound defensive maneuvers. Do nothing that will throw the center of gravity outside the area of the base.

8. If your opponent dribbles from your zone area to another zone, stick with him unless he can be shifted to a defensive teammate in that area without trouble.

9. After a shot, block out the offensive player in your area, and then go for the ball.

Drills to Coordinate the Zone Shifts

23. Shifting with the Ball: Diagram 7-25, Phase 1. There are many formations of zone defenses, but a common one is the 1-2-2 shown here. To begin, have the offense move the ball around the perimeter of the defense until the players get the various zone coverages. You would cover the shifts in a 2-3, 2-1-2, or a 3-2 zone the same way. In this defense the players shift as the arrows indicate. Player X1 must be very active and move constantly in covering the dotted area in front of the free-throw line. Player X2 should be the best rebounder, since most offenses will trigger to the right side.

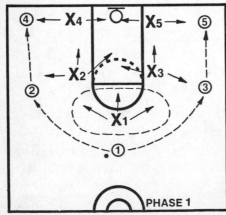
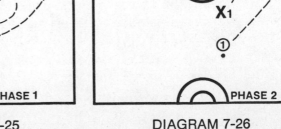

DIAGRAM 7-25   DIAGRAM 7-26

Diagram 7-26, Phase 2. When the ball is moved as shown here, the defense makes the shifts as indicated. The defense must always play in front of the pivot-post player when he is inside the vital scoring area.

Diagram 7-27, Phase 3. If a pass should be made direct from O1 to O4 as shown here, X5 must be prepared to move out early to be there, and X4 moves in to front O5. The other players move as shown. By moving the ball to the various positions, and positioning the offensive players in various situations, the defensive unit can learn to coordinate all their movements to meet offensive threats and thrusts.

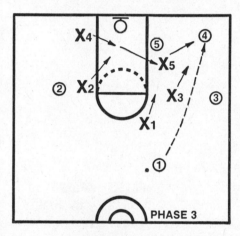

DIAGRAM 7-27

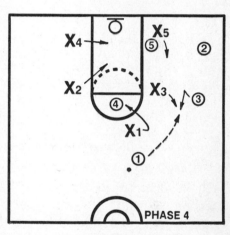

DIAGRAM 7-28

Diagram 7-28, Phase 4. If O4 and O5 are both in the vital scoring area, and the movement of the ball is as shown here, the defense must shift to front both players as shown. If the ball should move from O3 to O2, then X5 moves out quickly on O2, and X4 moves over to front O5. Player X2 falls in behind X4. Players X1 and X3 make adjustments in their zone area to meet the ball movements.

Diagram 7-29, Phase 5. When the ball is moved into the pivot-post position as shown here, the defense stops the ball handler by converging upon him.

24. Overloading the Zone Defense Drill: Diagram 7-30. A good drill to work against a zone is to place six and then seven offensive players on the floor, and overload the various zone areas while moving the ball around the court rapidly. This

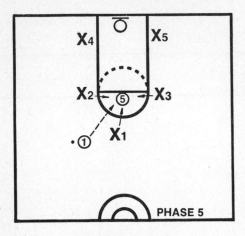

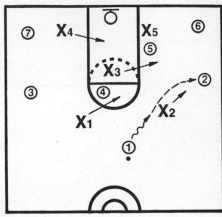

DIAGRAM 7-29   DIAGRAM 7-30

handicaps the defense, but helps them see the necessity of defensing the ball, and learning to shift in their zones, always to attack the scoring threat.

COMBINATION DEFENSES

Many teams combine the best features of a zone defense and the man-to-man fundamentals. The following are some drill situations to work out a combination defense. These combination defenses are hard for the offense to attack because they present many changing situations, and can only be solved by thoughtful free-lance attacks. Constant change is required to meet the different defensive combinations presented.

25. **Combination Defense Drills: Diagram 7-31, Phase 1.** Start with the offense situated in the perimeter as shown. When O1 has the ball, X1 plays him a tight man-to-man defense. Players X2 and X3 play O2 and O3 a loose man-to-man, sagging in toward the center and the basket. Players X4 and X5 play zone positions under the basket, but must be aware of the position of O4 and O5 only. If the ball should move from O1 to O3, the players shift as shown by the arrows. Now X3 plays O3 a tight man-to-man, X1 plays a loose man-to-man, and X5 shifts out into a loose man-to-man coverage on O5. Now players X4 and X2 play a zone position, but must not let O2 or O4 move into the scoring area ahead of them toward the ball—otherwise they straight zone their positions.

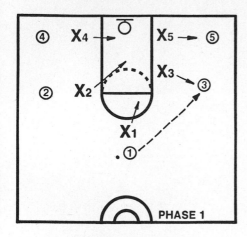

DIAGRAM 7-31

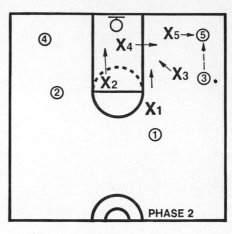

DIAGRAM 7-32

Diagram 7-32, Phase 2. When the ball is passed from O3 to O5, now X5 plays a tight man-to-man; X3 goes into a loose man-to-man and X2 and X4 zone their positions and shift as shown. The same principles apply, should the ball be moved to the left side of the floor to players O2 and O4. Do the drill with the offensive players moving the ball around the perimeter positions rapidly while reviewing the defensive players on their defensive shifts, and their responsibilities with each movement of the ball.

Diagram 7-33, Phase 3. Now have the offense move a pivot-post player, in this case O4, inside the dotted line area—Area A—the vital scoring zone. Player O4 is now a major scoring problem, so he must be guarded tight man-to-man, and as long as he plays within this area, X4 takes him and plays in front of him, and at the side toward the ball as it is being maneuvered. Allow no passes inside to O4. The other defensive problems are the point of the ball (player with the ball) and the wing player, or the player breaking from the weak side toward the ball handlers. Defensive players X3 and X5 play as deep as possible so as to give as much help to X4 as possible. Player X3 must use his judgment, but the deeper he can play away from O3, still being able to shift back to him rapidly when the ball is moved to O3, the better. Player X2 drops off to help X4 also. Player X1 plays to block any passes to O4 also. Actually now in this situation, X5 zones behind X4, while X2 and X3 are in loose man-to-man positions, with X1 playing to apply full pressure at the point of the ball.

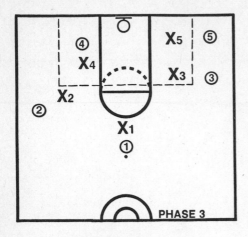

DIAGRAM 7-34

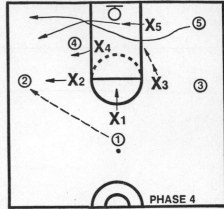

DIAGRAM 7-33

Diagram 7-34, Phase 4. If the ball moves from O1 to O2, and O5 cuts to the strong side toward the ball, X5 must take him, and as he does so, he should call to X3, "watch behind." Player X3 now zones and is responsible for the right side of the backboard area. Players X1, X2, X4, and X5 move as shown. Player X2 plays tight man-to-man at the point of the ball. Player X4 fronts O4 on movement of the ball, X1 is loose man-to-man, and X5 fronts O5 across Area A, but as he moves out toward the corner, X5 now drops into a loose man-to-man. Player X3 zones the right side, and makes sure no offensive wing player moves ahead of him toward the ball. The offensive situation here amounts to an overload, but the offensive players in the dangerous areas are properly defensed according to the principles of this defense.

Diagram 7-35, Phase 5. If O1 should pass to O3 and move in either of the paths shown, X1 and X3 switch, with X3 calling the switch. In this situation, as long as the offensive cutter does not go behind the defensive player, a defensive switch is made. This way X1 and X2 will maintain their floor positions out in front.

Diagram 7-36, Phase 6. If O1 should pass to O3 and cut behind him, X1 sticks on O1 in a tight man-to-man defense. But as O1 moves away from the ball, X1 will loosen up on him. Should O1 move to the opposite side of the floor, X1 could zone away from him, just making sure he does not move ahead of him toward the ball.

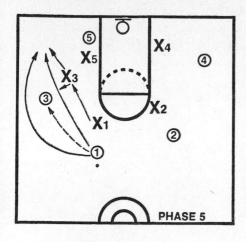

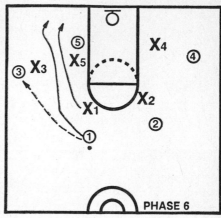

DIAGRAM 7-35   DIAGRAM 7-36

Diagram 7-37, Phase 7. If O1 should pass the ball and move as shown here, X1 must stick tight man-to-man on the cut through the middle, but as O1 moves to the corner, X1 will zone off. Should the ball be moved to O4, then X4 plays tight man-to-man, X1 and X2 loose man-to-man, and X5 and X3 would zone off on the left side—being aware of the wing players on that side only. In drilling to work out the positions on this combination defense, combinations, switches and variations can be worked out to fit any situation as it may arise.

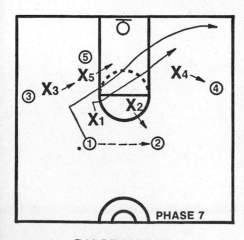

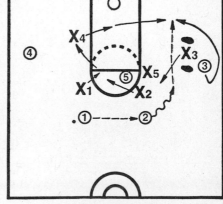

DIAGRAM 7-37   DIAGRAM 7-38

26. Rotation of Defense to Help Player on the "Hot Seat": Diagram 7-38. When the defense pressures the player with the ball, or works hard to deny the pass to a player inside, all players must be prepared to help the player who got beaten. Here, X3 pressuring to deny O3 the ball, gets beaten on a reverse, and O2 passes to O3 on the reverse and inside. Player X4, sagging off on the weak side, steps right in to take O3, X1 drops down to take O4, X2 shifts over to be on O1, and X3 adjusts his position to be able to cover O2. In some situations X5 might be able to drop in and take O3, in which case X4 would shift to O5, and the other players would rotate in the same way as before. Defensive rotation and help when a teammate gets beaten must be a way of life, and running drills to perfect the techniques is a must.

27. Stop the Fast Break Drill: Diagram 7-39. This drill is to develop efficiency in changing rapidly from offense to

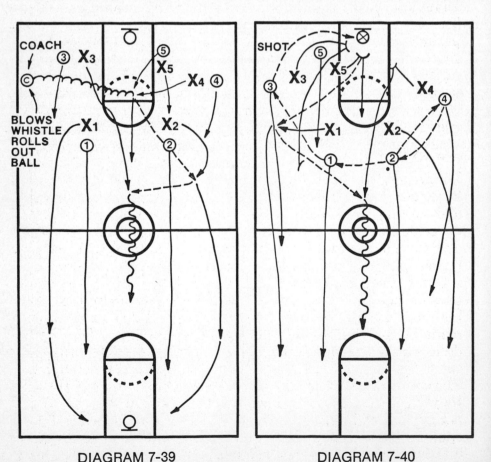

DIAGRAM 7-39   DIAGRAM 7-40

defense and learning to get back quickly to stop the fast break. The O's are on offense, and the X's on defense. The O's run through simulated or actual offensive patterns without the ball. The coach, standing on the side with a ball, picks an appropriate time to blow his whistle and roll out the ball to one of the defensive players. The X's now pick up the ball and fast break to the opposite end of the floor. The O's sprint back and go to the defense rapidly to stop the fast break. The two teams can go up and down the floor with this drill—teams alternating offense and defense.

A variation to this drill that could be used—instead of you holding the ball and rolling it out, have the offensive team run the offense with the ball, pass and cut, but allow no shots. When you blow the whistle, the offense drops the ball and sprints back on defense, and the X's pick up the ball and fast break.

28. Shoot, Rebound, Get Back on Defense Drill: Diagram 7-40. Cover the basket with a basket-covering device. The O's on offense pass the ball a few passes around the perimeter, and put the ball up on a shot. The O's follow hard on rebounds and if they secure the rebound, they put the ball back up and get credit for 1 point. The X's rebound the ball and immediately initiate a fast break. The O's now convert to defense and attempt to stop the fast break. If the X's score on the fast break, they score 2 points, and they get to stay on offense. The teams go back and forth for any length of time you choose.

29. Stopping the Fast Break at the Point of Origin: Diagram 7-41. Coaches differ on how to stop the fast break. Some advocate the simple "sprint-back" to defensive positions and getting there before the offense can get there. Others advocate attacking the fast break at its point of origin. This is a drill for that purpose. Cover the baskets. The offense, after a few passes, puts the ball up on a shot. If the defense secures the rebound, the two offensive players nearest him attack him in a two-timing maneuver, in an effort to delay and possibly deflect his outlet pass. In this case X3 secured the rebound on the shot made by O4. Immediately, O3 and O5 attack X3 to delay and deflect his outlet pass. The outlet pass will most likely be made out to the side and to the area of the free-throw line extended. Players O1 and O4 play for possible interceptions in these areas. Player O2 is the back man, and will be sure the fast break does not get behind him, but at the same time, he looks for possible opportunities to intercept a pass that might be made to the division court line area, and possible interceptions of passes that might be made from the side to the middle of the court. Many fast breaks can be stopped before they get under way by this method. The drill can be run up and down the floor to condition the defensive responses necessary to stop the fast break.

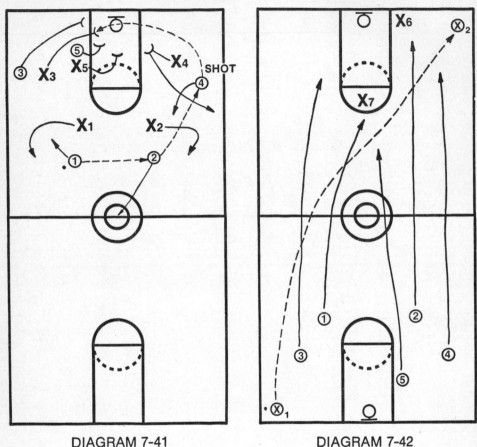

DIAGRAM 7-41   DIAGRAM 7-42

30. Beat the Long Pass: Diagram 7-42. The purpose of this drill is to teach the defensive player that, if he hustles, he can run as fast as a long floater pass travels when being made the length of the floor. Player X1 has the ball. He is to throw a long pass to X2 on the opposite corner of the court. The O's in positions shown, may start as soon as they can read X1's intention to throw. When X1 throws they must sprint back on defense, and their object is to beat the ball there, or at least get there before X2 can relay the ball to X6 or X7, for a score.

31. Help on Defense Drill: Diagram 7-43. You, as a

coach, must be realistic and realize that especially when tight pressure is applied to the ball handler, the defensive player will be beaten at times. A cover-up or "help" situation must be worked out for each defensive position when this happens. In this diagram, O1 is given the ball ahead of X1, the defensive opponent. As O1 starts dribbling toward the basket, X1 yells "HELP, HELP." When the rest of the team hears this, they loosen up to help X1. Then they make their shifts to cover up for him. Here X3 takes O1, X5 drops over to take O3, X4 moves in to take O5, while X2 slides into position to cover O4. Player X1 sprints back toward the 3-second area, and will pick up O2. Now work out similar cover-up situations for each position, and practice by giving the ball to the offensive player ahead of his defensive opponent.

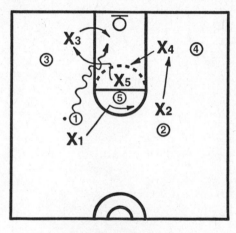

DIAGRAM 7-43

32. A Press Drill: Diagram 7-44. The players line up for a free throw, taking positions along the lane as usual. The player selected to shoot a free throw shoots until he makes the free throw. Immediately, the defensive team takes the ball out-of-bounds, and the free-throwing team puts on the pressing defense. By conversation prior to the throw, they have arranged their assignments. When X4 takes the ball out, O4 pressures him. Player O5 steps in to pressure X5, O3 takes X3, O2 takes X2, and O1 moves in to pressure X1. The X team attempts to bring the ball down the floor against this pressure. The O team applies full pressure the length of the floor. This is a good drill to teach the team to apply a quick and full pressure situation after a free throw is made.

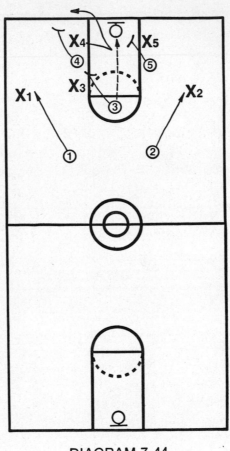

DIAGRAM 7-44

Defensive Rebounding Drills

DEFENSIVE REBOUNDING

When a shot is made by an opponent, the defensive player is already closer to the backboard than the opponent. If proper maneuvers are made, the player should be able to maintain this position and keep the offensive player from securing the rebound. When the offensive opponent shoots, every defensive player should block out the opponent. The only time not to "box-out" is when the offensive player is so far out that there is no threat in securing the rebound. The "blocking-out" should be followed immediately with three defensive players forming a triangle in front of the backboard, with one player in the foul lane and teammates on both sides of the basket. This defensive triangle prevents the offense from getting a "tip-in," a short follow-up shot, or a rebound.

Coaching Points for Defensive Rebounding

1. If the opponent cuts, the "block-out" should be made by making a forward pivot or a reverse pivot, placing your body between the cutter and the basket.

a. If the defensive player is in a boxer's stance (one foot in front of the other) and the cutter moves toward the side of the open stance (the back foot) it is usually better to block out by using the forward pivot. (Step with the front foot over the other in a spin toward the opponent.)

b. If the defensive player is in a boxer's stance and the offensive cutter moves toward the side of the front leg, the block-out can be made more easily with a reverse pivot (placing one foot behind the other in spinning toward the offensive rebounder).

2. Other rules on the block-out—if the offensive rebounder is close, a reverse pivot can be better to use in making contact. If the opponent is a step or more away, a forward pivot can be better to make the contact.

3. Inside the twelve-foot area, or in the triangle area, it is nearly always better to block out by using the reverse pivot.

4. Keep the opponent out as far as possible.

5. When the opponent cuts, it is important to make contact by making one of the pivots previously described. Keep this contact by ramming the buttocks into the upper part of the offensive player's legs, and then use short choppy steps to keep this contact long enough to keep the opponent out.

6. When contact is made, the defensive player should be in a semicrouch, with feet apart, arms up, elbows out, winglike, ready to jump for the ball. Make yourself as big as possible.

7. Players outside the defensive triangle area should retreat one or two steps from the opponent, then open up (give him a direction and locate the ball), then block out or step in front of him as he goes for the ball. The process here is (1) drop off, (2) open up, and (3) block out.

8. Locate the ball as soon as possible. Develop an awareness of where it is.

9. Keep the opponent far enough out so that when you go up for the ball, you can jump up and forward for the ball. This way the opponent will not be able to get at the ball with you. If you have to go straight up for the ball, the opponent can get at it as easily as you can.

10. Catch the ball—grab it—the defensive rebounds must be caught. Do not bat the ball in the air.

11. As you go up after the ball, *jackknife*, by throwing the legs apart and the buttocks out, catching the ball in front of you. This will keep the opponent a safe distance from you and prevent him from grabbing the ball.

12. Hold the ball well out from the body, and as soon as you catch it, snap it down and cover it with elbows out. (Snapping the ball will bring the elbows out.) Giving the ball a half spin so that one hand is above and the other below the ball will also protect the ball so that an opponent cannot reach over a shoulder and hook the ball away from you.

13. The good rebounder has to have *courage and determination to fight* for possession of that basketball. *Be mean and aggressive off the boards.* You have to hustle to get that ball. You are not going to get it by being timid or reluctant to make physical contact. A loafer shows up quickly by the lack of rebounds. A hustler—a hard worker—shows up quickly by the number of rebounds taken.

14. A good rebounder is an aggressive player who is not afraid of contact. Play clean, but hard. After getting the ball, keep the elbows out, and if you are pressured by an opponent close by, pivot away from this pressure, but in doing so, use your body in such a way as to make the opponent afraid to approach you.

15. Once you have possession of the ball, you must keep it. A quick pass or dribble should free you from the defensive player. Do not cross-court pass the ball under your defensive basket. This is an easy way to give the opponents two points.

16. Possession of the ball in basketball is equal to one point. Securing a rebound is equivalent to scoring one point. Constantly check rebounds and give credit for rebounding performances.

Habit Drills to Teach Defensive Rebounding

1. Since blocking out is an important factor in defensive rebounding, and forward pivots and reverse pivots are essential to making the block, these two moves should be well mastered.

These factors are determinants in whether the defensive player will make a reverse pivot or a forward pivot:

  a. The stance of the defensive player.

  b. The distance the defensive player is from the offensive player.

  c. The direction of the offensive player's move or cut to secure the rebound.

To teach these pivots or turns—have the players line up across the gym and face the coach. You, the coach, give the commands.

FORWARD PIVOT
REVERSE PIVOT

Do no blocking out on this drill. Just practice executing the turns.

After the players know the turns and have mastered them, you should emphasize making the turns quickly. Quickness is very important in basketball, and once a movement has been mastered, emphasize quick execution of all fundamentals. Also remember that good offensive rebounders are *quick*. The defensive rebounder must be *quicker* to contain them.

Since being low is important in blocking out, emphasize also in making the above turns or pivots that the player should stay as low as possible. If the defensive player stands up straight, good contact cannot be made with the offensive player. Contact is important. If the defensive player is low and his buttocks can make contact with the upper part of the offensive player's legs, good contact can be maintained.

Also, when executing these turns or pivots, have the players concentrate on spreading out. Tell them to make themselves as *big* as possible. Point the feet straight ahead, keep the arms up, shoulder-high, elbows out, and hands in the air.

Check the proper form on this drill.

2. Blocking Out on the Whistle: Diagram 8-1. Place the ball on the free throw line in the center of the circle. When the whistle is blown, the defensive players, the X's, are to keep the O's, the offensive players, away from the ball by blocking out. They are to block out for 5 seconds on this drill. The O's use any means possible to get to the ball. If one of the O players gets to the ball within 5 seconds, score 1 point for them. If the X's hold the O's out for 5 seconds, score 1 point for the defense. Change off the X's and O's after 5 tries.

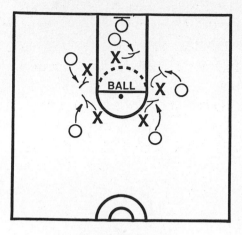

DIAGRAM 8-1

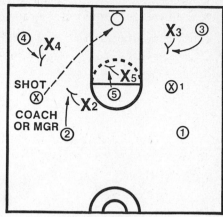

DIAGRAM 8-2

3. Blocking Out on the Shot: Diagram 8-2. The O's line up on offense as shown. Either the coach, manager, or one of the players puts a shot up, and all the X's block out, except X1, who sight checks to make sure his man does not sneak in for a rebound. The X's block out and secure the rebound. You, the coach, check form and techniques on the block out. The O's work hard to get the ball also. Scores could be counted, as in Diagram 8-1, with two points being awarded to the O's for each rebound, and one point to the defense for each rebound. The team to score six points first is the winner. Change offense and defense so that all can get work on blocking out.

4. Blocking Out on the Shooter: Diagram 8-3. On this drill, have the offensive player make his move and shoot a jump shot. The defensive player is to move with the offensive player and block out after the shot is taken. Have the defensive player use a forward pivot against the shooter on the block-out. Later designate the use of the reverse pivot so that the defensive player gets the feel of both turns. Remember that the stance, distance from the offensive player, and the direction the offensive player moves will be the determinants as to which pivot the defensive player makes for an effective block-out.

5. Blocking Out from the Seven Spots: Diagram 8-4. From the seven shooting spots outside, the players line up as shown, and each offensive player has a ball. Each offensive player, taking turns, makes his move, and gets off a shot and goes for the rebound. The defensive player blocks out. The coach checks the blocking-out techniques. The players rotate spots

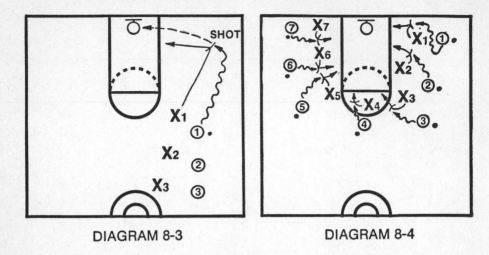

DIAGRAM 8-3   DIAGRAM 8-4

and positions on both offense and defense. If desired, a score could be kept—awarding two points for an offensive rebound, one point for a basket, one point for an effective block-out and one point for a defensive rebound. The player with highest total at the end of a designated time would be declared the winner.

6. **Weak-Side Block-Out Drill: Diagram 8-5.** The coach or the manager shoots the ball, while the weak-side, or "help-side" player goes out and puts a reverse pivot (if his opponent is aggressive) on the offensive player. This is a vital area, because the player in that area is usually sagging off on the weak-side defense, and will be caught away from the opponent. The

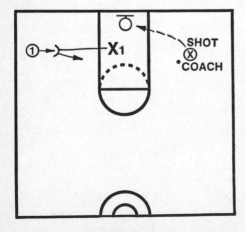

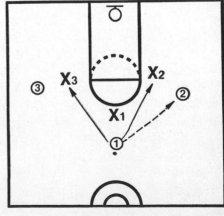

DIAGRAM 8-5   DIAGRAM 8-6

defensive player must go and get the offensive rebounder. If the defensive player does not move out in this manner to make contact, he will get caught under the basket and that is the worst place to be when trying to rebound.

7. **Three-on-Three Rebounding Drill: Diagram 8-6.** In this drill use three against three. The offense moves around, defense staying with them. After two or three passes, or some movement, put the ball up on a shot—either the players from offense, or the coach or manager can put the ball up. All rebound, and the coach checks the blocking-out procedure. Offensive players moving are harder to block out. When the defense secures the rebound, they outlet the ball and fast break to the court division line. Scores can be kept if desired.

8. **Five Against Five Rebound Drill: Diagram 8-7.** In this drill, set up your regular offense. Either the coach or manager shoots the ball up on the boards, or the offense can make two or three passes and put the shot up—rebound—defense blocks out, and fast breaks. The teams can go back and forth the full length of the court, or use half-court area to meet the needs of what the coach wants to emphasize. Check blocking out, getting rebound position, protecting the ball, timing on the jump, or whatever emphasis is needed.

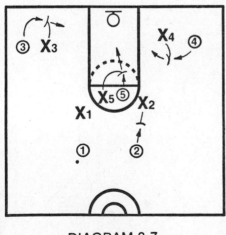

DIAGRAM 8-7

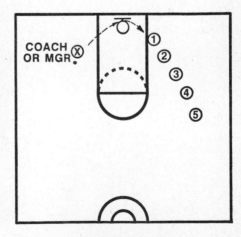

DIAGRAM 8-8

9. **Grabbing the Ball: Diagram 8-8.** Sometimes players go up to get a rebound, but somehow fail to hold onto it; this is an indication of weak hands. To overcome this, run these two drills.

  a. Have the players take a ball and slap it as hard as possible in each hand about 20 times. This will strengthen the hands.

  b. Do the drill shown in Diagram 8-8. You or the manager will throw the ball up on the board on the side opposite from the line of players. Have the players jump and *snatch the ball out of the air. Grab the ball* with either one or two hands, but emphasis is on getting the ball and holding on to it. Check other techniques—spreading out, timing height of jump, jackknife, and coming down with the ball and protecting it.

10. Full-Court—Continuous Movement Rebound Drill: Diagram 8-9. This drill emphasizes blocking out the shooter, defensive rebounding, releasing the pass for a fast break, and ball handling on the fast break. The drill moves along fast and players enjoy it, so it is a good idea to use it often. Begin the drill by first shooting the ball up from the free-throw circle area.

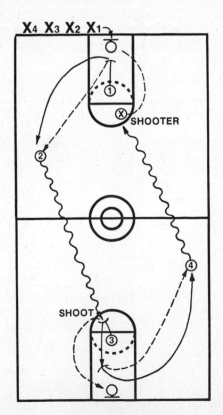

DIAGRAM 8-9

Player O1 screens the shooter out, gets the rebound and puts the outlet pass out to O2 on the side. Player O2 dribbles rapidly toward the opposite basket and O3. When O2 shoots, O3 blocks out the shooter, gets the rebound and puts the outlet pass out to O4. Now O4 drives toward the opposite basket, where he gets off a shot. Player X1 has moved in to replace O1. Meanwhile, O1 goes to the O2 position, O2 goes to the O3 position, and O3 goes to the O4 position. The drill keeps moving, and O4, after shooting and going for the rebound, will go to the end of the X line.

Work various passes on the outlet pass, such as the baseball pass, force out a dribble, and follow with a two-handed push pass. Also change the position of O2 and O4 from side to side so that the outlet pass will not always be to the same side. A point system can be worked out for the drill. Give a player 1 point for making a basket, a good block-out and a good offensive rebound. Subtract points for a poor block-out, any fundamental error, and letting the offense get a rebound. Total points at the end of the drill, and players with high points are rewarded, while players with minus total must run laps or do push-ups.

11. One-on-One, Rebound, Release Pass Drill: Diagram 8-10. The players line up as shown. Player O1 takes a ball and works to get off a shot. Player X1 goes with O1, and blocks out, then goes for the rebound, and does a release pass to either X3 or X2. Player O1 becomes the next defensive rebounder, and the X2 and X3 lines take turns becoming the next offensive player.

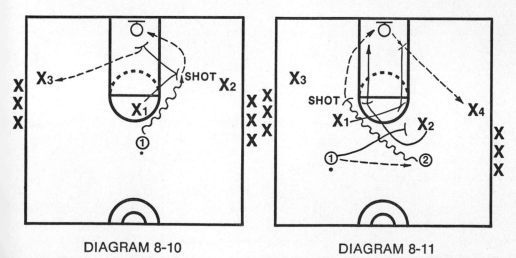

DIAGRAM 8-10   DIAGRAM 8-11

12. Two-on-Two, Rebound, Release Pass Drill: Diagram 8-11. Players O1 and O2 work the ball for a quick shot. Players X1 and X2 stick tight on screens, and when the shot goes up, they block out and go for the rebound. The offense follows hard for rebounds and if blocked out, they attack the defensive rebounder. The defensive rebounder makes an outlet pass to either X3 or X4. The offense now becomes the defense and X3 and X4 become the next offensive players.

13. Three-on-Three, Rebound, Release Pass Drill: Diagram 8-12. Players O1, O2, and O3 work two or three passes and get off a shot. Players X1, X2, and X3 block out and go for the rebound. The offense follows hard for the rebound also and puts the ball back up when they secure it. When the defense secures the rebound, they do a release pass to either X5, X4, or X6. The offense becomes the next defense, and X4, X5, and X6 next go on offense.

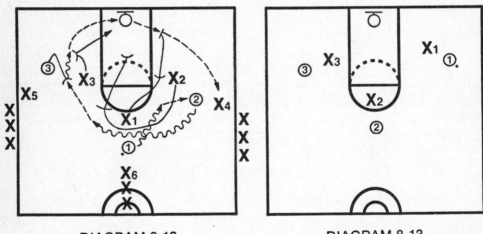

DIAGRAM 8-12   DIAGRAM 8-13

14. Twenty-One Rebound Drill: Diagram 8-13. The O's take turns shooting and follow their shots hard for the rebound. Player O1 shoots first, and may repeat the shot, if hit. When O1 misses, O2 shoots and then O3. When the O's hit a basket it counts 1 point. If the X's get the rebound, it counts 2 points. After the O's have all shot, the O's go on defense, and the X's take the offense. The side making 21 points first wins.

15. The Eagle Spread Drill: Diagram 8-14. The purpose of this drill is to teach the player to spread out as he goes up for the ball, jackknife on the rebound and turn away from the opposition. The players line up as shown, with the first player in the X line just in front of the basket and the first in the O line just to the left of the basket. You (or the manager) toss the ball up from the opposite side, and both lines go for the rebound. The O player with the better position should take the rebound, and spin away from the opponent, the X player. The X player will try to tie up the rebounder. The players rotate lines, and be sure to work both sides of the board.

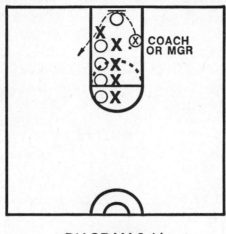

DIAGRAM 8-14

16. Holding onto the Ball Drill: This is a drill to teach the player to grab the ball and hold onto it.

   a. Attach an iron bar to a wall at a height of about 12 feet. The bar should project out from the wall about 2 feet.

   b. Attach a strong tire inner tube (or other elastic cord) to the bar, and attach a ball in a loop of the inner tube with a strong cord tied around the tube just above the ball to secure it. Fix the ball so that it hangs about 10 feet from the floor.

   c. Have the players take turns jumping up, grabbing the ball, and pulling it down until their feet strike the floor.

17. Wall Rebounding Drill: This drill can give a large number of players a rebounding-jumping drill in a short time.

Divide the squad into pairs, and have them spread out along a wall, or around the gym along the walls.

Each pair will take a ball. One player tosses the ball up on the wall at a height about equal to the backboard. The other player is to jump, grab the ball, in an eagle spread, and turn away from the tossing player, who will try to tie up the rebounder. They take turns tossing and rebounding.

18. Cross-Over Block-Out Rebounding Drill: Diagram 8-15. When defensing a player in the pivot-post area, it is important to play between the opponent and the ball. Often the opponents will put the ball up to give a player so defensed the inside position on a rebound. A cross-over block-out will protect on this—and the players need to drill on the maneuver. The players line up as shown—O's the offense, and X's the defense. The coach or manager puts the ball up on a shot, and X3, defensing the weak-side offensive player, calls "cross-over" and drops in to block O5 off the rebound, and X5 quickly spins over to block out O3 and to cover that side of the board. Work both sides of the floor on this drill.

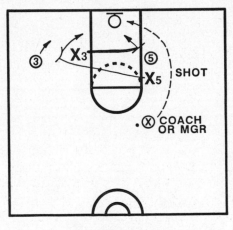

DIAGRAM 8-15

Fast Break Drills

THE FAST BREAK

Coaching philosophies concerning the fast break, what to do with it, when, how, and whether to do it, will be about as numerous as the number of coaches in the profession, especially in the high school and college ranks. The professional game doesn't leave the coach with much choice—the team has to get a shot off within 24 seconds. That is a lot of time, but it is a must, so the teams in the pro ranks almost have to be somewhat fast-break oriented. While the high school and college teams, on the average, put a shot up every 15 to 18 seconds, it is not mandatory, thus there is not the necessity to be so fast-break minded on the part of all teams. The style of attack at these levels will vary from the "all-out" fast-break system to those teams that never attempt a fast break, always preferring to bring the ball down court to use a five-player set attack system only. Here the coaches will vary from those that know "only the fast-break system" to those that know only a "set-attack system." Some coaches will be more versatile, and will use a fast break when the opportunity presents itself, and set up a five-player offensive attack when unable to gain a fast-break advantage.

Such coaches might be referred to as "limited fast break coaches."

The fast break is an attempt by the offense to gain an offensive situation in which they will have an advantage at the offensive end of the court by outnumbering the defensive players. Typical fast-break situations would be 2 on 1, 3 on 1, 3 on 2, 4 on 3, and 5 on 4. In some very unusual cases, it could even be 1 on 0, or 2 on 0, 3 on 0, etc. Such situations are rare, of course, and usually come from a steal that is unexpected, or that results from a pressing defensive attack that has been suddenly applied.

Fast-break situations arise from a steal or an interception, from rebounding a missed shot, a missed free throw, and possibly from shots that are made, and even free throws that are made. The fast break, to be successful, must be highly organized.

There is no doubt that fans love the fast-break game, and like to witness the lightning-like attack that strikes at once and scores. The players usually like to play the fast-break game more, but it requires that they be in perfect physical condition. Many coaches feel that they owe it to the fans and the players to coach the fast-break game, because it is both a crowd and a player pleaser.

Coaching Points for the Fast Break

1. The key to the fast break is control of the defensive rebounding. Most fast-break situations will arise from missed shots by the opponents, so the key to starting the fast break will be controlling the defensive boards.

2. Control of the defensive rebounding will require proper blocking out and checking the opponent off the boards. Chapter 8, "Defensive Rebounding Drills," gives techniques for this maneuver.

3. Occasionally use a long pass (sometimes called the "butterfly pattern") FAR down court on the fast break: Do this especially if the opponent tries to intercept the outlet pass to the side, or to the top of the free-throw circle. This will keep them worried about what you are going to do when you get the ball. On this "butterfly pattern," throw the ball FAR down court at the basket. Let the teammate catch up with it.

4. To start the fast break, the rebounder should look first to the side of his rebound area for an outlet pass. If there is no opening at the side, look next for an opening at the top of the free-throw circle. Always be alert for the butterfly pattern (a heave far down court).

5. Teammates must know who and where the rebounder is, and break to the outlet areas on the side and at the top of the circle so that the outlet pass can be initiated. Without the initial outlet pass, most fast breaks can never be gotten under way.

6. Always get three players into the fast-break pattern if possible. This means filling the three lanes as quickly as possible, and bringing in two trailers for other possibilities.

7. Get the ball into the middle lane before reaching the court division line if possible—if not possible, get it there as soon as possible, and keep it there unless another player is away out ahead.

8. The player in the middle lane must stop at the top of the circle, to feed the ball off, *and stay there* unless there is an opening for a clean drive to the basket.

9. The players coming down the side lanes should stay wide until they reach a point opposite the free-throw line extended. Here they cut direct for the basket, and if no opening occurs by the time they reach the basket, they continue on through and button-hook back out on the opposite sides. (This could mean players cross under the basket.)

10. Keep the ball in the middle. The player in the middle has two optional directions to go with the pass. Learn to fake one way and pass the other.

11. Insist that when the players come down the floor in a fast break, they pick up their knees and feet and RUN. Work hard at it. They must get out of pace and run—in fact—SPRINT.

12. The players must learn when there is a fast-break situation available—that is when the offensive players down floor outnumber the defensive players. When the offense does not have this situation and it is clear that it cannot be accomplished by a quick pass and a break for

the basket, the fast break must be called off and the set-offensive attack brought into play.

13. Anytime the ball is passed in to a player from out-of-bounds, this player should advance the ball as far as possible down court, either by a safe accurate pass, or a driving dribble. Always take the responsibility of advancing the ball as far as possible safely.

14. When a player secures the ball, look first for a pass, and dribble drive only if there is no one to pass to, or if the player open for a pass would be in a less advantageous position for the fast break than the passer.

Habit Drills for Teaching the Fast Break

1. Two-Line Passing Drill: Diagram 9-1. The players form two lines at one end of the floor. The first two players take a ball and while running at full speed, pass the ball back and forth. When the basket at the opposite end of the court is reached, one of the players will take a lay-up shot. They return to the starting point the same way and the next two players in line repeat the drill. The purpose of the drill is to develop the ability in players to handle the ball, to pass and catch it while running at full speed, as they will have to do while on a fast break.

2. Three-Line Passing Drill: Diagram 9-2. The players form three lines at each end of the floor. The first three in line at one end of the floor take a ball and pass it back and forth from the middle lane to the side lanes as they run full speed down the floor. When the opposite basket is reached a shot is taken. The first three in the line at the opposite end now pick up the ball, and run to the other end of the floor doing the same thing. The players go back and forth doing this passing, running at full speed. The purpose of the drill is to develop ball handling ability while moving at full speed, and to teach the players an awareness of the three fast-break lanes to be used on the fast break. The players in the two outside lanes should stay wide, and not crowd in on the middle lane. The two outside lane players stay wide until they reach an area opposite the free-throw line extended, when they then cut directly for the basket.

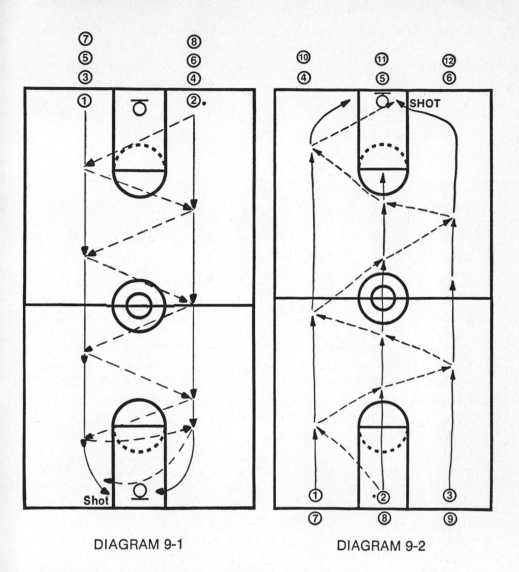

DIAGRAM 9-1   DIAGRAM 9-2

3. Continuous Movement Fast-Break Drill: Diagram 9-3. The players line up as shown in the diagram. Start the drill with two players at each end of the floor on defense, in this case X1 and X2 at one end and X3 and X4 at the other end. The other players form a line at the side of the court at each end as shown. Start the drill by putting the ball up on a shot at one end of the floor, and as shown here, at the X1 defensive end. The players X1 and X2 take the rebound off the shot, and outlet the pass to O6, who breaks inside to the free-throw line extended area to receive the pass. Now O6, X1, and X2 fast break to the opposite end of the floor where they are opposed by X3 and X4. Player O6 may dribble drive on the fast break, or pass to X1 and/or X2 in the outside lanes if it will enhance the speed of the fast break. Player O6 pulls up at the top of the circle, and then by passing off, and with a series of quick passes, attempts to score. They keep putting the ball up until they score, or until X3 or X4 secures the rebound. If a score is made, X3 or X4 will step out of bounds to throw the ball in to O1, who steps inbounds to receive it. Now O1, X3, and X4 fast break to the opposite end of the floor. If there is no score and the ball is rebounded by X3 or X4, the fast break is started from that position to the other end of the floor.

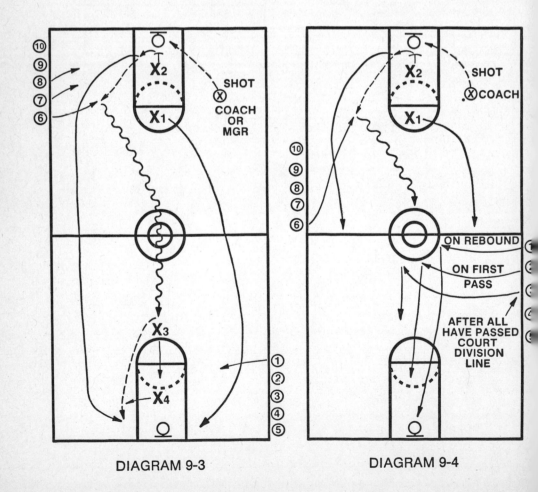

DIAGRAM 9-3   DIAGRAM 9-4

After O6, X1, and X2 go down the floor, the next two players in the line at the end of the floor, O7 and O8, replace them on defense. After coming down the floor on the fast break, O6, X1, and X2 go to the end of the O1 line. After O1, X3, and X4 fast break, O2 and O3 become the next defensive players to replace X3 and X4. The players now go back and forth on the floor with the drill working continuously. Players get offense, defense, ball handling (passing and catching, dribbling), shooting, rebounding, running, and excellent simulation of fast-break situations on the drill. It is a drill that players will enjoy. Several variations can be added to the drill, which will be shown in a later diagram. Run the drill often to relieve basketball practice monotony and boredom.

4. Three-on-Three Continuous Fast-Break Drill: Diagram 9-4. This is a variation of the continuous fast-break drill presented in Diagram 9-3. The players line up on opposite sides of the court near the court division line. Start the drill with X1 and X2 on defense. The coach puts the ball up on the boards. Player X2 rebounds, and O6 breaks to the outlet pass area to receive the release pass. Now O6, X1, and X2 fast break to the other end of the floor. When X2 secures the rebound, O1 sprints to touch the center circle, and retreats to a defensive position. When X2 makes the outlet pass to O6, O2 sprints to touch the circle, and then retreats to a defensive position to help O1. When O6, X1, and X2 have passed the court division line, O3 also sprints to touch the circle, and then sprints back to help O1 and O2, making it three-on-three, if O6, X1, and X2 have not scored by this time. If O1, O2, and O3 secure a rebound, they fast break to the other end of the floor, where this process is repeated by O7, O8, and O9. If a score is made by the offensive unit, the defense steps out-of-bounds to start the fast break, and to make the throw in. This drill is continuous, and has all the elements of the previous drill, plus added hustle of getting the defense there by stages for organizing against the fast break. It also causes the offense to try to take advantage of their fast break outnumbering the defense situation before the defense can get organized against them.

5. Five-on-Five Continuous Fast-Break Drill: Diagram 9-5. Three teams of five players go back and forth from basket to basket on this drill. Team O is on offense at one end of the floor to start the drill. Teams X1, X2, X3, X4, and X5 are situated as shown, with X4 and X3 inbounds on defense. You put the ball up on the boards to start the drill. Player O3 or some member of the

O team rebounds the ball and starts the fast break, and as shown here, O3 secures the rebound and outlets to O2. Now the fast break is underway with O1, O2, and O4 leading the break, and O5 and O3 trailing. At the other end of the floor, X8 and X9 are on defense. The other players are stationed outside as shown. When the fast breakers reach the top of the circle, and after one pass is made, X6 moves in to help on defense. After the second pass, X7 steps in, and as soon as a shot is taken, X10 steps in on defense. If the X defensive team secures a rebound, or if they are scored upon, they step out and inbound the ball, fast breaking to the opposite end of the floor, where X1, X2, X3, X4, and X5 repeat the defensive stages as the passes and shots are made. The three teams can keep the drill going continuously as long as you wish.

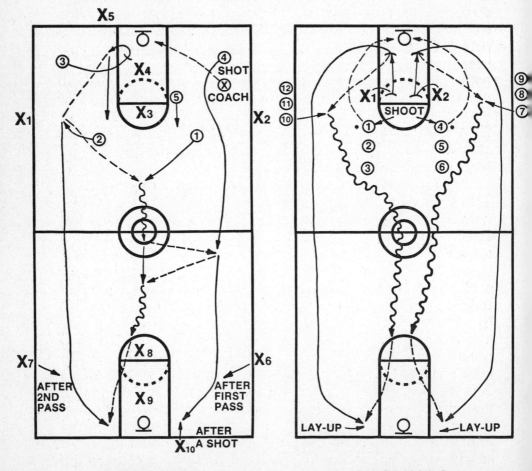

DIAGRAM 9-5   DIAGRAM 9-6

6. Rebound Hustle Drill: Diagram 9-6. Two lines of players line up at one end of the floor just to the right and left side of the free-throw circle as shown. The first players in line, in this case X1 and X2, become defensive rebounders, and the next in line shoot the ball and follow hard for the rebound. The defensive rebounder blocks out the offensive shooter, secures the ball, and turns in the air, if possible, and throws a release pass to a guard on the rebounding side of the floor, who has moved inbounds to the outlet pass area. If the shooter should make the basket, the rebounder takes the ball, and steps out-of-bounds to throw it inbounds. The guard receiving the ball, in this case O10 or O7, drive hard into the middle, and down the floor to the top of the circle at the other end of the court. In the meantime the rebounding player sprints down the outside lane to the area opposite the free-throw line extended, where he cuts directly to the basket to receive a pass from the guard to do a lay-up shot. One line goes first and then the other starts when the first line reaches the court division line. The shooter now becomes the next defensive rebounder, and the players work both sides of the floor. This drill gives the players work on blocking out, rebounding, release passing to the side, and emphasizes hustling down floor to get into the fast-break play for a score. The players return to the end of the line and alternate lines. It is also a good idea to work the forwards and centers into the guard lines, and vice versa.

7. Tip-Two-on-One Fast-Break Drill: Diagram 9-7. This drill starts by you or your manager tossing the ball up between two opposing jumpers. When the toss is made, O1 attempts to tip the ball away from X2, who commits himself toward one of the offensive forwards, O2 or O3. When the tip is successful, O2 and O3 advance the ball by passing and/or dribbling to the opposite end of the floor, where X3 is defending the basket. Player X3 attempts to force a shot or a loss of the ball by a turnover, while O2 and O3 attempt to convert a 2 point play by a clever two-on-one maneuver. If O2 and O3 score, X3 must remain on defense. If O2 or O3 lose the ball by a turnover, or they miss a shot, the player making the error must replace X3 on defense, and the drill continues. The jumpers are replaced at the designation of the coach, and O2 and O3 are replaced by the next players in line. The drill gives practice in jump-ball techniques, improves jumping, improves tip control, teaches how to defend on a two-on-one situation, improves ball handling while running down floor on a fast break, and scoring with two-on-one.

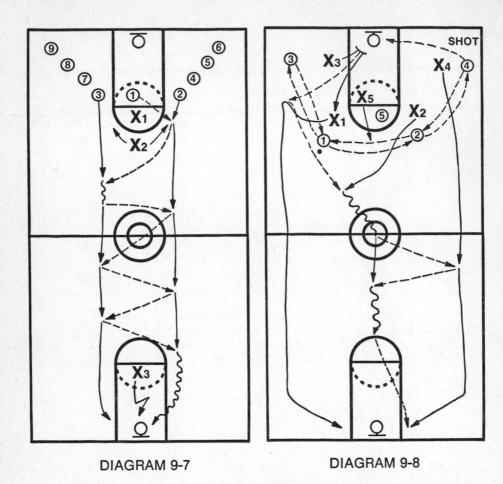

DIAGRAM 9-7   DIAGRAM 9-8

8. Switch from Defense to Offense: Diagram 9-8. To run this drill, put a ring reducer (a device that reduces the size of the basket circle) or a basket cover-up at O's basket. The X's are the first team of regulars and the O's are the substitutes or second team. The O's run the next opponent's offense. They are told what defense to use when the X's get the ball. If the O's score, they keep the ball. Anytime the O's get a good percentage shot, whether the attempt is successful or not, the defense has failed. Take steps with the defense to correct this. When the X's get possession of the ball by a rebound, an interception, or a loose ball, a fast break is attempted. If they do not get a good scoring opportunity off the fast break, they set up their regular offense, and then give the ball back to the O's or work on whatever pattern you designate. The situation here is controlled by you, and you can have the team rerun the patterns if they are sloppy, until correction is made. When X scores, or gives up the ball, they return to the defense. Any type of defense can be used in practicing the switch from defense to offense. This drill gives opportunity to improve the defensive work, defensive rebounding, the outlet pass, filling the lanes on the fast break, ability to make decisions as to whether the team has a fast-break opportunity, and when to go into the set offensive patterns.

9. The Butterfly Pattern: Diagram 9-9. This drill is designed to give practice in making the long baseball pass down court on the "Butterfly Pattern." To start the drill, you put the ball on the boards at one end of the floor. The players line up at each end as shown. The first player, O1 as shown here, starts at the free-throw line extended. The next player, O2, rebounds the shot, and makes the long pass to O1, who holds until O2 has the ball, and then takes off at full speed for the opposite end of the

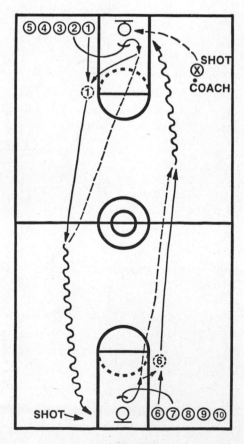

DIAGRAM 9-9

floor. Usually it is best if the pass is made so that the receiver gets it going straight away at full speed just beyond the court division line. After receiving the pass at full speed, the player dribbles to the other basket for a shot. Here the process is repeated with O6 and O7, and the drill moves continuously. Players O2 and O7 now go to the O1 and O6 positions at the free-throw line extended to become the next fast-breaking players, while O1 and O6 go to the end of the player line where they have shot. At times it is a good idea to throw the complete "butterfly-pattern" pass, and have the throwing player throw the ball FAR down the floor ahead of the breaking player. Let that player run hard and fast to catch up to the ball, pick it up and get footwork in order to drive in for the shot.

10. Half-Court Drills: Diagram 9-10. Half-court drills may be used to sharpen the players up on the patterns needed to get a shot off on a 3 on 2 advantage or a 2 on 1 situation. It also can be used to get the proper reaction from the defense needed to force a shot or a turnover. The players line up as shown, and O1 advances the ball by passing and/or dribbling to the top of the circle. Player O1 must stop at the top of the circle unless there is a clear, unmolested opportunity to go to the basket and score. A quick pass to O3, with the defense shifting as shown could bring a quick return pass to O1 for a good shot at the free-throw line area, or an opportunity to pass off quickly to O2 for a driving lay-up shot.

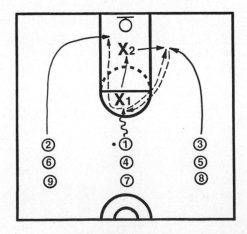

DIAGRAM 9-10

11. Three-on-One Fast Break Drill: Diagram 9-11. The players form in three lines at one end of the court. Two defensive players, X1 and X2 are placed at the top of each free-throw circle. Players O1, O2, and O3 advance the length of the court preferably by passing, and/or dribbling. The ball is to come back to the middle lane as the court division line is passed, and O1 advances to the top of the circle, where X2 forces him to stop and pass off to either O2 or O3, who go in for a lay-up shot. The ball is retrieved, and the three go to the other end by the same method, where X1 forces O1 to stop at the top of the circle and pass off again for the shot. After this the next three in the line repeat the drill. The drill gives ball handling while moving fast up and down the court and emphasizes the necessity for the player in the middle lane to stop at the top of the circle and pass off to one of the side lanes when this area is reached on the fast break.

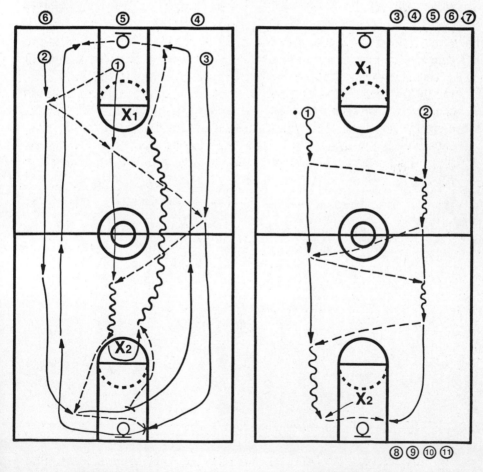

DIAGRAM 9-11   DIAGRAM 9-12

12. Two-on-One Drill: Diagram 9-12. The players line up at both ends of the court as shown. A defensive player is placed at both baskets, X1 and X2. Players O1 and O2 advance the ball the length of the floor by passing and dribbling until they approach the basket defended by X2. Now they attempt to get a declaration from X2 so that they can get a good shot. Player X2 attempts to force a shot or a turnover by faking to play one and actually defending the basket and the other player. The next players, O8 and O9 now go to the other end of the court the same way. The drill is continuous. Players X1 and X2 can be relieved of defensive duties if they force a turnover, or if one of the offensive players misses a shot—the erring offensive player replaces the defensive player.

13. Three-on-Two Fast Break Drill: Diagram 9-13. The players line up in three lanes at one end of the court. The first

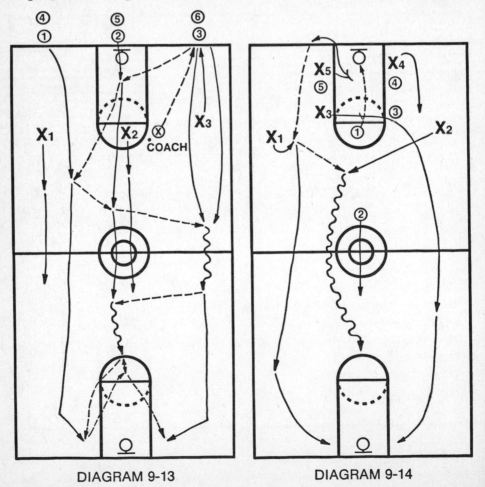

DIAGRAM 9-13   DIAGRAM 9-14

players in line step out on defense, in this case X1, X2, and X3. To start the drill, you pass the ball to one of the next players in line along the end line. The defensive players are to guard the offensive players, except that the defensive player guarding the one to whom you pass the ball must first go touch the end line before going down floor on defense. Players O2, O1, and O3 fast break down the floor, and will temporarily have a 3 on 2 advantage until, in this case, X3 can get back on defense after touching the end line. The offensive players O1, O2, and O3 now become the next defensive players, and hurry back to guard O4, O5, and O6, where the process is repeated on the next trip down the floor.

14. Fast Break from a Made Free Throw: Diagram 9-14. The players, both offensive and defensive teams, line up for a free throw. When the shooter makes the throw, the defensive player X5 grabs the ball, steps out-of-bounds and inbounds the ball to X1, who moves to the outlet pass area on X5's side of the floor. Player X2 breaks as shown to receive a pass from X1. Player X3, after blocking out the shooter, breaks down the outside on the left side of the floor, and the fast break is on. Player X4 trails the play and serves as an outlet pass possibly in case X5 cannot get an outlet pass inbounds to either X1, X2, or X3. The teams can go up and down the floor practicing this maneuver, and you can work out various outlet possibilities for the fast break. The play could go to the opposite side of the floor with X4 taking the ball out-of-bounds for the throw-in and X1, X2, and X3 can break to different positions for the throw-in. Many variations to the play can be worked out to fit your fast-break philosophy.

15. Fast Break from Missed Free Throw: Diagram 9-15. If the free throw is missed in the drill given in Diagram 9-14, the defensive team has the inside rebound positions and should be able to rebound and initiate a fast break from it. Here, with X4 securing the rebound, the outlet pass is made to X2 on the rebounder's side of the floor. Player X2 passes to X1 cutting to the middle as soon as he senses the rebound going to the opposite side. Player X3, after checking O2, the shooter, releases and drives down the outside lane on the right side, and with X2 filling the left side, the fast break is away. Player X5 holds for a release for X4 in case he cannot pass to X2, X1, or X3 to get the fast break under way, and then trails the play. Player X4 follows as the last trailer.

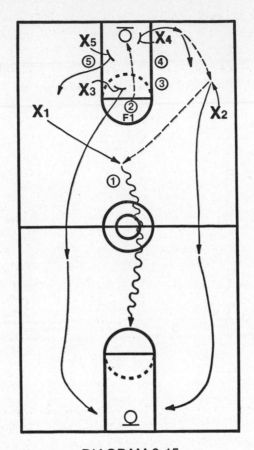

DIAGRAM 9-15

16. Two-on-One, Fast-Break Drill: Diagram 9-16, Phase 1. At least five players are needed for this drill. Players X4 and X5 are in the outlet pass areas, and X3 is defensing against O1 and O2. Players O1 and O2 drive against X3, who tries to force a shot or a turnover. If O1 or O2 score, X3 takes the ball out-of-bounds and fires an outlet pass to X4 or X5 in an effort to fast break the ball to the court division line. Players O1 and O2 try for interceptions and if successful, take the ball against X3 on another try. If X3, X4, and X5 successfully break the ball to the court division line, the drill now goes to Phase 2.

Phase 2. Players X3 and O2 now go to the outlet pass areas. Players X4 and X5 attack the basket with the ball, and O1 defends it. With 2 on 1 they should score, but if O1 gets a forced shot or a turnover, or rebounds a missed shot, he outlets to O2 or X3, and they attempt to fast break to the court division line. Players X4 and X5 play for interceptions. The drill can continue in this way for the length of time desired by the coach.

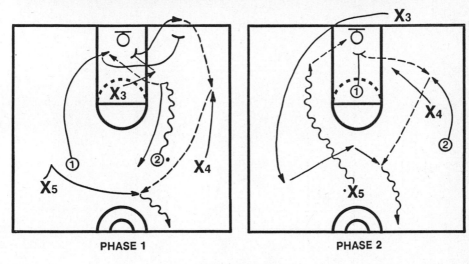

PHASE 1   PHASE 2

DIAGRAM 9-16

17. Continuous Outlet Pass Jackknife Rebound Drill: Diagram 9-17. Four players are needed for the drill. The players position themselves as shown, with X1 and X2 being outlet pass receivers, and X3 and X4 being rebounders. Player X1 starts the drill with a pass to X2, who passes cross-court to X3. Player X3 tosses the ball up and caroms it off the board for X4 to rebound. Player X4 eagle spreads in a jackknife approach to secure the rebound and while in the air, passes out to X2 who has moved out to the outlet pass area. Player X2 passes back to X1, who passes down cross-court to X4. Player X4 caroms the ball up off the board for X3, who likewise goes up in a jackknife spread after the ball, and passes it out to X1 who has moved to the outlet position. Now X1 again passes to X2, who has moved back to his original position, and the process can be repeated as many times as the coach desires. The next group can step in and do the drill when you decide. The passes are numbered in sequence.

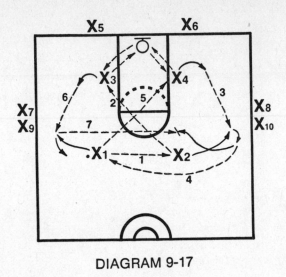

DIAGRAM 9-17

10

Offensive Rebounding Drills

OFFENSIVE REBOUNDING

Offensive rebounding has probably suffered some neglect at the hands of coaches due to the emphasis that has been placed on defensive rebounding and the necessity for blocking the offensive players off the boards in order to get the fast-break offense under way. Rebounding has come to mean "defensive rebounding" and so perhaps there has been a lapse in concern for the offensive follow up and rebound that could convert an easy two points. Although the fundamentals of offensive and defensive rebounding are similar, there are some significant differences—enough that the two need to be coached as different entities.

The first secret of offensive rebounding is simply to follow all shots with quick, hard-nosed aggressive play. Every shot should be considered missed and presenting an offensive rebound possibility. No less than three players should be on the offensive board. A fourth player should be ready to make a sweep for a long rebound when the opportunity presents itself. This player should be ready to get back on defense quickly if the rebound is not secured. This is often referred to as the three-and-one-half-player offensive rebounding strength and the one-and-one-half-player defensive situation. There are times when the offensive team may abandon defensive security completely and throw all five players at the offensive basket on a shot attempt in an aggressive manner in order to secure the offensive rebound. When the offense does secure the rebound, the opposition will not be able to get a fast break away.

To be able to follow well on the offensive rebounds, teammates must know when a shot is going up on the boards, and be on the way in for the rebound, even before, if not at the instant the ball leaves the shooter's finger tips. This is the second secret of offensive rebounding—knowing when the teammate is going to put the shot up, and from what position. Most of the time, a player will be in a position to follow his own shot, and should do so. The shooter will more likely know when and where to go on his own shot for a rebound, and can follow with abandon. The best rebounders are not necessarily the taller players, but can be players of average height who are always in position and ready to put the ball back up there, or if in a troubled area, to clear it out for the next action.

Most of the time the offensive player will be hindered in rebounding efforts by defensive players turning or stepping into the path to the basket and the ball. The offensive rebounder must learn to make quick movements and fakes to avoid these blocking-out efforts which obscure the path to the rebounding ball. Often a little fake to get the first movement from the defensive blocker will enable the offensive player to slide to an inside position. If in close, a fake that gets the blocker started on the turn can be followed by a spin in the opposite direction, enabling the offensive player to slide into an inside position that will take the defensive blocker out on the fight to get the ball. Sometimes, once the blocker has started a move, a simple "jab-step" to the inside will accomplish the trick.

Coaching Points for Offensive Rebounding

1. Consider every shot taken as a missed shot and follow hard and aggressively for the rebound.
2. Do not let the defensive player pin you in with contact. Avoid contact with the defensive player unless you can get the inside position.
3. When the offensive rebounder succeeds in getting past the defensive player, immediately assume a wide crouched position with knees bent, ready to spring into space to secure the ball.

4. If the ball is in close to the basket, attempt to score with the one-hand tip-in. Tip with a straight elbow, fingers spread wide, and with a pushing, snap-like motion of the wrist. DO NOT BAT AT THE BALL. It must be a controlled motion—a controlled tip.

5. When the ball is too far from the basket to tip, grab it with both hands, and go back up immediately with a power-lay-up shot. *Power it up!* This kind of an attempt often brings the three-point play.

6. Be aware of offensive and defensive responsibilities as an offensive rebounder. There must be defensive balance, so the player must know when his responsibility calls for staying back on defense.

7. If blocked off the boards and the opponent gets the rebound, don't foul in this area. It is foolish to foul in the back court area.

8. Keep hands high when going in for the offensive rebound. This will help avoid pushing fouls, and keeping the hands high will give a better offensive rebounding start.

Habit Drills to Teach Offensive Rebounding

Any drill or exercise that increases leg strength, jumping ability, and feet agility will improve the offensive rebounding potential. There are many drills, such as rope skipping, bench drills, dot drills, and wall drills. Many such drills can be done during the off-season by the players on their own. These drills can also be included in the season's practice routines, and will increase endurance as well.

1. Bench Drill. Have the player start by standing sideways next to a bench that would be from 18 inches to 24 inches high. The player, on a signal, jumps back and forth over the bench, jumping off the balls of the feet and using the arms to help in the jumping, lifting motion. You can start with a number that is appropriate for the condition of the individuals and the level of the competition, and work up to a higher number such as 40 or 50 jumps. This will improve leg strength, jumping ability, agility and endurance.

2. Jump at the Basket Drill. Divide the squad into groups of two at each basket. The players take turns tossing the ball up on the backboard and tipping the ball as many times as possible against the board. Competitive contests can be held to see which player can make the most controlled tips. While one player tips, the other counts. If there are not enough baskets in the gym to do this drill, spots on the walls can be marked at heights of 10 to 14 feet, and the spot can be used as a wall tipping drill to accomplish the same thing.

3. Sargent Jump Drill. Place a chart on a wall showing the various height measurements. Two or three times per week, have the players take 10 jumps with the manager recording the height of the best jumps. The difference between the player's reach and his jump is the vertical jumping ability. Usually a jump of 24 inches and above is considered good. By recording jumping records at intervals, competition can be generated to see who can improve his vertical jump the most during the season.

4. Barbell and Bounce Jumping Drill. Three players will be needed to work together on this drill. A barbell with as much weight as the player can handle is placed on the shoulders. A sponge or towel is placed across the back of the neck to cushion the weight of the barbell. Two players, one on each side of the jumper, act as spotters and steady the barbell to keep it from falling and to protect the player doing the exercise. To do the exercise, the player stands with feet parallel and about shoulder width apart. He jumps up and crosses the feet, first bringing the right foot across in front of the left foot. On the next jump come back to the original position. Now on the next jump, bring the left foot across in front of the right, and then jump returning to the original position. Repeat the drill in a rapid rhythmical manner until the jumper is exhausted. This drill is a great developer of balance and leg strength in the player. The players take turns spotting and jumping.

5. Jumping at the Basket Drill. The squad lines up and running single file at the basket, runs five times down each side and five times down the middle. When running and jumping at the basket, do it in this way. When going in from the right side, take off on the right foot (high jump) and reach for the basket with the left hand. This will turn the players so that upon landing, they will be facing back up the floor. Now go back up the floor, and come in from the left side. Here, take off on the left foot and reach for the basket with the right hand. Again the body turn will face the player up-court. Now come down the middle, and jump at the basket with both hands, doing the take-off on whichever foot the coach designates.

Follow this by dividing the players into groups under each basket. Standing directly under the basket, with hands held high over the head, each player jumps continuously to see how many jumps he can make without stopping, and without bringing the hands down. *On all jumps—stress the high jump.*

6. Two-Line Tip Drill: Diagram 10-1. A simple two-line tip-in drill. Form two lines on opposite sides of the court as shown. Player O1 dribbles in to the basket and throws the ball up on the board. Player O6, on the opposite line, comes in and tips the ball into the basket. If not successful on the first attempt, O6 tips until successful. Player O1 secures the ball and passes the ball to O7 who dribbles in and throws the ball up for O2. The players exchange lines and positions so that all get tipping turns.

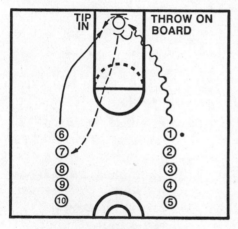

DIAGRAM 10-1

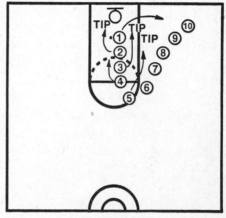

DIAGRAM 10-2

7. Single Line Continuous Tip Drill: Diagram 10-2. The players form a circular single line in front of the basket as shown. The first player tosses the ball on the board. The second, O2, follows and tips up on the board, and so does the third, O3, etc. After a certain number of tips against the board, (a number called by one of the players or by you) the ball is tipped into the basket. This can be repeated, or run to the opposite side of the basket.

8. Three at the Basket: Diagram 10-3. Put three players at a basket in the rebound triangle as shown. You or the manager put the ball up on the boards. All three players go for the rebound. The other two attack the player who gets it, and who must put it back up on a POWER SHOT. They keep this up until a basket is scored. This gives the players practice in powering the ball up off the boards, and helps in developing the ability to bring about the three point play.

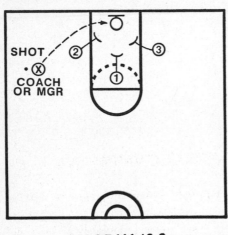

DIAGRAM 10-3   DIAGRAM 10-4

9. Triangle Rebounding Tipping Drill: Diagram 10-4. Players O1 and O2 take positions at the side of the basket as shown. Players O3, O4, and O5 line up at the top of the free throw circle. Player O3, the first player in the line, takes a shot from the circle, and follows on the rebound with O1 and O2. All three tip and keep at it until the shot is good. The ball is then passed back to O4, the next in line. Player O1 moves to the end of the line, O2 replaces O1, and O3 replaces O2. Now O4 shoots, and the process is repeated. The drill is excellent to develop the ability to shoot, follow, and tip the ball into the basket.

10. Two at the Basket Drill: Diagram 10-5. Place two players at the basket on either side or in front. Work all positions. The coach or manager throws the ball up on the board. The players fake, spin, or jab-step to get the inside position and hold the opponent out. The player who gets the ball is to put it back up in an attempt to score. The other attacks the player who secured the rebound. The drill is to teach the player the technique of attaining and securing the inside position.

11. Carom Tip Drill: Diagram 10-6. Five players line up as shown. Player O1, the first in line with a ball, tosses the ball high on the board so that it caroms across off the board to O3 on the opposite side, and then moves quickly over to the end of the

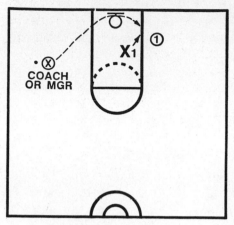

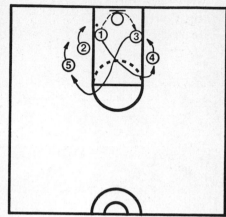

DIAGRAM 10-5   DIAGRAM 10-6

O3 and O4 line. Player O3 rebounds the ball at the height of the jump and tosses it back across the board to O2 who has moved up to replace O1. Player O3, after the toss, moves quickly in behind O5. Player O5 moves up to replace O2 after he has made his toss. The drill is continuous with each rebounder going quickly to the end of the opposite line as soon as the rebound is tossed back across the board. The players time their jump so as to get the ball at the height of their jump and flick it back across the board while in the air.

12. One-on-One Offensive Rebounding Drill: Diagram 10-7. Players O1 and X1 both line up a comfortable distance from the basket and facing it. Player O1, with the ball, shoots at

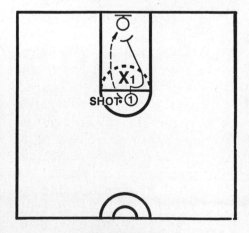

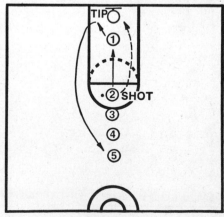

DIAGRAM 10-7   DIAGRAM 10-8

the basket, and must step around X1 to recover the rebound and score. At first X1 is to be instructed not to resist O1 in his movements to rebound, and O1 is instructed to slide to both the right and the left in going around X1. Later, allow X1 to try to stop O1 in his rebounding efforts. The drill teaches the offensive rebounder to be aggressive and to meet resistance from the defensive player who is blocking out.

13. One-Tipper Drill: Diagram 10-8. Player O1 takes a position in front of the basket. Player O2 shoots until he misses, and on the miss, O1 tips the ball back up with one or both hands until he hits it. The players then rotate positions with O3 shooting next, and O2 tipping next. Player O1 goes to the end of the line. The drill can be made more effective and more difficult by placing a ring reducer on the basket.

14. Team Rebound Drill: Diagram 10-9. Divide the squad into three teams in any manner the coach may decide—at random, players choosing sides, etc. The teams line up as shown, and you or the manager put the ball up on the board. The first player from each line attempts to rebound the ball back up for a score. After a player has scored three baskets, he goes to the end of his team line, and the next player in line replaces him. Each player remains in the rebound area until three baskets are scored. The first team to have all its players score three baskets is the winner. The drill will develop competitive aggressiveness, and will accustom them to the give-and-take ruggedness needed for offensive rebound play. The players also enjoy the competitive drill.

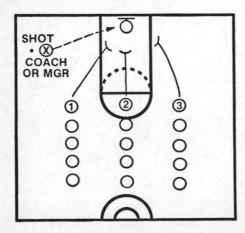

DIAGRAM 10-9

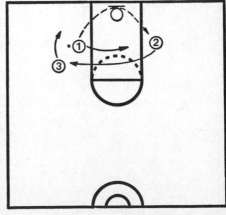

DIAGRAM 10-10

15. Five Time Rebound Drill: Diagram 10-10. The players position themselves at a basket as shown. Player O1 tosses the ball high on the board so that it caroms off to O2, who times the jump to take it high, and toss the ball back high so that it caroms back to O1. They keep the ball in play until each has rebounded the ball five times. Now O3 replaces O1. Player O1 moves over to replace O2, and O2 replaces O3, and watches while O3 and O1 repeat the drill. Then they rotate again and continue as long as you wish.

Individual and Team Offensive Drills

INDIVIDUAL OFFENSIVE MANEUVERS

Every basketball player must learn and have a repertoire of individual offensive maneuvers that will free him for a shot in the battle against the defenses that are encountered during a game. A player may be the finest shot in the game when open, but if that player lacks power or knowledge of individual maneuvers necessary to get open when the defense is applied tightly in one-on-one situations, such a player will be unable to take advantage of any shooting prowess that has been developed.

Most situations in the game of basketball today eventually come down to a one-on-one, two-on-two, or three-on-three at the most. The coach of players of high school age or younger is faced with the problem of teaching the individual offensive maneuvers necessary to get free for the shot and the score in these situations. This can be done by the drill process, of course, and the coach at higher levels of maturity needs to reinforce these patterns of learning in maneuverability. This calls for the drill process too.

Habit Drills to Teach Individual Offensive Maneuvers

1. The Rocker Step: Diagram 11-1. The first offensive maneuver to teach the player is the *rocker step*. Have the players line up in the guard and forward operational areas as shown in this diagram. The first player in each line is given a ball and a defensive player guards the player with the ball. Have the player with the ball just rock back and forth by stepping at the defensive player, and then stepping back as far as possible. The player with the ball will get the feel of moving against the defensive player and of protecting the ball. If at any time the defensive player moves at the ball or with the offensive player, and in such a manner that the center of the defensive player's gravity is moving at the ball, the offensive player must burst by the defensive player with a driving dribble. Following the simple rocker step routine, you should teach the player to *fake a shot, and drive* from these moves, and to *fake a drive*, and step back and shoot.

In developing the rocker step, the player establishes one foot as a pivot foot, and steps forward and back in the rocker move with the other foot. Teach the "rocker move" with both the right and left foot, and from all positions on the floor. The players rotate lines, and from offense to defense. When the "rocker step," the "fake-a-shot-drive," and "fake-a-drive-shoot" have been mastered, the player now has the basic foundations for other individual moves.

DIAGRAM 11-1

2. Walking Step or Hesitation Step: Diagram 11-2. The next movement to teach is the walking step or a hesitation step from the rocker movement. In this movement the player, after taking a step forward, and then back, takes a slow hesitation step of about half a step in length, or a half a step forward, then bursts on by the defensive player with a driving dribble. The player may also work the hesitation step in this way—after the forward step at the defensive player, fake back with head and shoulders as if going to step back again, or even take a half step back. If the defensive player moves his weight forward to stay with the offensive player or at the ball, then the burst of forward speed by the offensive player will be a surprise that will make the movement successful. Diagram 11-2 illustrates the step ideas. Use the same formation as that given in Diagram 11-1 and work on the "walking step" or "hesitation step." The secret of this move is to get the defensive player moving with the ball, and then to burst by him with a "change-up" when the offensive player can catch the defensive player with a forward thrust of the body weight.

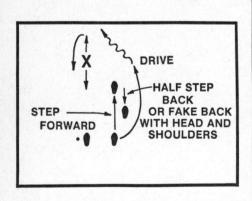

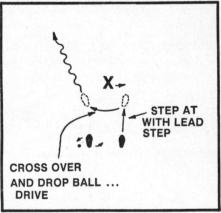

DIAGRAM 11-2   DIAGRAM 11-3

3. The Cross-Over Step: Diagram 11-3. This move also comes off the rocker step. The player with the ball steps at the defensive player in what might be termed a "lead step." If the defensive player does not respond, then the offensive player is home free and can drive on by. If however, the defensive player shifts his defensive position to meet the forward step or thrust, the offensive player should step across the pivot foot with the forward foot quickly, and while protecting the ball, drive in the direction away from the defensive player's movement. This move can be enhanced many times by making the forward step just a "jab-step" (half a step) to draw movement from the defensive player. Then a quick execution of the cross-over can put the offensive player by the defensive player free. Work the cross-over step in both directions and use the formation given in Diagram 11-1 to teach the players this movement from the various player operational areas on the floor.

4. Opening Up the Offensive Player Drill: Diagram 11-4. The offensive player has to learn to shake the defensive player to get open for a pass from teammates in the player operational areas. If the defensive player is tight and plays a denial position, the offensive player must employ special footwork to get open. Work the drill here to teach this footwork. Player O2 takes the position shown and wants to work free for a pass at the free-throw line extended. Take a position facing inside, or to the middle, and position the feet as shown. This position enables the player to see the movements of all teammates as well as the opponents, and should enable the player to get free to receive a pass without being any farther toward the center of the floor than the free-throw line extended. To shake the defensive player, O2 takes a lead step with the near foot, faking a drive, then steps out to receive the ball from the guard, O1. Have X2 play a strong denial position. This footwork usually frees O2 for the pass. However if there are problems, other maneuvers can be employed as will be shown in later diagrams. Work both sides of the floor and different positions on the floor so that the players learn to maneuver from all positions.

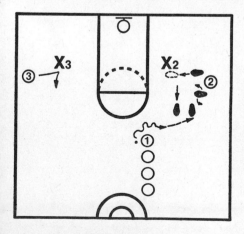

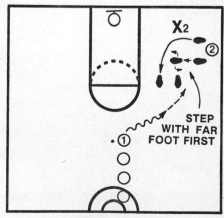

DIAGRAM 11-4   DIAGRAM 11-5

After receiving the ball, the offensive player then turns to face the opponent and to maneuver from the moves learned in the "rocker step" series.

5. Far Foot Lead Step Drill: Diagram 11-5. If the player has trouble getting free from the maneuver shown in Diagram 11-4, and if the denial position of X2 is strong, have the offensive player try the move shown here. Player O2 steps at the defensive player with the FAR FOOT, and then throws the body across in front of the defensive player with the inside foot, and then moves out to receive the ball from the guard. Now the player can turn and use the rocker-step moves to get his next move going. Work this drill from both sides of the floor and from the various positions used as operational areas in your offense.

6. Pivot to the Inside, Block Out Drill: Diagram 11-6. If X2 plays such a strong denial position as to make reception difficult by using footwork shown in previous footwork maneuvers, teach the footwork shown here. Have X2 play a very strong denial defense. Player O2 advances to meet the ball, and stops in the position about where the ball is usually to be received, and with the outside foot forward, makes a good fake to receive the ball from O1 who is dribbling toward him. Now O2 turns or pivots to the inside, crossing over with the outside foot and using the inside foot as the pivot foot. This turn should place O2 inside X2 and now O2 immediately extends the inside arm outward toward the middle so as to hold X2 back and to block him out of the play. Player O2 now dashes toward the basket to receive a pass from O1. Work the drill from both sides of the floor, and rotate the players from offense to defense so that all play all positions.

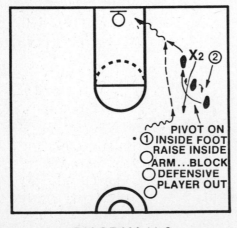

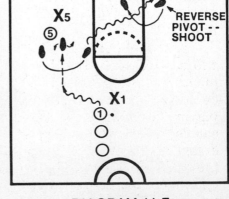

DIAGRAM 11-6   DIAGRAM 11-7

7. The Inside Pivot Drill: Diagram 11-7. This is an offensive maneuver by a player with the ball in the pivot-post area to get the defensive opponent on the inside hip, or the hip nearest the opponent. It gives the shooter the advantage of a step away from and by the defensive opponent. The move combined with a hook shot can be deadly, and also at times gives the shooter a shot close enough that no hook is needed. The move is little more than a reverse pivot on the foot next to the opponent. It can be executed in any number of positions in and around the pivot-post area—all that is required is that the offensive player get the defensive opponent moving to counter the offensive move. Once the offensive player gets the opponent moving and can see no clear drive for an opening, the offensive player stops, plants both feet, and if necessary fakes a shot. Any declaration on the part of the defensive opponent should enable the offensive player to execute the pivot on the foot nearest the defensive player, stepping backward and in toward the basket, thereby placing the opponent on the offensive player's hip in such a manner as to cleverly spin by him and get an almost unmolested shot. Combining the hook shot with the maneuver can add to the scoring power of the player. Run the drill as shown in Diagram 11-7. At first O5 need not be opposed on defense, or only with passive defense. Player O1 passes to O5 in the area shown. Player O5 spins on a cross-over and drives toward the basket. At the end of the dribble, plant the feet, fake if necessary to get a commitment from the defensive player, and then execute the footwork shown and described to get off the shot. Work the drill from the various areas and directions in and around the pivot-post area to familiarize the players with the approaches that can be made from the maneuver. Have all players work both the offense and defense on the drill, and from all positions. The drill at times may be limited to the forwards and the pivot-post players.

8. One-on-One Drill: Diagram 11-8. The players pair up and scatter about the floor. A ball is given to each pair. One player takes the ball, as an offensive player—the other, as a defensive player, tries to take the ball away from the offensive player. The offensive player is not allowed to dribble or pass, but can use the one step and pivot advantage to protect the ball. The defensive player is to be rough and aggressive in efforts to get the ball. The offensive player using the one step and pivot, and with one hand above, one below, protects the ball by stepping, turning, pivoting, and giving the ball tough protection. The object of the drill—to teach the player that one defensive player should not take the ball away from him.

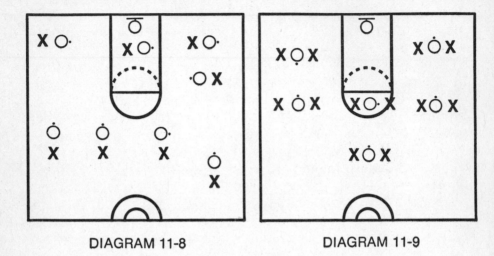

DIAGRAM 11-8   DIAGRAM 11-9

9. Two-on-One-Drill: Diagram 11-9. Have the players divide into groups of threes. One player takes the ball—the other two defensive players try to take the ball away from the player with the ball without fouling. For a stated number of seconds, such as 5 or 10 seconds, the player with the ball cannot dribble or pass, but protects the ball by shielding it with extended elbows, hands and arms above and below the ball, and by using the one step and pivot advantage. The two defensive players aggressively try to steal the ball without fouling. At a stated time interval, the offensive player may dribble or pass out of his predicament. The object of the drill—to teach the player with the ball that two defensive players should not be able to take the ball away from him without fouling.

FAKES AND FEINTS

Fakes and feints are very necessary maneuvers to develop in the basketball player. As with all things, the coach needs to drill more and work harder to ingrain the moves in the younger players. Drills are very necessary. A fake is split-second motion designed to get the defensive player momentarily off balance, or to get him to commit himself so the offensive player can go around him, or gain shooting room. To be a good one-on-one player the individual should develop some good fakes and feints.

The following are examples of fakes and feints that should be developed.

1. Fake a shot—drive
2. Fake a drive—shoot
3. Fake right—drive left
4. Fake left—drive right
5. Fake right—shoot
6. Fake left—shoot
7. Fake right, fake left, drive right
8. Fake left, fake right, drive left
9. Fake right, fake a shot, drive left
10. Fake left, fake a shot, drive right
11. Fake left, fake a shot, drive left
12. Change pace—slow down—then when opponent slows down, give a burst of speed by the opponent.

A "change of pace" is actually a "fake" or a "feint" movement. The change of pace is a change of speed. It is one of the most lethal weapons a player can use. The player cannot operate at top speed constantly in basketball, but even if he could he could not accomplish as much by constant top speed as would be possible by working a change of pace.

The faster a basketball player is, the greater the advantage. Sometimes a player can get by with sheer speed, but if the player can combine speed with a clever change of pace, that player becomes more difficult to defense. Since the opponent is not used to seeing the player operate at full speed, this change of pace will make him seem faster than he really is.

Basketball requires quick starts and a rapid pickup, and players who are slow in speed, but who possess a quick start, are more difficult to guard than faster, but slower-starting players. Along with a change of pace, the player should be able to execute a quick change of direction. The player should develop the ability to do this with or without the ball. This change of direction maneuver is really a fake—the player fakes a move to go in one direction, but goes in another. Often a change-of-pace dribble or a change of direction will permit the player to score. The change of direction from left to right, and right to left should be mastered.

It is not necessary to have the ball to fake one direction and go in another, although a better chance of evading the defensive player is afforded in this situation, since usually the player with the ball is more closely guarded, and tighter play will afford a better chance of getting free with a fake movement. Usually the closer the opponent plays, the greater the opportunity the offensive player has of losing him.

Kinds of Fakes

Several kinds of fakes are possible by a player. They are ball fakes, head fakes, shoulder fakes, body fakes, foot fakes, and fakes that are combinations of these. Usually head, shoulder, and body fakes are better than ball fakes. A ball fake is the weakest type of fake to be made, but when combined with a head, shoulder, body, or foot fake, it may be a very effective weapon. The experienced defensive player will not fall for a ball fake, a head fake, or even a shoulder fake, but will concentrate on the offensive player's hips and midsection and go in the direction in which those body parts move.

As a "faker," the player should remember that faking movements must be made quickly, appear to be genuine, and be followed by explosive moves. The quick, but long initial step will usually enable the player to elude the defensive player.

A fake-a-shot—drive, is a maneuver in which the offensive player with the ball fakes a shot at the basket in an attempt to draw the defensive player closer to him so that he can dribble around him. If the guard falls for the fake and starts to jump, or moves high toward the shooter with weight shifted forward, it will be easy to make a drive around him. The guard does not have to leave his feet to make himself vulnerable to this move. As soon as the player moves forward or lifts upward, he is off balance for the offensive player's next move. When the offensive player eludes a defensive player in this move, great pressure is immediately put on the defense behind the player who has been a sucker for the fake.

Sometimes a double fake is required, especially after the defensive player has become familiar with the offensive player's moves. A double fake is a fake before a fake. Example: Fake right, fake left, then go right. Such fakes have to be made quickly, and the get-away move must be very explosive.

All a player does with a fake is attempt to get the defensive player to make a movement in one direction so that an opening can be afforded to the offensive player. The *dummy* play is another excellent fake maneuver to be used by the offensive player who does not have the ball. In this move the player pretends to do nothing, to see neither the passer nor the ball. The moment the defensive player relaxes, the "dummy" breaks toward the ball or the basket to receive the ball and possibly score.

Habit Drills to Teach Faking

The following are drills that can be used to teach the various fake movements.

1. The Dozen Fakers Drills: Diagrams 11-10 to 11-19. These diagrams give a drill in which a series of fake movements can be taught. Each will have a brief explanation of the fake and the move. On these drills you pass the ball to the players and call out the fake and move that the player is to make just before each drill is started.

Diagram 11-10. You feed the ball to the players breaking into the basket area as shown. The player receives the ball near the basket, plants the feet, fakes with head and shoulders as if to shoot from the left side, then pivoting on the right foot, reverses to the left to turn and shoot a right-handed shot in front of the basket. Run the drill from both sides of the basket.

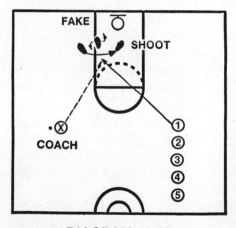

DIAGRAM 11-10

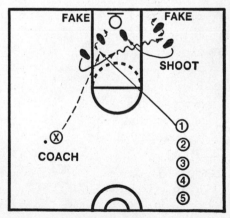

DIAGRAM 11-11

Diagram 11-11. The player starts and makes the first fake as in Diagram 11-10. When the pivot or turn is made the player puts the ball on the floor for a dribble across the lane, plants both feet, fakes a shot from the right side, and now does a reverse pivot with the left foot as the pivot foot, placing the right foot as shown, and shoots. The shot could be a left-handed hook, or any shot you select. Work both sides of the lane on the drill.

Diagram 11-12. This move is almost the same as in Diagram 11-11, but made from a different approach in receiving the ball. The players break from an area deep near the baseline to the free-throw line to receive your pass. Upon receiving the ball, the player plants both feet, fakes a movement to the right with head, shoulders, and eyes. This is followed by a cross-over spinner, pivoting on the left foot, and a dribble drive down the lane near the basket. The player again plants both feet, fakes a shot to the left, but pivots on the left foot with a reverse pivot to swing into and in front of the basket for a shot. Work the drill from both sides of the basket.

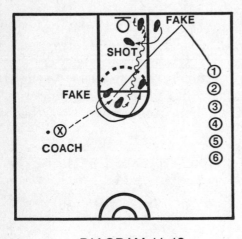

DIAGRAM 11-12

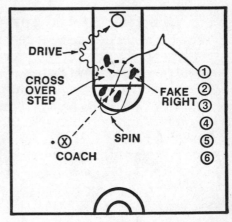

DIAGRAM 11-13

Diagram 11-13. This approach is the same as in Diagram 11-12. The player, upon receiving the ball, does a spinner or cross-over move, pivoting on the left foot, crossing over with the right, and fakes a drive with a lead step or a "jab-step"—to the right. This is followed with a cross-over again with the right foot (hold the left foot in pivot position), protecting the ball on this move, then drop the ball and dribble drive down the outside of the lane for the basket and a shot. Keep the ball well protected on all turns, and be sure to practice the drill coming in from both sides of the basket.

Diagram 11-14. This drill uses the same approach as in Diagram 11-13, but a different fake move. When the player receives the ball, he spins to face the opponent, fakes a drive to the right, then fakes a cross-over move to the left, then drives right to the basket. Be sure to work all drills going both directions and from both sides of the basket.

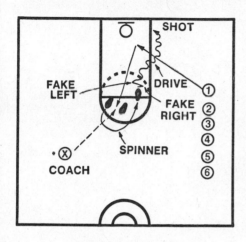

DIAGRAM 11-14

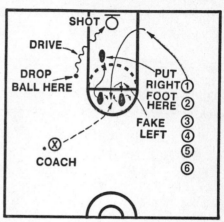

DIAGRAM 11-15

Diagram 11-15. The player here receives the ball in the same position as in the three previous diagrams with back to opponent and the basket just above the free-throw line. Upon receiving the ball, the player fakes to his left with head and shoulders, and then steps as far back as possible with the right foot, pivoting on the left foot, and at the same time drops the ball in a well-protected position as the turn is made, to start a driving dribble to the basket. This turn executed quickly will leave the opponent on the hip, especially if any declaration is made on the first fake to the left.

Diagram 11-16. The players line up as shown, and as the player comes down into the scoring area, you feed the ball. Upon receiving the ball, O1, in this case, fakes a shot. If the defense moves at him, he drives for the basket. If no move is made by X1, the defense, to guard O1, and he is free, then he shoots. Two fakes should be practiced on this drill—fake a shot, drive, fake a drive, and shoot. Player O1 should be fed the ball within a comfortable shooting range of the basket. The players change off on offense and defense, and work both sides of the court.

Diagram 11-17. Player receives the ball in scoring area. Fake left and drive right, or fake right and drive to the left for a shot. Then use this same drill to teach and practice the double

DIAGRAM 11-16

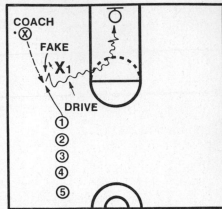

DIAGRAM 11-17

fake. First fake left, fake right, drive left. Then fake right, fake left, and drive right. Practice from both sides of the floor and all the team operational areas.

Diagram 11-18. In this drill, a change of pace is practiced. When the player approaches the scoring area and the defensive player moves to the defense, O1 slows down, almost to a walk, or maybe even stops. When the defensive player slows to the offensive move, a sudden burst of speed is exerted in a "change-of-pace" and "change-of-direction" drive to the basket. You feed the ball to the player when an opening comes.

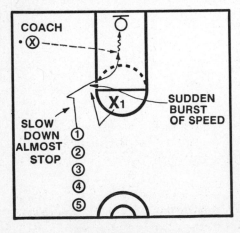

DIAGRAM 11-18

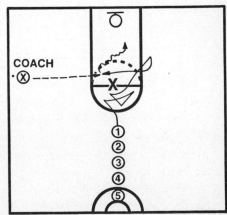

DIAGRAM 11-19

Diagram 11-19. In this drill the player approaches the defensive player near the free-throw circle. When the defense declares, the offensive player makes a series of flutter moves, faking right, left, making moves, changing direction, fluttering back and forth or button-hooking out. You feed the player when he gets open, and then the player executes fakes, spins, jab-steps or cross-over moves to get the drive to the basket. This concludes the dozen fakers drills.

2. Stop Short, Shoot Drill: Diagram 11-20. Many times a player will be on a dribble drive to the basket with a defensive player in hot pursuit. This drill is to teach the player to stop, fake, and let the defensive player go on by when playing close behind in hot pursuit. Player O1 is given a lead and X1 pursues O1 in an attempt to catch him and block the shot. Player O1 stops and fakes, or fakes and stops at the same time, letting X1's momentum carry him on by O1. Player O1 puts the shot up. Change from offense to defense. The defense rotates to the end of the line.

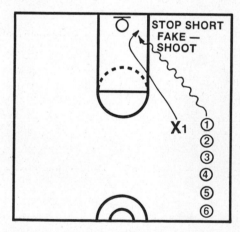

DIAGRAM 11-20

3. Change of Pace and Cross-Over Dribble Drill: Diagrams 11-21 and 11-22. This drill is to teach how to get ahead of the defensive player by a change of pace or a cross-over dribble.

Diagram 11-21. Player O1 starts out on a fast dribble, then slows down to get the defensive player slowed in the pursuit. When the defensive player slows to match O1's speed, O1, by a sudden burst of speed, drives to the basket in an effort to lose X1.

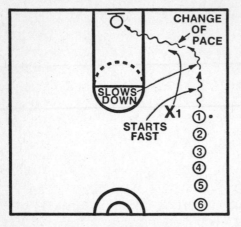

DIAGRAM 11-21

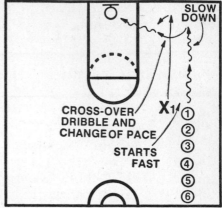

DIAGRAM 11-22

Diagram 11-22. If X1 should overrun or overplay O1 when the slow-down change of pace is made, O1 may do a cross-over dribble maneuver shifting the dribble from the right to the left as the shoulder is ducked and the body used to protect the ball. Player O1 will now be inside X1, and can drive on in to the basket. When the cross-over dribble is made, O1 can effect a change of pace to make the move more effective. The players rotate from offense to defense, and the defense goes to the end of the line. Run the drill to both sides of the floor.

TEAM OFFENSIVE DRILLS

Most coaches are faced with a shortage of time. They never have time to get all the things done that they need to get done within the allotted practice time schedule and the available space. With the Title IX programs now being brought into all the athletic programs, this situation will be even more acute, and with the sharing of time and facilities by men's and women's programs, few will have time to accomplish all that they will want to get done. Better planning and organization of practice sessions will be one way to get more done within the allotted time and space scheduled.

One of the ways to better take advantage of this time schedule is to incorporate as many of the fundamental drills as possible into team offensive and defensive patterns. The team offense can be broken down into parts, and can be run as ball handling drills. While improving upon the skills of passing, dribbling, shooting, pivoting, stops, starts, and change of direction, the team offensive patterns are also being improved and rehashed. You can sit down, break your offense into parts and then run these parts as drills. There will always be a need for some drills, but many "just drills" can be eliminated with this kind of planning. The following are some drills that can be used to build a team offense, or used as team offensive drills.

1. Offensive Guard Drills: If you use a two-guard offense, drills can be devised that include the movements these two guards would make in executing the offense. Diagrams 11-23 through 11-25 give such drills.

Diagram 11-23. Player O2 fakes a deep cut, and comes back to receive a pass from O1. Player O1 follows the pass and receives a return hand-off from O2 as he goes over the top. Player O2 pivots and rolls toward O1's move toward the basket in a dribble drive. Player O1 may pass back to O2 on what amounts to a "slip and roll" movement. The drill should first be run without a defense. Later when the moves are mastered, add defensive opposition.

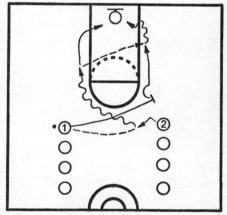

DIAGRAM 11-23   DIAGRAM 11-24

Diagram 11-24. The guards now proceed to work all the guard options in the offense. Here O1 passes to O2 and moves inside to screen O2's opponent as O2 dribbles close behind O1's screen. Player O1 rolls on a pivot to the inside and toward the ball, and peels off on a cut to the basket. Player O2 may return the ball to O1.

Diagram 11-25. Here the move is slightly different. Player O1 passes to O2 and O2 dribbles diagonally towards O1, who cuts off the dribble to receive a pass back from O2. Player O2 pivots and rolls toward the basket as O1 dribble drives to the basket. Player O1 now feeds O2 on his move to the basket. Incorporate all the two guard moves into the drill.

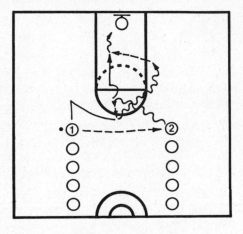

DIAGRAM 11-25

2. Guard-Forward Drills: Break down the guard-forward moves in the offense and include these moves in offensive drills. Diagrams 11-26 and 11-27 show such drills.

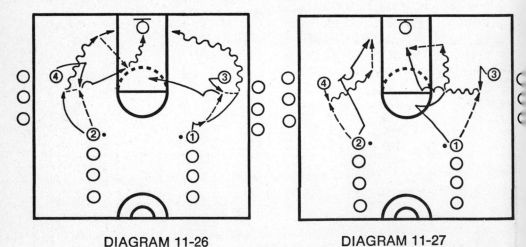

DIAGRAM 11-26   DIAGRAM 11-27

Diagram 11-26. The guards and forwards line up in their respective operational areas. Player O1 passes to O3, and moves outside to receive a return pass. Be sure O3 does the fake and footwork necessary to shake the defensive player. Player O1 can dribble in for a shot or he may pass back to O3, who rolls on a pivot toward the ball and fans out toward the free-throw line. This variation is shown in the movement involving O2 and O4. Work all the various guard-forward options in the offense on this drill. Work both sides of the floor.

Diagram 11-27. This diagram gives two options to the guard-forward moves. The one on the right side is called the "Inside-Outside" option. Player O1 passes to O3, and O3 dribbles toward the free-throw line and O1 faking to the left, cuts over the top of O3 who has stopped, pivoted and posted for the cutter. Player O1 receives the ball, drives toward the basket and may pass back to O3, who pivots and rolls toward the basket and always toward the ball and the cutter. On the left side, O2 passes to O4, and moves to screen to the inside for O4. Player O4 dribbles tight off the screen, and may pass back to O2 on a roll-off move. There are many option possibilities in the guard-forward movements. Drills on all these are to be a part of your offense.

3. Guard-Guard-Forward Drills: Diagram 11-28. Now with two guards and one forward, run as ball handling drills all the patterns that would include these positions in the offense. This diagram gives an option possibility called the "double" or the second guard through. Run all the play options as a ball handling drill including these three player options possible in the offense. Run all drills to both sides of the floor.

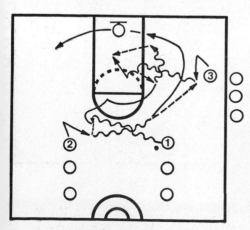

DIAGRAM 11-28

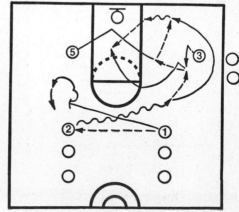

DIAGRAM 11-29

4. Two Guards, Forward and Center Drill: Diagram 11-29. Now put in the pivot-post player and run the offensive options involving two guards, one forward, and the pivot-post player. This diagram gives one such option. Drill on all the options to be included in your regular offense. Next, to complete the offense, add the other forward, and run all the offensive patterns as ball handling and offensive drills. The offense is now complete, and through drill situations, you have built your offense. Any offense of your preference can be built with similar drills.

5. A Reverse Action Offensive Drill: Diagrams 11-30 and 11-31. These two diagrams show a reverse action offense that can be run as an offensive drill.

Diagram 11-30, Phase 1. Player O1 passes to O2. Player O2 passes to O4, and cuts outside to the baseline. Player O5, playing about midway between the free-throw line and the basket on the left side of the lane, acts as a screen for O3, who cuts in such a manner as to manipulate his opponent into O5. Player O3 moves across the lane for a possible pass from O4. Player O3 may cut over the top of or behind O5.

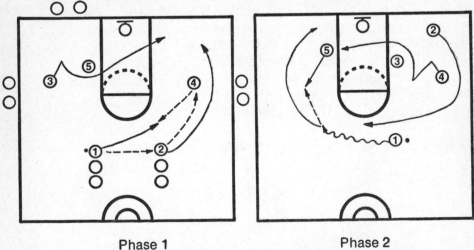

Phase 1

DIAGRAM 11-30

Phase 2

DIAGRAM 11-31

Diagram 11-31, Phase 2. This shows the position of the players at the end of the Phase 1 movement. If no opening is chosen, O4 has passed the ball out to O1, who moved over to replace O2 when O2 cut to the base line. Now O1 moves the ball to the left side, and O5 moves out to the forward position. Player O2 moves back out to the guard position. Player O1 passes to O5 and cuts outside to the baseline. Player O3 adjusts to a screening position on the lane similar to O5's previous position, and O4 cuts across the lane to screen the opponent off on O3. The movement has been reversed from the right side to the left side. The passing and movement may be repeated from side to side with O3, O5, and O4 interchanging positions in the moves shown, and O1 and O2 cutting to the baseline, and back out again for as long as you desire. The movements shown here are the foundation moves of a simple reverse action offense, and you can add to the basic movements to develop the offense to meet the development of the team and to fit available talent. The drill can be run with or without an opposition defense.

DRILLS FOR OUT-OF-BOUNDS PLAYS

During the course of a game the team will receive the ball out-of-bounds often enough that it will pay rich dividends to have out-of-bounds plays from every possible out-of-bounds situation. The defense may not always respond so that a play can be run from every spot, but the team should be prepared in case it does. There is something devastating about an out-of-bounds play that gets a quick score. It demoralizes the opposition. The team must be very well prepared for out-of-bounds plays along the front court side lines, and the offensive end line. The out-of-bounds plays should fit into the regular offensive patterns as much as possible. Their perfection calls for drills and drill practice.

Drive, Hook, Screen, Slide Series

This is a series of out-of-bounds plays that can be run from the front court side line and can be used against all types of defenses with little variation. The plays can be run as drills during practice sessions. They can be used as a part of a regular offense, with the offense beginning from the out-of-bounds throw-in spot.

1. **The Drive: Diagram 11-32.** The guard next to the out-of-bounds sideline always calls the play. Player O1 calls "DRIVE," and then power drives through with a burst of speed in the path shown. Player O4 breaks from the weak side over and by O5 to screen off his opponent. Player O3, taking the ball out-of-bounds, passes the ball into the open player and cuts hard for a return pass and the basket. Many options to the play can be

worked out to fit the offense and the defensive adjustments. The important thing is to drill until the players react to the situations as they should.

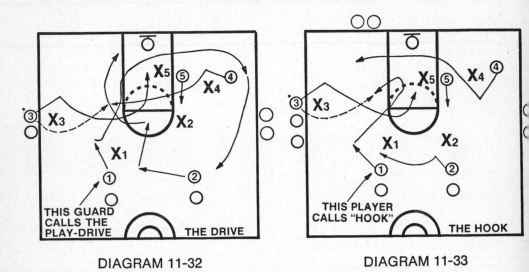

DIAGRAM 11-32   DIAGRAM 11-33

2. The Hook: Diagram 11-33. The guard, O1, calls "HOOK" and starts a drive through, but button-hooks back to receive the ball in the area shown and to post up for cutting players. Player O3, with the ball out-of-bounds, has options of playing to O1, O4, possibly O2, and breaking hard for a return pass.

3. The Screen: Diagram 11-34. Here O1 calls "SCREEN," and starts a drive through, but cuts over to create a double screen for O4 breaking across the lane. Player O3 passes to O4 and breaks over the top. Players O5 and O2 break as shown and are options for O3 on the throw-in also. Player O2 may cut through just off O3's tail, creating a split off O4's post play. Player O1 returns to the guard position.

4. The Slide: Diagram 11-35. Player O1 calls "SLIDE" and fakes the screen on O5 and O4, but slides to the corner as shown. Player O3 may pass to O1, O4, and O2 for various options and cuts. Run and drill all plays to both sides of the floor.

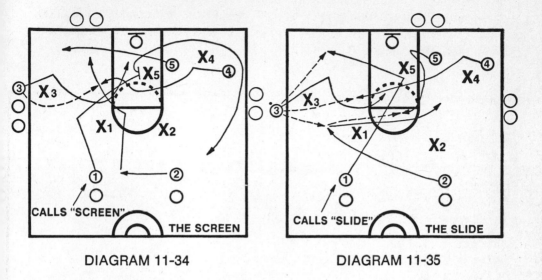

DIAGRAM 11-34   DIAGRAM 11-35

Out-of-Bounds—Offensive End Line

Plays from along the offensive end line should have quick scoring possibilties. Most teams will throw up a zone defense against such plays. The offensive team should be prepared to get a quick shot against the zone or the man-to-man defense.

1. Opposite Side Opener, Against a Zone: Diagram 11-36. The players line up in the box formation shown. Player O3 is the best shot along the baseline and from the side from 14 to 18 feet. Players O4 and O5 fake as shown, and move to positions indicated, while O1 and O2 cut to the outlet pass positions. Player O3 passes in to O4 and breaks the opposite direction. Quick passes from O4 to O1 to O2 to O3 should get O3 a good shot from the area opposite the first shift of the zone, and about 12 to 15 feet from the basket. If the defense starts shifting to meet the threat, look for quick openers to O5, and O4 inside by reversing the pass pattern.

2. Quick Opener Against Man-to-Man: Diagram 11-37. Players line up in the diamond formation as shown. Player O1 takes the ball out-of-bounds. Player O3 may screen for either O4 or O5, but here selects O4. Player O4 cuts off the screen for a possible opening. If the defense switches, O3 quickly rolls on a reverse, and should be open right under the basket. Player O1 has pass possibilities as shown to O4, O3, O5, and O2. When O1 inbounds the pass, he moves in as shown.

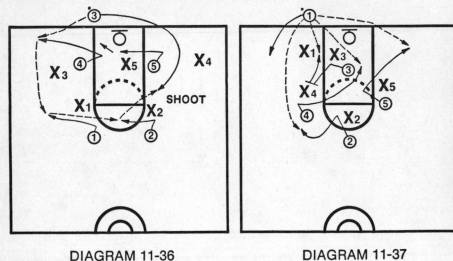

DIAGRAM 11-36   DIAGRAM 11-37

12

Pregame Warm-Up Drills

IMPORTANCE OF THE PREGAME WARM-UP

The pregame warm-up has two purposes really—to prepare the team psychologically and physiologically for the ensuing contest. Before the team arrives on the floor, the Coach should have made some psychological preparation in the dressing room. It may be a continuation of an ongoing process that has been going on for days preceding the contest and the arrival of the teams upon the floor. The pregame warm-up will provide the final touches.

Another consideration to be remembered in selecting pregame warm-up drills is the all-important fact that an athletic contest is a public demonstration—an exhibition for the viewing taxpayers, fans, and team supporters. The drills should make the team look its very best. Drills selected with pride, consideration and thoughtfulness can not only be a source of prideful public demonstration, but can also influence the mental attitude of the players about to enter competition. A slothful warm-up can carry over to become a slothful game. A warm-up that exhibits pride, enthusiasm, and that fits in with the whole team pattern of offense and defense can do much to properly prepare the players while presenting a public display that enhances the team's community image.

The pregame warm-up should include every activity and fundamental that a player will be expected to execute in the ensuing contest. During the game the player will be expected to pass, dribble, shoot, screen, pivot, cut, change direction, play defense, shoot free throws—all of which should be included in the warm-up process. Many teams have adopted the practice of coming on the floor and running through all the team offensive patterns, and then engaging in a short offensive-defensive scrimmage at a somewhat slowed down pace. This practice is sound.

Most teams in high school will be allotted a 15 to 20 minute warm-up period. College and university contests can usually use more time if they want. The 15 to 20 minute period is sufficient if properly planned. The team should never dash out on the floor and hurry the warm-up. A fast warm-up could hurry the process of energy reserves being emptied into the blood stream too soon, thus causing the player to be lacking in last quarter drive because of depleted energy reserves. Then too, a team that comes dashing out on the floor and goes quickly into a fast warm-up is liable to be kept running scared all night. The floor entry should be made with deliberateness, and with the players feeling confident.

The tempo of the warm-up should start slowly, and gradually work up to a three-fourths speed. After reaching a three-fourths tempo, the players should at some time do a brief part of the warm-up at full game speed. This point should be reached about five minutes before tip-off time. The players should break a sweat. The peak of the warm-up period should be followed by a relaxing slow down until the game starts.

Drills for the Pregame Warm-Up

Many of the drills previously presented in this book could be used in the pregame warm-up. Many of the passing drills, and dribbling and shooting drills, would be appropriate for this purpose and could be used in this way. For instance, the double exchange passing drills presented in Chapter 1, Diagrams 1-5 and 1-6 could very easily be used as slow and leisurely passing drills for the pregame warm-up. Likewise the 3-player and 5-player grapevine drills presented in Diagrams 1-7, and 1-8 used on half-court could be very appropriate for this purpose. The 1-4 lay-up shooting drill presented in Chapter 3, Diagrams 3-5, and

3-6 are excellent for pregame shooting procedures. The drills given for the jump shot from the seven basic spots in Diagrams 3-10, and 3-11 are good for a warm-up on the jump-shooting procedures. Many of the other basic drills given in the other chapters can be so used for the pregame warm-up. Some other warm-up drills are presented next.

1. Cut by the Pivot-Post—Shoot Drill: Diagram 12-1. This is a simple and easy warm-up drill. The players line up as shown, with one player in the outer half of the free-throw circle. Two or more balls can be used in the drill. The first player in line passes to the pivot-post, fakes one way with a good cut, changes direction and breaks over the top of the pivot-post to receive the return pass, and dribbles to a spot somewhere within shooting range, stops, shoots a jump shot and follows for the rebound. Roll the ball out to the next in line. The second player in line repeats the process, but fakes and breaks opposite the direction of the first player. The other players repeat the process, and others take turns as the pivot-post passer. Variations to the drill can be worked out, with the pivot-post player doing various ball handling stunts, if desired. The drill involves passing, cutting, change of direction, receiving a return pass, dribbling, shooting, and rebounding.

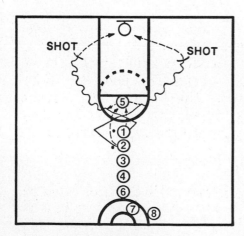

DIAGRAM 12-1

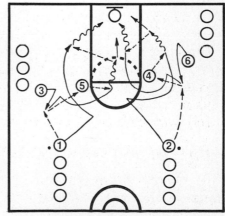

DIAGRAM 12-2

2. Split the Post—Two Sides: Diagram 12-2. The guards, forwards, and two pivot-post players line up as indicated in the diagram. Both sides of the floor work the drill, first one side, then the other. The guards pass to the forwards. The forwards pass to the pivot-post player, and then, after a good fake move, the guard and forward split over the top of the pivot-post player. The pivot-post feeds one of the cutters, who may pass to the other cutter, and one will drive for a lay-up shot, or stop and jump shoot from a comfortable shooting range. With both sides working the ball, and with the pivot-post player doing some extra ball handling stunts, it is a good interesting pregame warm-up drill.

　　3. Split the Post—One Pivot-Post Player: Diagram 12-3. This drill is the same as Diagram 12-2, except that only one pivot-post player is used. This player takes the pass from a forward on one side and then breaks to the other side to repeat the process there. The players break and cut by the pivot-post as shown. After O1, O3, O2, and O4 pass and break by O5, the next players in line repeat the process. Player O5 can be replaced by the next in line also. Passing variations and ball handling exhibitions can be added, if desired.

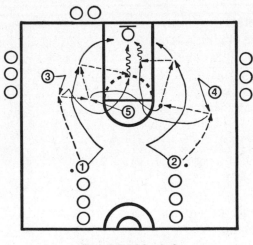

DIAGRAM 12-3

　　4. The Double X Drill: Diagram 12-4. This drill will have to be explained in two phases. **Phase 1**—the players line up as shown. Guard O1 passes to O2, and O2 starts a diagonal dribble drive and returns the ball to O1 breaking behind him. Guard O1, after a short dribble drive, whips the ball into the pivot-post player, O5, and now after executing a good fake, O1 and O2 execute a split over the top of O5, and fan out to replace O3 and

O4. Players O3 and O4 move out toward the guard positions, and O5 tosses the ball out to one of·them as in this diagram, O4.

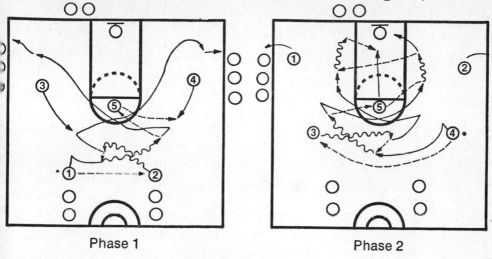

Phase 1   Phase 2

DIAGRAM 12-4

Diagram 12-4, Phase 2. The ball starts here in possession of O4 just after O5 has tossed the ball out to that position. Player O4 passes to O3, and they do an exchange exactly as O1 and O2 previously did, and pass the ball into O5 again, and do a split over the top of O5. Player O5 feeds one of the cutters, and passing variations can be added with one doing a lay-up. Player O5 may turn and receive a pass from one of the two cutters to do the shooting. The guards and forwards now exchange positions, with O1 and O2 going to the end of the O3 and O4 line, and O3 and O4 going to the end of the O1 and O2 line. The next pivot-post player in line now enters the court to replace O5 and O5 goes to the end of the pivot-post line. The next guard and forward players in line step inbounds and repeat the drill.

5. The Three-Player Weave with a Tail Out: Diagram 12-5. The players form three lines in the mid-court as indicated. The passes go from O1 to O3 to O2 to O1 for the first lay-up shot. Player O2, after passing to O1 for the lay-up shot, moves toward the corner, and then times his cut back to take a pass from O3 who has retrieved the ball. Now O1 returns to retrieve O2's shot, and passes to O3 who has gone toward the corner and returned for the lay-up shot. Now the ball is rolled out to the next three who repeat the drill. Remember all three players will shoot a lay-up shot.

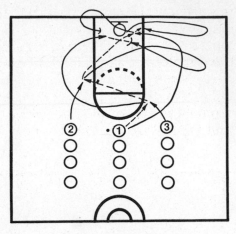

DIAGRAM 12-5

6. The Special: Diagram 12-6, Phases 1, 2, 3 and 4. This drill is a special drill that was developed from a combination of several other warm-up drills, namely those used by St. Louis University, Drake University, Iowa University, and others who showed intricate pregame warm-up drills. The drill involves many of the game's fundamental maneuvers, and has moves, cuts, and patterns that fit into many offenses. The drill has been called "THE COACH'S SPECIAL" (name it after the coach—the players will). Most squads enjoy doing the drill, and it is spectacular to watch. Done properly it is a fine exhibition. Use it, and the opposing scouts and coaches will be taking notes to see what you are doing, and unless you show them, they may never figure it out. It is not that complicated, however. The drill will have to be explained in diagrams giving four phases.

Diagram 12-6, Phase 1. The players line up in a single pivot-post two-guard, two-forward offense as the diagram indicates. The ball starts with the guard on the same side of the floor as the pivot-post player, O5. Player O1 passes the ball to O2, O2 starts a cross-court diagonal dribble toward O3, and O1 cuts over the top behind O2 to receive a return pass. Now O1 dribbles toward O4, and O4 faking to shake the defense meets a pass from O1. Players O1 and O2 now pull up to positions just outside O3 and O4 as indicated.

Diagram 12-6, Phase 2. Now the players are in the positions shown here; O4, with the ball, does a double exchange with O3, and they exchange positions exactly as in the double exchange passing drill, with O4 passing to O3 as O3 moves to meet the ball. Player O4 follows the pass, and O3 passes it back to O4, and then cuts over the top of O4 to receive a flip pass back. Remember in the double exchange, the ball always returns to the side from which it originated. After receiving the flip pass back from O4, O3 passes the ball to O1, and pulls up behind O1, while O4 pulls up behind O2. In the meantime, O1 has moved into O4's spot, and O2 moved into O3's spot.

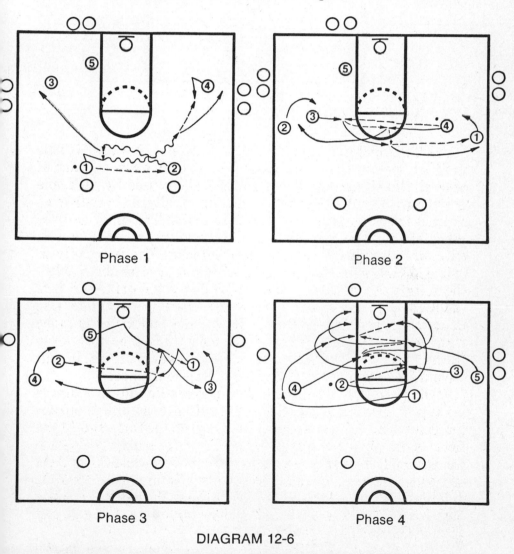

Phase 1

Phase 2

Phase 3

Phase 4

DIAGRAM 12-6

Diagram 12-6, Phase 3. The players are now in the position shown here, with O1 having the ball. Now O5 fakes a deep cut, and breaks to the opposite side of the lane to receive a pass in the pivot-post position, just below the free-throw line, and outside the lane. Player O1 passes to O5, and cuts over the top for a return feed pass. Player O1 now passes to O2 on the opposite side of the floor, O3 steps into the area vacated by O1, and O5 now pulls up behind O3.

Diagram 12-6, Phase 4. When O2 receives the ball from O1, the players are in positions shown, O1 calls out the number of passes to be made before a shot is taken, and the players go into a flat 5-man weave pattern. Player O1 moves behind O2 and O4, and comes back into the middle again. Player O2 passes to O3, and goes behind O3 and O5, and the pattern continues until they have completed the number of passes called, and the player coming up on that pass number shoots the lay-up shot. The 5-man weave (grapevine pattern—pass to one—go behind two) can be flattened and any number of passes can be made. It is not wise to make over four to six passes. The drill is now complete, and the next group steps up and repeats the drill. The drill is a crowd pleaser, and most teams will enjoy doing it a great deal. It has many of the movement patterns of a two-guard, single pivot-post offense, and requires the execution of most of the game's offensive fundamentals.

7. All Purpose Warm-Up Drill: Diagram 12-7. This is a very fine practice and pregame warm-up drill. The drill involves most of the offensive fundamentals and techniques of the game, and if executed well, can be a fine exhibition. It will require four phases to explain the drill with its variations.

Diagram 12-7, Phase 1. The drill requires four balls—two in each line at the guard or mid-court positions. Players O3 and O4 are high post players; O6 and O5 are outlet pass players to start; O1 and O2 pass to the high post position on their side, and the player on the left (O1 in this case) cuts through the lane to receive a flip pass from the opposite post player, O4, while O2 cuts through to take the hand-off from O3 on the other side. The player on the left *always* cuts first regardless of the order of the passes. Players O1 and O2 drive in to shoot, and the high post players follow their passes and rebound the shot of the player to whom they passed.

Diagram 12-7, Phase 2. The players are now in the positions shown. Players O3 and O4, the rebounders, pass to the outlet positions to O5 and O6; O1 and O2, the shooters, break up to the high post positions to take the passes from the next mid-court players. The player on the left side should not make the pass until both high post players are ready. The outlet passers, O6 and O5, pass to the next players in line and go to the end of those lines. Players O3 and O4, the rebounders, go to the outlet pass positions. Now the drill is repeated with the players doing this rotation of positions.

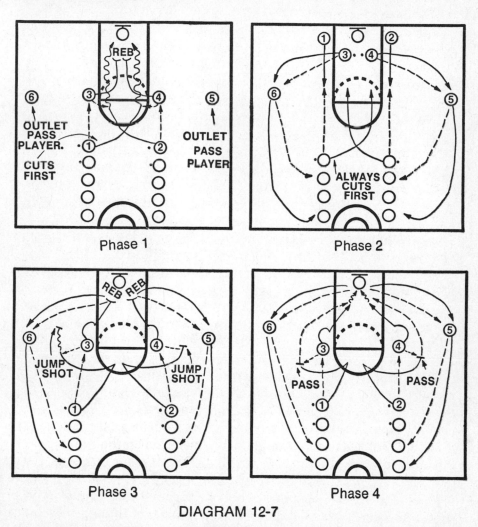

DIAGRAM 12-7

Diagram 12-7, Phase 3. Here the players start the same cut as before, but cut back to go over the top of the post player they passed to, take a flip pass in return and do a jump shot. The high post player pivots and rolls to the basket facing the shooter and rebounds the shot. Emphasize proper form and technique on the rebound. The players rotate the same as on the previous lay-up shot drill, except that when the outlet pass goes to the line in the mid-court, the outlet pass player should go to the opposite side of the floor so as to get practice from both sides of the floor.

Diagram 12-7, Phase 4. This phase is executed exactly the same as the jump-shot phase shown in the previous diagram except that the player doing the jump shot drops the ball to the high post player who is rolling to the basket. The high post player does not roll until the jump shooter goes up to shoot. After going up for the shot, the shooter drops the ball down to the high post rolling toward the basket. The player should develop the technique of either passing or shooting while in the air. The high post players, after taking the pass and doing a lay-up shot, rebound their own shot, pass the ball to the outlet player positions, and the rotation is the same as in the jump-shot drill. Players O1 and O2 become the next high post players, and O3 and O4 become the next outlet pass players. Players O6 and O5 go to the end of the mid-court lines.

8. Three-Spot Pivot, Three-Man Weave Drill: Diagram 12-8. This makes an excellent pregame warm-up drill. The players line up in three lines in the mid-court area as indicated. Player O1, in the middle, starts the drill by dribbling in a shallow diagonal direction toward one of the side lines. Upon reaching a point about even with the outside line, O1 stops, pivots, and posts for O2. Player O2 fakes a cut by, but veers over to receive a feed from the post, and then dribbles in a shallow diagonal direction toward the other line. When he reaches a point about even with the O3 line, O2 stops, pivots and posts for O3 cutting by. Player O3 now dribbles in the same manner to a point near O1, and stops, pivots and posts. Player O1 cuts off the post set by O3, and passes to O2, and now the three players do a 3-man weave grapevine passing routine to the basket. Player O1 will call out the number of passes to be made before the shot—in this case six. When the sixth pass is executed, the player receiving it will shoot a lay-up shot. Usually four to six passes are adequate, and the weave can be flattened to accommodate the number of passes needed for the number called.

9. Double-Line Lay-Up Drill: Diagram 12-9. This drill furnishes lots of movement and action, and for that reason makes a fine pregame warm-up drill. The players line up in two lines as indicated. Player O1 in the left line passes to O2 in the right line for a lay-up shot. Player O2, after shooting, turns back onto the court along the base line left of the basket. Player O4 follows O2, and rebounds the ball, and passes it to O2 on his return to the court. Player O2 passes to O1 now driving in for a

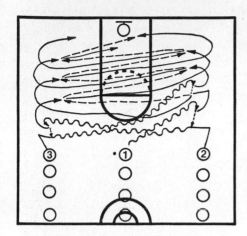

DIAGRAM 12-8

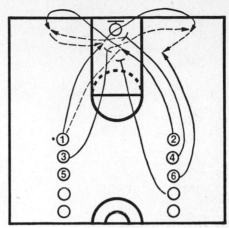

DIAGRAM 12-9

lay-up from the left side. Player O3 follows and rebounds O1's shot and passes to O1, who has returned to the court on the right baseline. Player O1 now passes to O6 cutting in for a lay-up from the right side, and the drill now continues from one side to the other in this same way. The players rotate lines and positions taking turns shooting and rebounding from each line.

10. The Blooper Warm-Up Drill: Diagram 12-10. This is a take-off from several pregame warm-up drills you have all seen. The players line up in the team offensive formation shown. Player O1 starts with a pass to O2 and O1 and O2 make a dribble exchange. Player O1 then passes to O4, and cuts outside as shown. Player O4 passes to O5 moving across the lane. Player O5

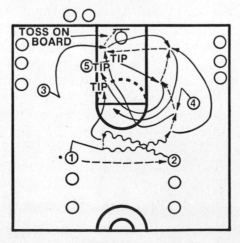

DIAGRAM 12-10

passes to O1, and O1 passes the ball to O3 moving in to the basket area from the left side. Player O3 now tosses the ball high on the board, and O4 cutting over the top of O5 comes in to tip the ball back up on the board. Now O5 swings in the line to tip, as do O2, O1, and O3, and they tip the ball on the board until a name or a number is called. Then the ball is tipped into the basket. The next group steps up to repeat the drill. Run the drill to both sides of the floor.

11. Drills given in Chapter 10, Diagrams 10-1 and 10-2, are very fine warm-up drills that involve offensive rebounding and tipping drills.

Combination Drills (All-Purpose)

Most drills require the execution of more than one fundamental or technique in basketball. Some drills, however, are such that more emphasis is placed on one particular fundamental, and those drills have correctly been placed under such classifications as shooting, passing, dribbling, pivoting and footwork, defense, rebounding, etc. There are many drills that require the execution of several fundamental techniques, and such drills can be called combination drills. You, the coach, can place the emphasis on all phases of the drill, or on one particular fundamental to meet the specific needs of the squad at hand.

Usually combination drills can best be used by a squad of experienced players. You will have to select such drills carefully to meet the needs of the squad and to match the skill level of the team. Although many of the drills previously given under other specific categories might be considered combination drills, we present the following additional drills under this classification.

1. Pressure Defense Rebound Drill: Diagram 13-1. Place three players in the triangle rebound position near the basket, and two lines of players on each side of the floor—one on offense, and one on defense—and about 20 to 25 feet from the basket. To start the drill, one sideline offensive player with the ball, in this case O1, moves against the defensive player X1 and

245

tries to get off a shot under tight guarding pressure by X1. Player O1 must work to get off a good shot in the scoring area, and X1 works hard to prevent O1 from scoring. One of these two players will run two laps—O1 if he misses the shot, or X1 if O1 scores. Player O1 will always go under the basket to one of the rebound positions after the shot. Laps, if assessed for missing the basket, are to be run after the turn as a rebounder. When the ball comes off the board or through the net, it is to be grabbed by one of the three players in the rebounding position. The rebounding player that gets the ball is to be attacked by the other two rebounders who will try to make it tough for that player to pass the ball out to one of the offensive sideline players being guarded. If the rebounder loses the ball or makes a bad pass, that player must stay under to rebound again, and the defensive player X1 will go out to a side line position. If the offensive player on the side cannot get free within 5 seconds for a pass, that player must run two laps before getting a turn to shoot. If the ball is passed out successfully, then the rebounder comes to a sideline position. The drill now starts again. Players rotate offensive and defensive positions. The drill involves offensive maneuvering, shooting under pressure, blocking out, rebounding, and passing the ball out on the outlet pass—all under pressure situations.

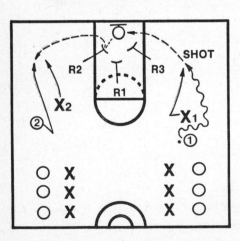

DIAGRAM 13-1

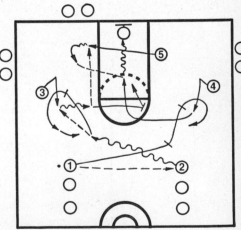

DIAGRAM 13-2

2. All-Purpose Special Drill: Diagram 13-2. This drill involves passing, dribbling, screening, cutting and shooting from an offensive two-guard, single-pivot-post formation. The players line up in the guard, forward, pivot-post positions as shown. Player O1 passes to O2 and screens inside for him and then continues on to screen inside for O4, who fakes and moves up as shown. Player O2 dribbles close behind O1's screen, passes to O3, and screens inside for O3. Player O3 dribbles close off the screen, toward the outer half of the free-throw circle. Just before reaching the circle, O3 passes to O5 who has cut across the lane and is moving deep toward the corner. Player O3 continues on across the circle and sets another screen for O4, who has just come off O1's screen. Player O4 cuts sharply behind O3's screen toward the basket to receive a pass from O5, who after a short dribble, has stopped and pivoted to execute the pass. Player O4 may shoot or pass off to O3, O5, and tipping and passing variations can be worked out with O4 tossing the ball on the board, with the other players lining up to tip the ball as many times as desired.

3. Pass-Off Dribble Drill: Diagram 13-3. This is an excellent drill to teach passing off from the dribble. The players line up as indicated. Player O1 starts a diagonal direction dribble as indicated, and O2 moves toward the basket, breaking out deep from the corner. Player O1, while moving rapidly with the dribble, whips the ball to O2 who goes in for the shot. The players change lines, and be sure to run the drill coming from both sides of the floor—right to left, and left to right.

DIAGRAM 13-3

4. The Three-on-Two Down, Two-on-One Back, Defense Fast-Break Drill: Diagram 13-4. The players line up

in three lines as indicated at one end of the court. At the opposite
end, two defensive players, X1 and X2, are ready to defense
against the three-line fast break. The first players in the three
offensive lines at the far end of the court take the ball down the
floor, passing back and forth, and always forward, quickly
working for a shot against the two defensive players. Now X1
and X2, when they recover the ball, either from a rebound or out
of the net from a scored basket, break for the opposite end of the
floor, and O2, the center player in the three-line fast break now
retreats to the other end to defense against X1 and X2's fast
break, making it a two against one situation. Players O2, X1,
and X2 go to the end of the three lines when they finish, and now
the next players in the three lines break down court against O1

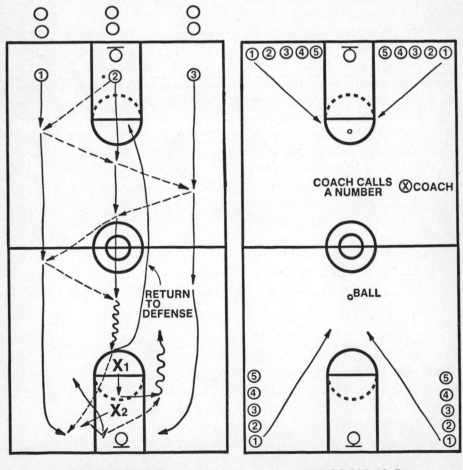

DIAGRAM 13-4   DIAGRAM 13-5

and O3 who replace X1 and X2 in the three-on-two defensive situation. The players rotate lines so as to get a chance at all positions. The drill is continuous and the players break back and forth with first three-on-two and then two-on-one situations.

5. Free Ball Hustle Drill: Diagram 13-5. This drill may be run on half court, or at both ends of the court at the same time as indicated. The players line up as indicated and in either manner shown on both ends. The squad should be divided evenly with half the players on one side, and half on the other. Then have each line count off. Each line should be equal in number, and have corresponding numbers. You can place the ball in a spot or roll it out to a spot on the floor, and then call a number. The player on each side whose number is called hustles to get the ball. The one who gets the ball immediately goes on offense, and the other goes on defense to prevent the score. If the offensive player scores, that team gets 2 points. If the defensive player successfully prevents the score, then that team gets 2 points. The team ahead at a given time wins, or the team that reaches a certain point total first wins. After the players learn the drill well, the coach can call two numbers, and the drill will involve two-on-two, and later three numbers can be called out for a three-on-three hassle and score. You should rotate the numbers to be sure all the players get in on the drill, and keep team scores.

6. One, Two, or Three Ball—Shoot Drill: Diagram 13-6. The players line up in four lines near the four corners as indicated. Player O1 in the first line dribbles in to shoot a lay-up shot, retrieves the ball from the basket, passes it to the O2 line, and then goes to the end of that line. Player O2 does a short dribble and passes to the O3 line, and goes to the end of that line. Player O3 passes to the O4 line, and follows to the end of that line. Player O4 now passes to the next player from the O1 line breaking for the basket, and a shot. Player O4 now goes to the end of the O1 line, and the drill is repeated. Later add a second and a third ball to the drill, and it can be a very interesting and challenging passing, dribbling, cutting, and shooting drill.

7. Pass, Return, Pivot, Dribble, Shoot Drill: Diagram 13-7. The players line up as indicated. Player O1 starts the drill by passing to X1, and follows the pass on the run. Player X1 passes back to O1, and then goes to the line behind O4. Player O1 now passes to X2, who returns the pass, and moves to the position vacated by X1. Player O1 passes to X3 who returns the pass and moves to the position vacated by X2, as O1 passes to X4, who holds the ball. Player O1 runs past X4, stops, plants the feet,

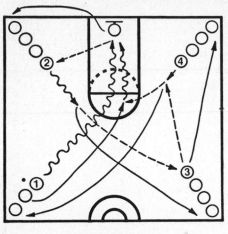

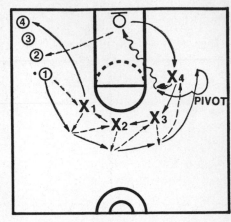

DIAGRAM 13-6   DIAGRAM 13-7

does a reverse pivot on the inside foot, and then cuts over the top and inside X4 to receive the ball back, and dribbles in for a lay-up shot. Player X4 now goes to the position vacated by X3. Player O1 recovers the ball after the shot, passes to O2, and goes to the X4 position. Run the drill at full speed, and X2, X3 or X4 may keep the ball, but when either of them keeps the ball, O1 must stop after running past the player, plant the feet, reverse pivot, and cut back for the return pass and the drive to the basket. The O line players will always go to the end of the X line, no matter who hands off for the dribble drive on the lay-up shot. Player O1 should run as close to the X players as possible. Also run the drill from the opposite side of the floor so as to learn to pivot from either foot.

8. Passing, Pivoting, and Shooting Drill: Diagram 13-8. To start the drill, some one puts the ball up on the board. Player O8 rebounds the ball and passes to O7. Player O7 meets the pass, pivots and passes to O6 moving in toward the basket and in such a manner as to receive the ball near the top of the free-throw circle. Player O6 must decide to take the ball to the basket, or to stop and pivot to the left. If O6 stops, pivots, and posts, O1 breaks over the top of the post, takes a pass, and shoots or dribbles for a position jump shot. Player O5 is the defensive player, must defense either O6 or O1, and is faced with the dilemma of taking either O1 or O6—whichever one decides to go for the basket. Player O8 rotates to the O7 position, O7 to the O6 position, O6 to the end of the O1 line, O1 to the O5 position, and O5 to the O8 position. Vary the drill by having either O1 or O6 go for the shot, thus making O5's defensive task more difficult.

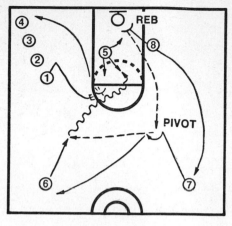

DIAGRAM 13-8

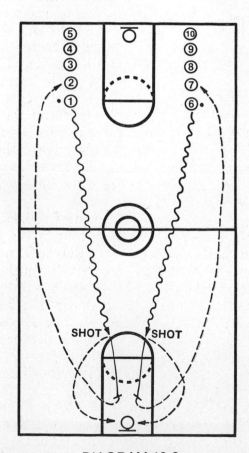

DIAGRAM 13-9

9. Relay Shooting Drill: Diagram 13-9. Two teams line up at one end of the floor as indicated. The first player in each line has a ball. Upon a starting signal from the coach, the first player in each line dribbles to the top of the free-throw circle at the opposite end of the floor and shoots a jump shot. If the shot is missed, the player must retrieve the ball, go back to the top of the circle and shoot until the shot is made. After making the shot, the player passes a length-of-the-floor baseball pass to the next player in line who repeats the process. The team to finish first is the winner. Winners can be rewarded or losers can be penalized.

10. The Buddy Drill: Diagram 13-10. The players line up as indicated and operate in pairs, with each pair having a ball, if possible. To start the drill, O1 dribbles in to shoot, and is closely followed by O2 who pretends to defense O1 by yelling, stomping feet, and doing anything to distract O1 on the shot. Player O2 rebounds the ball and passes to O1 who returns quickly to the playing floor. Players O1 and O2 now pass the ball back and forth with short quick passes as they return to the end of the line.

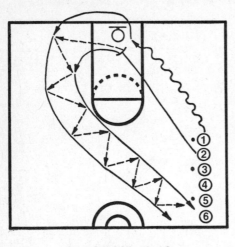
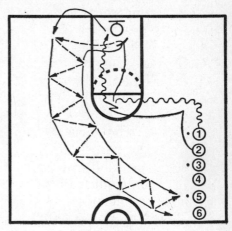

DIAGRAM 13-10   DIAGRAM 13-11

Now O3 and O4 repeat the drill, followed by O5 and O6, until all have done the drill. Players O1 and O2 reverse positions at the end of the line so that on their next turn, O2 will shoot, and O1 will defense and rebound. Change the positions of the line formation so that the players get practice coming into the basket from all angles, positions and sides.

11. The Buddy-Dribble, Pivot, Hand-Off, Lay-Up Shot Drill: Diagram 13-11. This drill uses the same buddy system as the drill in Diagram 13-10, except that O1 fakes a drive to the basket, but dribbles to the area somewhere near the free-throw circle, stops and pivots and posts. Player O2, following, drives by to receive a hand-off and drives for a lay-up shot. Player O1 rebounds the shot, and passes to O2 who returns quickly to the court, and they buddy the ball back to the end of the line with a series of short quick passes. Now O3 and O4 repeat the drill, and then O5 and O6, etc. Players O1 and O2 exchange positions the next time they come up for the shot so that they get turns shooting, dribbling, and pivoting. Again change the position of the line on the floor, so that all the angles are worked coming into the basket. The dribbler should also vary the position where the stop is made for the pivot, and the player following the dribbler should vary the cut off the pivot-post by faking one way, driving the other, or fake driving by, then stepping back and shooting from in front of the screen set by the dribbler when the pivot-post is made.

12. Get the Ball Down the Floor Drill: Diagram 13-12. The players line up in the four positions indicated. Player O1, at one end of the floor, starts down the floor with a driving dribble, and when reaching an area of about the free-throw line extended, passes to O2 who has moved to meet the ball. Player O1 follows the pass as shown to the outside lane and O2 immediately passes to O3 who breaks diagonally across from the court division line as shown. Player O3 now passes to O4, who has come out from the low post position to receive the ball somewhere near the free-throw line extended. Players O1, O2, and O3 break into the lanes as shown, and O4 may pass to any of these players for a quick passing session that leads to a lay-up shot. The ball now goes to the next player in the O4 line, who repeats the drill in a reverse action to the other end of the floor. The players rotate positions numerically, that is from O1 to O2, to O3, to O4 and from O4 to the O1 position. The drill is continuously moving from one end of the floor to the other.

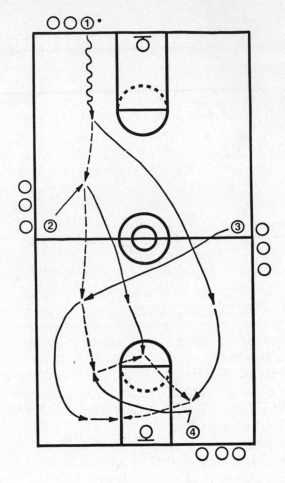

DIAGRAM 13-12

Drills for Special Situations

$\widehat{14}$

There are many special situations that occur during a basketball game that the coach must prepare the team to meet. Preparation means being ready, and being ready requires drilling and rehearsal. Some drills for such situations are presented in this chapter.

1. Stick 'Em Keep-Away Game: Diagram 14-1. There are situations in many games where the team needs to maintain control and possession of the ball for specific periods of time. To prepare the team, use this drill every night in practice—it is usually better to use it at the end of practice. Put two teams on the floor, one on offense, the other on defense. Play a keep-away game using the rules of basketball exactly, except scoring. The team does not attempt to score—just keep the ball. If fouled, the offense keeps the ball. Keep time to see which team can keep possession of the ball the longest. Use a stop watch to do this. The winning team can be rewarded or the losing team penalized. For the defense you should start with a man-to-man and later work on zoning principles. Warn the players to keep away from the corners and the trap areas indicated by the shaded areas.

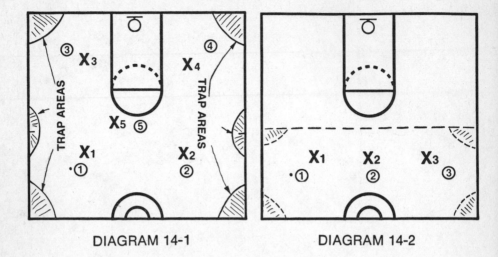

DIAGRAM 14-1   DIAGRAM 14-2

2. Stick 'Em Keep-Away—Mid-Court Area: Diagram 14-2. This drill could be used in the same way as Diagram 14-1, except that the players are limited to the mid-court area, and play three against three in a keep-away game, timing with a stop watch to see which team can keep the ball the longest. The mid-court area can be more clearly defined by putting down masking tape on the floor. Keep away from the trap areas and pass the ball quickly and rapidly in a keep-away maneuver. Apply the 5-second count rule, and allow a limited dribble. If the offense is fouled, they keep the ball. The team with the longest possession is rewarded, or the losers penalized.

3. A Special Press Drill: Diagram 14-3. Place the ball at O1's feet. Player O1 must stand with back to players X1 and X2. The drill starts when O1 picks up the ball. Players X1 and X2 attack O1, and O1 is to attempt to pass the ball to either O2 or O3. Players O2 and O3 are assigned spots just at the end of the free-throw line extended, and they cannot move from the spots assigned. Player X3 is to attempt to intercept the pass if possible. The drill teaches the players to react properly when two-timed by pressure defense, and also to anticipate where a pass is going when applying a pressure defense.

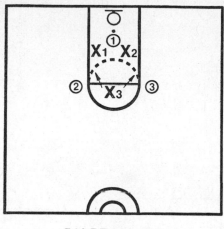

DIAGRAM 14-3

4. Ball Full Length of Court Quickly: Diagram 14-4.

This play would be used usually against a tight pressing man-to-man defense to move the ball quickly the full length of the court, and following a score—when the team has passing rights along the base line out-of-bounds. Players O2 and O3 break toward the ball and O2 steps out-of-bounds to receive the pass from O1 along the base line. Player O1 then cuts inbounds off the screen set by O3 to receive the ball from O2. Player O1 now sends the ball on down court to either O4 or O5 as shown. Player O3, after screening for O1, moves quickly down court, and may receive the ball from O4 or O5 on a drive to the basket. Variations in the pass patterns may be worked out.

5. To Increase a Lead: Diagram 14-5.

Many times a team has a small lead late in the ball game and is being subjected to intense defensive pressure. Proper drill can enable the well-coached team to exploit this situation and increase the lead. This play will do it! The opponents have just scored. The defensive pressure is intense. The team calls a time out. Review the play at this time. Play is resumed by having the players take the positions as indicated. Just prior to the signal to begin play, the coach jumps up and yells loudly, "Line up, line up." Players O3, O4 and O5 quickly position themselves in a straight line,

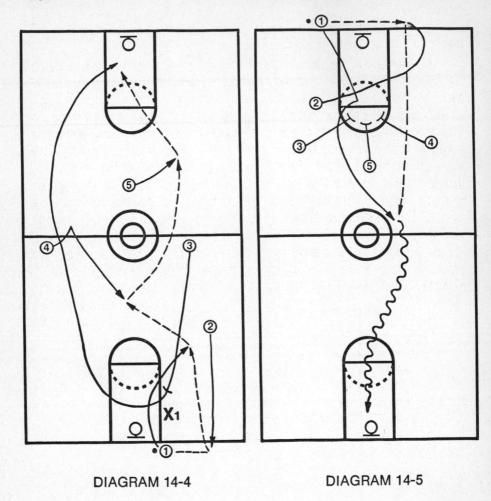

DIAGRAM 14-4   DIAGRAM 14-5

standing almost shoulder to shoulder just at the outer half of the
free-throw circle or line, and facing O1, who has the ball out-of-
bounds. Player O2 fakes a move toward the line formation, but
dashes quickly out-of-bounds on the opposite side of the free-
throw lane from O1. Player O1 passes to O2 behind and along
the baseline out-of-bounds. Player O1 now drives straight at the
three teammates lined up at the free-throw line, then suddenly
veers to his right and moves around them in such a way as to
screen the defensive player off in the pocket formed by the triple
screen set by O3, O4, and O5. Player O1 should be free as a deep
cut is made toward the basket at the opposite end of the court. A
long "butterfly pass" to the mid-court area or beyond should
send O1 dribbling home for an easy 2 points. This play can be
used for short time situations of 4 seconds or more any time the

defense is pressing. The play can be executed in less than 5 seconds if the timing is good.

6. Defensive Mental Lapse to Increase a Lead: Diagram 14-6. Here again the defense is exerting pressure—the lead is slim and the team is attempting to control the ball and run down the clock. Take a time-out with the ball near the court division line. Review the play. When play is resumed after the time-out, the players line up as shown in the diagram as if going for the wrong basket. The defensive players, having a mental lapse, take position to guard the offensive players going the wrong way. If this happens, (and it has happened many times), all O2 has to do is to elude his defensive opponent, using a fake, and then dash for his own basket to receive a pass from O1, and dribble in for an easy 2 points. The players have to be good actors on this play. Rehearse it often. If the defense is playing tight, only one defensive player needs to make a mistake to give the

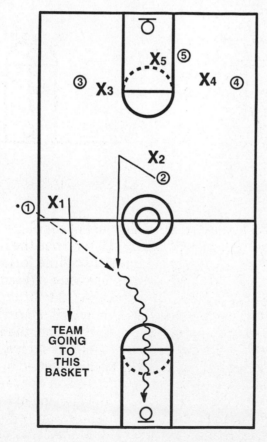

DIAGRAM 14-6

offensive player a chance to dash for the basket. This play has been used successfully with a small lead, with a tied score, and even when the team was behind. If the play works, it not only is an easy two points, but can be a morale-breaking factor for the opponents—especially the coach. It has been known to upset even the officials.

    7. Three-Second Score from the Court Division Line: Diagram 14-7. This play can be executed within a 2- to 3-second time limit, however it is safer to use with a 3- to 5-second time limit. It is best to use the play after a time out and giving it a good review. Player O1 takes the ball out-of-bounds at the court division line and the players start from the positions indicated. Upon the signal to begin, O2, O5, and O3 move to form a triple screen near the free-throw circle, or near the free-throw line. Player O4 breaks toward the ball, and then swings around the screening players, O2, O5, and O3, as close as possible. As O4 clears the screen, he should be free for a pass from O1 underneath the basket area. An option to the play is to have O2 break toward O1 and the ball as soon as O4 cuts by O2. Player O2 should be open for a pass, and O1 may take the option of passing to O2, if all is not clear for O4. Player O2 can relay the pass on to O4, who should be positioned underneath the basket. This option requires a little more time to execute, but is more accurate, and perhaps more successful. The pass from O1 to O4 must be long and accurate. The relay from O2 to O4 can be safer, especially if O1 is not strong on executing the half-court baseball pass.

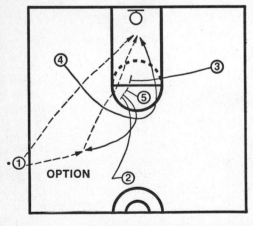

DIAGRAM 14-7

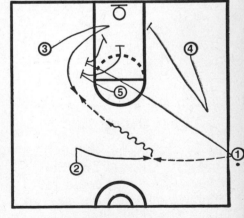

DIAGRAM 14-8

8. Three- to Five-Second Time Limit for a Shot: Diagram 14-8. Two passes and a maneuver just about hits the 3- to 5-second time limit. The ball is out-of-bounds and the players line up as indicated. Upon signal to begin, O1 passes inbounds to O2 and dashes off to help set a double screen for O3, who is the best outside shooter on the team. Player O3 fakes first on a deep cut underneath, and then comes off the double screen set by O5 and O1 to receive a pass from O2. Player O3 puts the ball up from behind the screen as O1, O5, and O4 all break for the rebound position in case of a miss, and time for a second shot off the rebound. It is important to hit the last shot of the game—many games are won or lost with the accuracy (or lack of it) of the last shot taken in the game. Drill and rehearsal will stress the importance of this shot.

9. Three to Five Seconds for a Shot: Diagram 14-9. Players line up as indicated. Player O1 passes inbounds to O2, who maneuvers to pass to O3. Player O3 passes to O1, breaking off the double screen set by O4 and O5 just at the free-throw line extended. Player O1 could be free for an easy shot.

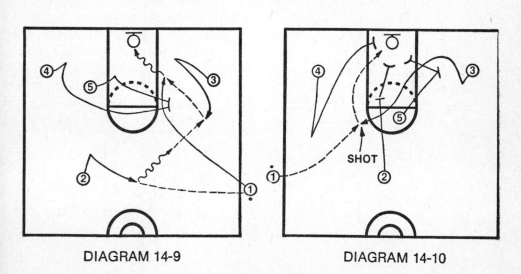

DIAGRAM 14-9   DIAGRAM 14-10

10. One to Two Second, Last Shot Situation: Diagram 14-10. This play could get that LAST SHOT needed with one or two seconds left. Player O1 has the ball out-of-bounds. Player O3 is the best shooter from the outside. The players line up as indicated, and when the signal to begin is given, O5 screens down for O3. Player O3 breaks behind this screen low-side, then up toward the free-throw line to break high off the screen set by O2 just below or at the free-throw line. Player O1 passes to O3 for the shot. The others position for rebound possibilities.

11. Two Passes—Length of Court—Three to Five Seconds: Diagram 14-11. Two passes can be used to move the ball down court well within the time limit of 3 to 5 seconds. Players line up as indicated. Player O5 takes the ball out-of-bounds for the throw-in after taking a time-out following a basket or a scored free throw. Player O5 passes to O4 after O4 steps out-of-bounds along the base line. Player O3 screens for O5 and O2 screens for O1. Player O5 breaks inbounds for a return pass from O4 at mid-court area, and O1, breaking off O2's screen, has gone far down court. Player O5 passes to O1, who has

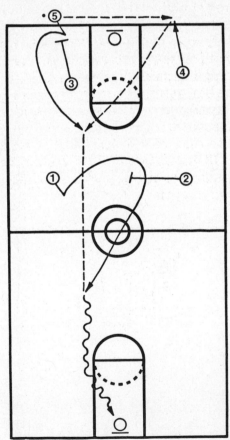

DIAGRAM 14-11

a short drive to the basket. This action can all take place well within the 3- to 5-second time limit.

12. Special Talent Situation: Diagram 14-12. This play has been devised to utilize the special talents of players on the team and to take advantage of extreme height if such tall players are available. It could be a good out-of-bounds play any time during the game, but with a time situation of 1 to 3 seconds left in the game, and the ball out-of-bounds at this particular location, it could pay rich dividends. Players O4 and O5 line up in a V position with inside feet together. They face away from the basket and partially face each other with backs to O1. They hold up their outside hands as a target for O1. (If defense demands a position between them, they must comply—if official says so.) Players O4 and O5 are your tallest players, of course. Player O1 can toss a high lob pass to either one of them, and they can move immediately toward the basket, or execute a turn-around jump shot from this position. They could also be drilled to take the ball high in the air and shoot while in the air. Player O1 could toss the ball against the back of one of these players (or the defensive player) and quickly step inbounds to retrieve it for a shot. This maneuver would require at least 3 seconds since the time will start as soon as the ball touches a player inbounds. Players O2 and O3 line up in a vertical position as indicated, and on the signal, break as shown. They can take the inbounds pass, if there are no other options.

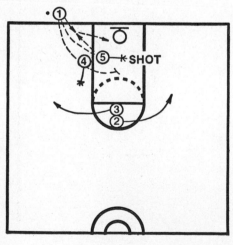

DIAGRAM 14-12

15

Preseason Conditioning

The rigorous and lengthy basketball season necessitates a preseason conditioning program. The team that is the strongest and in the best condition will have the margin necessary for victory in the games that are decided by close scores. The coach who claimed that his team would be in better condition than any opponent they would meet—and prepared his team accordingly—was a winner. The necessity of physical conditioning for the basketball team still exists today.

Conditioning really starts with the preseason program. During this time most coaches cannot get inside the gym and hold formal practice. Most collegiate and high school conferences and state association rules prohibit practice before a certain date. This means the players, if not out for another sport, will have to carry out such a program informally and on their own, although coaches today manage to carefully control such programs.

The conditioning program should be based upon sound physiological principles. To play a basketball game the athlete has to call upon two energy systems that the body has—the aerobic system and the anaerobic system. Aerobics literally means "with oxygen" while anaerobics refers to exercise without oxygen, or while accumulating an oxygen debt. Aerobic exercise refers to exercise of the endurance type, or exercise over a prolonged period. Since basketball games require movement on the part of the player over a period of 32 to 40 minutes, certainly the preseason conditioning program should contain some aerobic exercises, such as running long distances—one mile or farther.

Basketball also consists of movements of quick sprints, such as on a fast break down floor at full speed, or a quick cut or a break for shorter distances. These can be interspersed with stops, starts, and change of direction. These are repeated constantly, so the conditioning program should include anaerobic exercises, such as the 50-yard to 100-yard dashes and sprints.

The following is suggested as a preseason conditioning program for the high school and college teams. Start the program with three days a week, and work gradually into four, then five, and later, six days a week.

1. Warm up with a light distance run of five to eight minutes. Follow this with stretching exercises and calisthenics. These can vary from toe touches to trunk twisters, jumping jacks, push-ups, pull-ups, and whatever else the coach feels meets the loosening-up and muscle-stretching process.

2. Include in the calisthenics exercises to strengthen thigh muscles, inner and outer knee ligaments, ankle ligaments, muscles of the arms and chest, front thighs, hamstrings, and muscles of the abdomen and back.

3. *Sprints:* Start with 4 to 6 50-yard sprints. Work this up to 10 to 12 sprints. Later increase the distance to 75 yards, and then to 100 yards.

4. *Jump-the-Rope:* Start out with 5 minutes per day. Work up to 15 minutes per day. This will not only increase the leg spring and strength, but will strengthen the wrists—so essential to good passing and shooting.

5. *Run One Mile:* As the preseason workouts progress, set a time schedule for the run. The time to be made should be set to comply with age and abilities of the level being coached.

6. End the workout with weight-lifting exercises appropriate for the basketball player. Such a program

should include dead lifts, squats, toe raisers, a clean and press, pull-ups, biceps curls, forearm curls, and bent-over rowing. If modern day weight machines are available, they can be used for the above weight training exercises. If leaper machines are available, use them to increase leg strength and jumping ability. If such machines are not available, simple bar bells, with weights and bench jumps can be used for the same purpose.

7. If "toss back" machines are available, use them to work up drills that sharpen reaction abilities of the players in relation to ball handling abilities.

8. If the basketball floor is available for free play, let the players go awhile on their own with shooting and free play.

9. Set standards for the mile run, the sprints, and the various weight and jumping events.

Such a program should have the team in proper physical condition to begin the season at hand.

In-Season
Conditioning

Research has shown that if a basketball team does nothing but practice basketball during the season, as the season wears on, the actual physical strength and endurance of the team will deteriorate. This is because all muscle tissue acts according to basic physiological principles. One of these basic principles, simply stated, is that in order to promote a gain in strength, the work load for a muscle group must be greater than that to which the person is accustomed. Contracting the muscle against a load greater than normal increases muscle strength. Contracting against loads less than normal results in loss of strength, and atrophy of the muscle. This principle is commonly known as the "principle of the overload." This means that the continuation of basketball practice alone, without increased work or an extra effort, could find the team approaching the crucial point in the season—tournament time—with less endurance and strength. Thus it behooves the coach to have some kind of in-season conditioning program that will at least prevent the deterioration of endurance and strength.

While there is no limit to programs that a coach might use for conditioning and endurance, the following three drills are suggested and should be done at the end of practice at least three times per week. They are:

1. THE SPOT RUN
2. SIT-UPS
3. PUSH-UPS

THE SPOT RUN

The spot run consists of running in place for 10 seconds with a 10-second rest. Repeat this ten times. In doing the run the feet are raised just high enough to clear the floor. The cadence is as rapid as the player can move. When a standard of eighty steps per 10 seconds can be maintained for the duration of 10 repetitions, the player has sufficient endurance to meet the demands of a basketball game and more. If the coach desires greater endurance, more repetitions or innings may be added, or the length of the inning may be increased

SIT-UPS

The sit-ups are to be performed with the hands clasped behind the head. The legs are kept horizontal on the floor with the feet being held by a teammate. On each sit-up, the elbow touches the knee, that is the right elbow touches the left knee, and on the next sit-up the left elbow touches the right knee. Working in pairs, when one finishes, the players exchange positions so that the other can do the sit-ups. The exercise is carried on for two minutes at as rapid a pace as possible. A standard of ninety sit-ups should be attained by each player. To do this exercise it is wise to lie on the sweat clothes or to have some padding on the floor so that the player does not incur abrasions on the back.

PUSH-UPS

This exercise should be performed on the finger tips for a period of 30 seconds. The chin should touch the floor on each push-up. A standard of 25 push-ups in 30 seconds is the goal. Some players will do better than this.

The above program should be administered to the entire squad at the end of practice. You or another person can act as timekeeper. A whistle can be blown to start and stop each inning of the spot run and the sit-ups and the push-ups, with each player counting his own performance. Each player should keep a record of his development and performance. A card or sheet can be drawn up for this purpose. (See Figure 1.) The cards or sheets can be distributed before the exercises begin. The records will help motivate the program, and competition can be introduced to liven the work, a champion being recognized for each period in the exercises. Do the program on alternate days three times per week. Do not go all out on the program at first, but work into it gradually with at least three periods of exercise being done before an all-out effort is attempted.

This program should always be done at the end of practice. The deadening effect of the pressure on nerve endings in the finger tips would adversely affect shooting results if the push-ups were done before or during practice.

It will take 12 to 15 minutes to administer the above program.

A suggested alternate to the above program is the following:

1. Endurance drills on the basketball floor that involve intensive pressing drills the full length of the floor— done at least three times per week.

2. A light weight-lifting program done three times per week that would include the following: Squats, toe raisers, clean and press, biceps curls, and forearm curls.

Such programs conducted on alternate days three days per week should prevent deterioration of strength and endurance in the basketball player during the season.

BASKETBALL CONDITION RECORD											
NAME_____					SEASON OF _____						
DATE	1	2	3	4	5	6	7	8	9	10	SIT-UPS	PUSH-UPS

FIGURE 1

Post-Season Conditioning

What the player does after the season is over and between seasons could be a very important factor in the player's development. The basketball season is a long one, and usually a period of rest is needed when the player can be free of game and coaching pressures. Usually though, players play the game because they love and enjoy it. When the season is over, it is amazing how soon they return to the gym and start playing some intense free-lance scrimmage games on their own.

Some time after things settle down, and before the player gets away, the coach should sit down with each player and discuss the program that could best serve the needs for that player's future development. A folder should be prepared for each player, outlining the player's needs, and what the player needs to do to accomplish certain goals and objectives. This way the player gains an insight into his problems and will be more likely to feel that an interest is being taken to help him improve and accomplish more.

Usually such programs for off-season and between-season work for the individual should include the following:

1. A weight-lifting and strength-building program.
2. A running program that includes both sprints and distance runs.
3. A rope-jumping program
4. Fundamental weaknesses should be pointed out, and the player told what is necessary to eliminate such weaknesses as shooting, dribbling, defensive shift, free throws, etc.
5. Summer leagues are available to some players. If they can play in such leagues without endangering eligibility, they should do so.
6. Basketball camps are now common—if possible have the players attend at least one.
7. Any program should include lots of shooting and work on all shots.

The player who conscientiously follows the program outlined by the coach during the off-season months will return in the fall a better athlete, an improved basketball player, and a more mature and coachable person.

Index

A

All-purpose drills, 245-253
All purpose warm-up, 240-242

B

Balance, body, 113, 114
Ball full length of court quickly, 257
Barbell and bounce jumping drill, 204
Baseball pass, 33-37
Baseball pass fast break drill, 36-37
Bench drill, 203
Blind passing, 24
Blocking out, 173-177, 182
Blooper warm-up, 243-244
Body balance, 113, 114
Bounce pass, 41-43
Buddy, 252
Buddy-dribble, pivot, hand-off, lay-up
    shot, 253
Bull in the ring, 33
Butterfly Pattern, 193-194

C

Carom tip drill, 206-207
Catch dribbler, 137-138
Chair maze dribbling drill, 55-56
Change of direction, 113, 114, 115, 116,
    118
Change of pace, 112-120
Change-up drill, dribble, 61
Chest pass, 22
Circle dribbling drill, 59-60
Combination defenses, 162-170
Combination drills, 245-253
Conditioning:
    in-season, 267-270
    post-season, 271-272
    preseason, 264-266
Continuous movement fast-break, 187-189
Continuous outlet pass jackknife rebound
    drill, 199
Cross-over block-out rebounding drill, 182
Cross-over step, 212-213
Cut by pivot-post—shoot, 235

D

Dead ball, 23
Defense and dribble, 132
Defense the side line hook pass, 40
Defensive drills:
    individual, 121-141 (*see also* Individual
        defensive drills)
    rebounding, 171-182 (*see also* Rebound-
        ing, defensive)
    team, 142-170 (*see also* Team defensive
        drills)
Defensive pivot drill, 107
Direction, change, 113, 114, 115, 116, 118
Double exchange on double line, 26-27
Double exchange on single line, 25-26
Double-line lay-up, 242-243
Double X, 236-237
Dribble, 50-67
Dribble, jump-turn hook pass drill, 38
Dribble change-up drill, 61
Dribble-drive the defense drill, 61-62
Dribble lay-up relay, 58
Dribble—meet opposition drill, 53-55
Drive, 229-230

E

Eagle spread drill, 180-181

F

Fakes and feints, 216-224
Far foot lead step drill, 214
Fast break drills, 183-199
Five against five, 150-151
Five against five rebound drill, 177
Five-man weave, 29
Five-on-five continuous fast-break drill,
    189-190
Five time rebound drill, 209
Flip, 46-48
Follow the coach, 56-57
Forward pivot, 171, 172, 173-174
Forward pivot—hold-out drill, 117-118
Forward spin, 42
Four against four, 150

Four ball, four-corner dribble drill, 62-63
Four-corner dribble-pivot drill, 59
Four-corner hook pass drill, 39-40
Four-corner passing drills, 29-30
Four-corner pivot drill, 108-109
Four-line pivot drill, 107-108
Free ball hustle, 249
Free throw, 94-101
Full-court—continuous movement rebound drill, 178-179

G

Get ball down on floor, 253
Grabbing the ball, 177-178
Grapevine drill, 29
Guard-forward drill, 47
Guard drills, offensive, 225-226
Guard-forward drills, 226-227
Guard-guard-forward drills, 227
Guarding:
   player without ball, 151-157
   weak-side cutter, 141

H

Half-court drills, 194
Hand-off pass, 46-48
Hesitation step, 212
Holding onto ball drill, 181
Hook, 230
Hook pass, 37-41
Hook shot, 89-94

I

Imaginary meet ball-reverse drill, 119-120
Increase a lead, 257-260
Individual defensive drills:
   attitude, 124-125
   catch dribbler, 137-138
   coaching points, 127-128
   defense and dribble, 132
   defensive footwork, 133-134
   defensive lateral glide, 136-137
   defensive one-on-one close-out, 139-140
   defensive shift, 130
   formulating philosophy, 122-123
   guarding weak-side cutter, 141
   ideas to emphasize, 125
   importance, 121-122
   knee tag, 135-136
   mistakes to avoid, 129
   1, 130

Individual defense drills (con't)
   one-on-one, 131
   one-on-one—full length of court, 134-135
   one-on-one from guard-forward positions, 132-133
   poor play and teaching, 123-124
   quick hands, 136
   reaction one-on-one, 139
   seat-tag, 135
   sprint-glide, 138
   sprint-glide, return, 138
   3, 131
   2, 130-131
   two-on-one, 140-141
Individual offensive drills, 210-224
Inside pivot drill, 215

J

Jump at basket drill, 203-204
Jumping at basket drill, 204-205
Jump shot, 79-86
Jump stop and stride stop drill, 114
Jump stop and stride stop dribbling drill, 114-115
Jump-turn pass, 37

K

Knee tag, 135-136

L

Lay-up shot, 70-79
Lead, increase, 257-260
Lob passes, 48-49

M

Meet ball-reverse drill, imaginary, 120

O

Offense:
   individual drills, 210-224
   rebounding, 201-209
   team drills, 224-232
One, two, or three ball—shoot, 249
One-hand push pass, 31-33
One-hand set, 86-88
One-on-one, 131, 215-216
One-on-one, rebound, release pass drill, 179

One-on-one from guard forward positions, 132-133
One-on-one—full length of court, 134-135
One-on-one offensive rebounding drill, 207
One-tipper drill, 208
One to two second, last shot situation, 261-262
Opening up offensive player drill, 213-214
Opposite side opener, against a zone, 231
Out-of-bounds plays, 229-232

P

Pace, change of, 112-120
Pass, pivot, shoot, 250-251
Pass, return, dribble, drive drill, 62
Pass, return, pivot, dribble, shoot, 249
Passing, 20-49
Passing reaction drill, 30-31
Pass-off dribble drill, 247
Pass-off from dribble at full speed to player on reverse, 66-67
Pass-off while dribbling at full speed, 65-66
Pivot drills:
  coaching points, 103
  defensive, 107
  formation, 106
  forward, 102
  four corner, 103, 108-109
  four-line, 107-108
  reverse, 103
  single line pivot and pass, 106
  three-line pivot-post, 106-107
  three-spot, 105-106
  toss back and recover, 109-110
  truck and trailer, 104-105
Pivot to inside, block out drill, 214
Pregame warm-up drills, 233-244
Pressure defense rebound drill, 245-246
Push pass, 22
Push-ups, 268

Q

Quick hands, 136
Quick opener against man-to-man, 231-232

R

Reaction one-on-one, 139
Rebound, hook pass drill, 40
Rebound, pass, shoot drill, 35-36

Rebound hustle drill, 191
Rebounding, defensive:
  blocking out, 173-177, 182
  coaching points, 171-173
  cross-over block-out, 182
  eagle spread, 180-181
  five against five, 177
  forward pivots, 171, 172, 173-174
  full-court—continuous movement, 178-179
  grabbing the ball, 177-178
  holding onto ball, 181
  one-on-one, rebound, release pass drill, 179
  reverse pivots, 171, 172, 173-174
  three-on-three, 177
  three-on-three, rebound, release pass drill, 180
  twenty-one, 180
  two-on-two, rebound, release pass drill, 179-180
  wall, 181
Rebounding, offensive, 201-209
Receiving, 16-20
Relay shooting, 252
Reverse action offensive drill, 228-229
Reverse pivots, 171, 172, 173-174
Reverse spin, 42
Rocker step, 211
Roll ball out—dribble in shoot drill, 60-61

S

Sargent jump drill, 204
Screen, 230
Seat-tag, 135
Shooting:
  free throw, 94-101
  hook, 89-94
  important things, 68-69
  jump, 79-86
  lay-up, 70-79
  one-hand set, 86-88
Side line hook pass drill, 40
Single line continuous tip drill, 205
Single line hook pass drill, 38-39
Single line pivot and pass, 106
Sit-ups, 268
Slide, 230
Snap pass, 23
Special, 238-240
Special passes, 49
Special press drill, 256
Special situations, 255-263
Special talent situation, 263

Speed dribble relay drill, 63-64
Split the post, 47-48, 235-236
Spot run, 268
Sprint-glide, 138
Sprint-glide, return drill, 138
Square and triangle passing drill, 45-46
Star passing drill, 45
Starts, 113, 114, 118
Stick 'em keep-away game, 255
Stick 'em keep-away—mid-court area, 256
Stops, 113, 114, 118
Switch from defense to offense, 192-193
Switching, 157-159

T

Tag dribble drill, 57-58
Talent, special, 263
Team defensive drills:
   coaching points, 143-145
   combination defenses, 162-170
   five against five, 150-151
   four against four, 150
   guarding player without ball, 151-157
   habit drills, 146-151
   switching, 157-159
   three against three, 149-150
   two against two, 146-149
   zone defenses, 159-162
Team offensive drills, 224-232
Team rebound drill, 208
Three against three, 149-150
Three at basket, 205-206
Three-line passing, 32, 186
Three-line pivot-post, 106-107
Three-man grapevine passing drill, 27-28
Three-on-one fast break drill, 194-195
Three-on-three, rebound, release pass drill, 180
Three-on-three continuous fast-break drill, 189
Three-on-three rebounding drill, 177
Three-on-two down, two-on-one back, defense fast-break, 247-249
Three-on-two fast break drill, 196-197
Three-player weave with tail out, 237
Three-second score from court division line, 260
Three-spot pivot drill, 105-106

Three-spot pivot, three-man weave, 242
Three to five seconds for shot, 261
Three- to five-second time limit for shot, 261
Tip-two-on-one fast-break drill, 191-192
Toss back and recover drill, 109-110
Trail the dribbler drill, 64-65
Triangle rebounding tipping drill, 206
Truck and trailer drill, 104-105
Twenty-one rebound drill, 180
Two against two, 146-149
Two at the basket drill, 206
Two guards, forward and center drill, 228
Two-handed overhead pass, 43-46
Two-handed push pass, 22-31
Two-line drill, 19-20
Two-line passing drill, 24-25, 186
Two-line tip drill, 205
Two-line whistle drills, 53
Two-on-one, 140-141, 196, 216
Two-on-one, fast-break drill, 198-199
Two-on-two, rebound, release pass drill, 179-180
Two passes—length of court—three to five seconds, 262

W

Walking step, 212
Wall drill, 18-19, 44
Wall rebounding drill, 181
Warm-up drills, pregame, 233-244
Weak-side block-out drill, 176-177

Z

Zone defenses:
   after a shot, 160
   attack player with ball, 159
   center of gravity, 160
   communicate with voice, 160
   hands shoulder high, 160
   more than one player in your zone, 159
   no player in your zone, 159
   overloading zone defense drill, 161-162
   principles, 159-160
   shifting the ball, 160-161